LOTIONS, POTIONS, PILLS, AND MAGIC

D1712043

Lotions, Potions, Pills, and Magic

Health Care in Early America

Elaine G. Breslaw

NEW YORK UNIVERSITY PRESS
New York and London

NEW YORK UNIVERSITY PRESS
New York and London
www.nyupress.org

References to Internet websites (URLs) were accurate at the time of writing.
Neither the author nor New York University Press is responsible for URLs that
may have expired or changed since the manuscript was prepared.

LIBRARY OF CONGRESS CATALOGING-IN-PUBLICATION DATA
Breslaw, Elaine G., 1932-
Lotions, potions, pills, and magic : health care in early America / Elaine Breslaw.
p. cm.
Includes bibliographical references and index.
ISBN 978-0-8147-8717-5 (cloth : alk. paper)
ISBN 978-0-8147-8718-2 (e-book)
ISBN 978-0-8147-3938-9 (e-book)
1. Medicine—United States—History—18th century. 2. Medicine—United States—History—19th century. 3. Medical care—United States—History—18th century. 4. Medical care—United States—History—19th century. 5. Physicians—United States—History—18th century. 6. Physicians—United States—History—19th century. 7. Public health—United States—History—18th century. 8. Public health—United States—History—19th century. 9. United States—Social conditions—To 1865. I. Title.
R152.B725 2012
362.10973—dc23
2012016648

New York University Press books are printed on acid-free paper,
and their binding materials are chosen for strength and durability.
We strive to use environmentally responsible suppliers and materials
to the greatest extent possible in publishing our books.

Manufactured in the United States of America
10 9 8 7 6 5 4 3 2 1

In few of the civilized nations of our time have the higher sciences made less progress than in the United States.

Democratic institutions generally give men a lofty notion of their country.

—Alexis de Tocqueville,
Democracy in America,
vol. 2, 1835

To all the Breslaws: Karl, Theresa, Rachel, and Alec
And to my husband, John

CONTENTS

LIST OF ILLUSTRATIONS

ACKNOWLEDGMENTS

The writing of this book was a collaborative process. Except in a few instances, the original research supporting my conclusions is based on the more detailed investigations of other scholars. Many of those students of history and medicine who contributed important data are probably unaware of their significance for this work. They are, however, acknowledged in the bibliographic essays that accompany each chapter. Like most historians, I am eternally grateful for such scholarship and hope that I have given sufficient credit to those studies and have not distorted any conclusions. But of all those whose analysis and research have been most rewarding for me, I give special thanks to Alfred Crosby, Charles C. Mann, John Harley Warner, and the late John Duffy, all of whom have been instrumental in the formulation of my own ideas and understanding of the health problems in early America. Of that quartet I have met only Professor Duffy who participated in my Ph D orals at the University of Maryland. I also owe a debt of gratitude to the late Helen Brock with whom I had many conversations and sharing of information that stimulated my interest in the history of health and medical care. It is unfortunate that the bulk of her research has never been published and thus her name does not appear in the bibliographic essay.

The idea for this book began during the bicentennial celebration of the mid-1970s when I prepared a course on Health in Early America at Morgan State University. It was subsequently offered at Johns Hopkins University and attracted students preparing for medical degrees. Questions and comments from students stimulated more thought and consideration on the role of medical care on the status of health before modern medicine. Other friends and colleagues continued to express an interest in the subject and encouraged the writing of a book on the state of health and medical care in early America. I am always grateful for the kind words from Thomas Cripps, my colleague at Morgan State, and from my cohorts at the University of Tennessee. Conversations with David Grimsted of the University of Maryland were illuminating, as always, and brought some lesser-known figures to my attention.

Many libraries and their librarians were essential for the research or providing pictures, but I am especially in debt to Anne Bridges of the University of Tennessee (Knoxville) and Richard Behles of the University of Maryland Health and Human Services Library (Baltimore). That library's photographer, Thom Pinho, provided excellent images from their collection. The National Library of Medicine website was especially helpful in locating and providing illustrations. The site was easy to navigate and the system for requesting images quite efficient, making the search for visual material that much smoother. Thanks also to Nicole Joniec of the Library Company of Philadelphia, various staff members of the John Carter Brown Library at Brown University, Marianne Martin of the Colonial Williamsburg Foundation, Evie Santana-Nola of the Harvard College Library, and the staff at the Library of Congress for locating and providing other images from their collections. And finally, I must acknowledge the Internet as a source of information and, in particular, Google books for making nineteenth-century published works so easily available. Those sources saved many a trip to distant archives.

Several friends were willing to read selected chapters. To John Neff, Edward Rogers, and Daniel Feller, I say thank you for your comments. I am also grateful to the anonymous reviewers who helped me refine my thesis as they insisted on more "fleshing out" to support my ideas regarding the conflict and tensions about health care in early America. Insightful comments from David Miller of the Garamond Agency (who decided not to take it on as a project) and then Debbie Gershenowitz of NYU Press helped to develop that thesis. The careful editing from NYU Press cleared up some fuzzy writing and brought about a much needed clarity of expression.

Members of my family have contributed each in his or her own way to encourage my writing. To my granddaughter, Rachel Breslaw, whose budding interest in history and writing is a special inspiration; to my grandson, Alec Breslaw, whose enthusiasm for life and innovation has been an added inducement to come up with new ideas; and to my son and daughter-in-law, Karl and Theresa Breslaw, who were always willing to listen to my latest proposal over shared meals. I am especially grateful to my husband, John Muldowny, whose patience during the writing process and presence during the research phase is so very much appreciated. To all of them I dedicate this book.

Introduction

Good health in the twenty-first century depends on diet, exercise, and the right genes. Good health in early America depended on diet, exercise, and the right genes. That much has not changed. But there is a world of difference between those two eras, both in the quality of life we expect in the modern age and our ability to overcome genetic obstacles and epidemic diseases. We have insulin for diabetes, chemotherapy and radiation for cancers, diagnostic imaging to pinpoint health problems, and a grab bag of drugs and treatments for the ills that have plagued people for eons. We have more effective methods of purifying water and preserving food to prevent those ailments of the gut that often killed when they did not disable. Even more important, we have antibiotics to cure contagious diseases and vaccines to prevent them, and our food supplies are safer, more abundant, and more varied. As a result, life expectancy has almost doubled from forty years in the early eighteenth century to more than seventy-eight years in present-day United States. In those distant years infant mortality was so high—about one-third of babies born died in infancy—that only those who were the most resistant to germs lived to adulthood. Childhood was rife with diseases that handicapped or killed even more: measles, diphtheria, whooping cough, scarlet fever, and the pathogens in the cow's milk. There were no cures or means of preventing these life-threatening conditions even though doctors claimed to have the power to cure all.

Adults faced another barrage of ailments especially if they lived in cities. Incoming vessels invariably brought smallpox, venereal diseases, and the mosquito-borne ailments like malaria and yellow fever. Only natural immunity, sometimes genetic and sometimes born of previous bouts with those diseases, provided protection. Most of all, complete ignorance of the cause of diseases prevented an effective means of curing or even easing some symptoms. The idea that a germ—a pathogen, a living substance in the environment—could cause an ailment was a strange and unacceptable notion, a fantasy on the same level as believing in fairies. The medical world did not know that vectors such as mosquitoes or fleas could communicate disease. Early Americans blamed it on an invisible miasma in the air. At times disease was blamed on sinful behavior or, in the case of Africans and Native Americans, on violating taboos. Ignorance about disease was universal and not confined to any ethnic or national group.

As often happens today, a certain number of people recovered from the most life-threatening conditions or went into remission without medical intervention. Some health problems, like the common cold, resolve even if nothing is done. Some, like cancer, may go into remission or seemingly disappear without any interference by a medical practitioner. So too, in those old days, people survived the most inappropriate therapies. That a few patients did recover was taken as proof of the power of the healer to cure. Failure did not count. In those few cases of recovery, doctors could tout their successes even though they were in fact helpless to bring about a cure with their lotions, potions, pills, or heroic depletion procedures. After all, such therapies demonstrated visible signs of change in the body. Bleeding or purging or vomiting were obvious reactions and could be taken as curative if the patient survived.

Nonetheless, the real power in the doctor's arsenal of cures was in his or her aura of authority and omniscience. Whether physician (university-educated or apprentice-trained), midwife, folk healer, shaman (Native American), or obeah or conjurer (African), the medical man or woman conveyed a sense of his or her ability to heal. That ability in reality had less to do with the prescribed potions and procedures than the power of suggestion: the placebo effect. Patients endowed their medical practitioners (whether orthodox or folk) with enormous authority; they believed in that person's power to cure. The very suggestion of such a power worked to relieve symptoms. Medical personnel wrapped themselves in an aura of magical talent; their medicines were imbued with supposedly powerful antidotes to the ills of mankind. Their advice carried the authority of centuries of belief about the nature of good health and sickness, wrong as it was. Who could dispute the virtue of those prescriptions? There was no science ready to question the medical assumptions of the healer before the middle of the nineteenth century.

The physician has held an ambivalent place in Western society. Lampooned in seventeenth-century England and France as monopolistic, pompous asses who, according to the author Roy Porter, were accused of growing rich off the "fat of human misery," their services, for those who could afford their fees, were in continual demand to cure human ills. This was especially so for the upper class that considered the physician a symbol of their social status and therefore more worthy of their custom than other sources of medical care. On the other hand, the bulk of the population in America as in England depended on the less respectable folk healers, the self-taught, or those using their own home remedies. Such "folk empiricism" was not necessarily inferior to regular medical practice although it was usually less dangerous. Their supposed cures or explanations for disease and ill-health were very similar for all groups. All drew on the same theories of medicine and read the same books. In practical terms, not much divided the folk healer from the physician except for formal education—but that formal education was crucial to the doctor's attraction. They may have been unable to cure, but they could inspire more confidence and were the fashion among the more affluent. Making use of an educated physician's services drew a line between the upper class and the rest of the population. This was especially so for women who turned to the "man midwife" for assistance during childbirth, not just because they thought it was safer but because it was more prestigious, conveying a sense of superiority over the bulk of the population. In actual practice the more affluent were deluding themselves in much the same way everyone did who called on a medical practitioner in the days before scientific medicine. There was little that medicine in any form could do except to alleviate some symptoms. Whenever a patient recovered it was most likely because the body was healing itself and because confidence in the doctor aided that process. But it was not the therapy: that was at the best useless and at the worst deadly. By the nineteenth century, as American doctors came to rely even more than those in Europe on the heroic therapies of bleeding and purging, their procedures became a greater threat to life and health.

All physicians were, as David Wootton insists in his controversial 2006 book *Bad Medicine*, actually "doing harm" and not good. In time the amount of harm done by those medicine men and women grew fastest among the educated medical establishment. The more orthodox among the established physicians came to depend more and more on their extreme heroic depletion methods. The lancet, the glister (enema), and mercury were the major tools. The followers of folk medicine, the midwives, and other non-academic practitioners favored herbal therapies and diet more than depletion (although they never gave up purging their patients), and they grew in popularity among all segments of the population by the end of the eighteenth century. That growing disenchantment with the medical establishment encouraged the newer unorthodox practices of the nineteenth century and the favoring of the "sugar-coated pill."

This is the story of the American experience with health conditions in the early period of its history: of medicines used, of nutrition and food habits, of ethnic borrowings, of the treatment of diseases and training of doctors, of public health problems and solutions, and of the interplay of social change and medical views. It is also the story of how the medical profession in America failed to improve health and often became a stumbling block to advances in medicine. Traditional medicine in America, which was held in such high regard in the earlier centuries, lost its status and power long before the germ theory of disease finally discredited old-fashioned therapies. Doctors in the United States, unlike those in Europe, resisted change or innovations that violated their traditional theories of disease, in spite of scientific advances in France and Germany that contradicted those therapies. Instead of the established professional, it was the layman or the scarce and often obscure scientifically inclined doctor, who introduced new ideas and took the lead in experimentation. When a forward-looking novice physician like Dr. Adam Thomson advocated a new method of smallpox inoculation in 1750 Philadelphia, he faced a formidable obstacle from the old-style practitioners who continued to reject both inoculation as well as the idea of a specific disease.

In 1985 Ronald Numbers prepared an essay titled the "Fall and Rise of the American Medical Profession." His section on the "fall" was very short, and he spent most of his space describing the "rise," the emergence of a scientific medical profession that began in the years after the Civil War and was mainly due to the new model of medical education that began with Johns Hopkins University Medical School in 1893. For the first time a medical school required a bachelor's degree for entry and, with financial independence, could focus on research rather than attracting students with few qualifications. Like most historians of American medicine, Numbers's concern was with the extraordinary record of research and technological advance in the United States that followed in the twentieth century. His essay reflects minimal interest in the reasons for the "fall" of the profession, which he traces to the short period between 1830 and 1850, and blames on poorly trained doctors and competition from sectarians who opposed their traditional remedies. This, he says, left the system in "shambles." But the fall was due to many other factors, some inherent in the profession and some integral to American culture of the time. Evidence of the decline can be found in the tensions between physicians and the public in the colonial and revolutionary eras; it reached its nadir during the second quarter of the nineteenth century with the rise of alternative medical practices that competed with the more orthodox. This study tackles the issue of the "fall" to consider the state of medicine and health in the years before the loss of public confidence, which effectively undermined the significance of the doctor in the care of health and treatment of disease. Those years represent a culmination of distrust on the part of a disgruntled population.

There is little evidence to support the assumption that the seeds of later scientific developments in American medicine lay in the earlier period. It was a lack of interest in science as a source of knowledge in health care that was the defining characteristic of medical professionals in this country. Indeed, as late as 1860, Dr. Oliver Wendell Holmes, who as a medical student in Paris in the 1830s was in awe of the statistical-scientific approach of French medicine, and was one of the few who accepted the idea that a doctor's hands could cause infection, scoffed at the idea that laboratory science could have any practical value for medicine and health. Theories based on what was thought to be rational wisdom combined with experience were the essentials of medical knowledge. As a result any attempt to standardize practice failed in the face of the individual's experience. And if there had been uniform standards for treating health problems, they would have been useless based on a faulty understanding of the body and the cause of disease. Diagnostic tools like the stethoscope and thermometer were ignored, and those like X-rays had not yet been invented. The existence of cells, bacteria, or viruses was not known nor were the functions of most organs understood. As European anatomical and statistical studies progressed, they were rejected by Americans who thought of themselves as exceptional and above such crass experimentation. Not until the end of the nineteenth century, when there was again a direct link between European medicine and the United States, would there be any improvement in American medical science. Finally, any commitment to science was due to the recognition that Europeans were making discoveries regarding the causes of some diseases: that individual diseases had specific causes and were not an upset of bodily humors. Europe provided a newly objectified concept of disease that would eventually lead to real progress in medicine and the development of preventive vaccines. But such was not the case in the United States until long after the Civil War as the orthodox American medical profession rejected European ideas and thus contributed to its own downfall.

But change did come. The epilogue provides a brief overview of the tremendous and far-reaching advances in American medicine in the modern era. However, a newly energized alternative medicine movement reflecting a growing disenchantment with those very benefits has begun to question those advances. There are, therefore, some parallels between what happened to the medical profession in the mid-nineteenth century and what is happening today. Many drugs as well as surgical procedures promoted by physicians are, as they were in early years, often useless and many times as dangerous. Modern medicine may well be a positive good for the world, but it too has its deficiencies and its critics. Although most people retain their faith in the physician's dicta, there is still a defiant tension between the medical profession and the public reminiscent of those prescientific days.

There are many works on the history of medicine in America, on specific diseases and epidemics, on agricultural practices and foodways, on population trends, on Native American medicine, on the role of slavery, on the self-help movement of the nineteenth century, and many other topics treated in this book, but there is nothing published that brings all these issues together to focus on how they contributed to the loss of confidence in and sometimes outright hostility to orthodox medicine. This book follows the declining role of the physician in American society from its heyday in the colonial era (1607–1776), to the gradual loss of medical authority in the early National period and its failures during the cholera epidemics of the mid-nineteenth century. Topics discussed include the demographic disaster of the early European-Indian contact, the treatment of and changing concepts of diseases, childbirth practices, the training of medical personnel, food habits and nutrition, military medicine, alternative medical practices, and public health problems as they intersected with the major political, economic, and military affairs of the time.

The description of the practice of medicine and the state of health in early America will also be instructive for those who are nostalgic for what they think of as the "good old days." It will be useful to know something of the nitty-gritty of everyday problems, of the perils of orthodox medicine, of the pain and discomfort of life in early America, and finally of why many people turned away from those types of health care, and why some continued to follow those unpleasant practices. This is the story of what it was like to be sick or in pain before the scientifically advanced medicine of the twentieth century and how people struggled to alleviate their ailments.

1

Columbian Exchange

The winter had started when the Pilgrims, religious exiles from both England and Holland, arrived at the Massachusetts coast on November 11, 1620.
The *Mayflower* had been at sea for sixty-five days and no terrible diseases
had seized them during the crossing. Dr. Samuel Fuller, the ship's surgeon
had lost only one passenger and a seaman who had been sickly from the
beginning, leaving one hundred men and women passengers and forty-seven
crewmen. While anchored and deciding where to go from this point, a few
more passengers and three of the remaining crew died. A decision was made
not to proceed to Virginia, their original destination, but to settle in what had
long been a fishing area for many Europeans—Portuguese, English, Italians,
French, and possibly others since the 1480s, long before Columbus. Massachusetts was not an unknown land and had been mapped by John Smith a
few years before the arrival of the Pilgrims. The Pilgrims would be the first
Europeans to successfully plant a settlement in New England. A small party
left the ship and began to explore the area known as Cape Cod.

C. Smith taketh the King of Pamavnkee prisoner 1608

In this illustration of John Smith's encounter with Opechancanough, the Pammunkey chief in Virginia in 1608, we see the Indians as stronger, healthier, and more muscular than the English. Here Smith is demonstrating his mastery over his much taller captive. Most commentaries at the time of first contact describe the Indians as healthy, a condition that would change dramatically shortly afterward. From John Smith, *General Historie of Virginia, New England, and the Summer Isles* (1624). (Courtesy of Houghton Library, Harvard University, STC 22790)

Other Europeans who had explored along the northeastern coast had failed to create any permanent colonies. Giovanni de Verrazzano, an Italian acting for the French king, traded with the locals in 1523, but his crew was driven away, he reported, by a large number of hostile Indians. About eighty years later Samuel de Champlain visited Cape Cod in the hopes of setting up a French base, but the thickly settled villages discouraged him. Well armed and with large populations spread along the New England coast, the Indians successfully prevented any permanent European settlements, accepting only the sojourners, fisherman, who came for a few months, fished and traded for furs, and then went home. In 1614 John Smith appeared on the coast but soon left after arranging for his lieutenant Thomas Hunt to dry the fish they had caught before returning to England. But Hunt antagonized the locals by kidnapping some of the Native Americans; he was initially driven off but retained a few of his victims to take back to England, including one man named Tisquantum (better known as Squanto) of the Wampanoag tribe. Shortly afterward, Sir Fernando Gorges tried to found an English community in present-day Maine, but his group too was driven off by the Natives who, after the experience with Hunt, considered Europeans to be extremely dangerous people. In the following years, others who landed on the soil found the Indians violently hostile, determined to prevent any more foreigners from appearing on their shores. Sometime during 1616 a shipwrecked French ship was attacked; the Indians killed some of the crew and others were carted off to replace those men lost to the English. Shortly afterward, another French ship appeared in the vicinity of Boston. It was set afire and everyone on board was killed. European settlement was not wanted and was easily discouraged by the large number of native people in the area.

Unwilling to be intimidated by potential threats from the local inhabitants, the Pilgrims sent a small group of armed men to search the land and find a place to settle. They saw a few Indians who ran away but did not come across the large number of thickly settled villages described by others, nor were they threatened in any way. In one deserted village, the scouting party saw tools scattered and fields cleared but no sign of inhabitants. They dug up some graves and found a few objects, which they took back to the *Mayflower,* and a cache of corn that could be used for seed. On December 16, 1620, the passengers disembarked and began to build houses and a fort for a permanent town on the site of the old village. But where were the great numbers of Indians noted by earlier visitors? The Pilgrims decided that God must be on their side and had cleared the land for His chosen people.

Without assistance from the natives, the Pilgrims suffered terribly that first winter. Insufficient food had been brought on the boat, and there was little nourishment to be had from the land before the spring. Between December 16 and the end of the following March forty-four more Pilgrims died, and the crew lost half their number to a variety of illnesses. Dr. Fuller blamed the deaths on scurvy, a nutritional deficiency that was not recognized as such at the time but was believed to be an infection like other diseases. A handful of Indians watched their suffering from a distance but did not approach except for the theft of some tools. More Pilgrims arrived that spring of 1621, further stressing the food resources. But none left to go home on the returning *Mayflower*. Their decision to stay was born of their determination to establish a Godly community separate from the taint of either Dutch influence or that of the English Church in spite of the deprivations in the wilderness.

The mystery of the missing Indians was soon solved; in the middle of March 1621 the Wampanoag chief, Massasoit, sent an emissary, Samoset, an Abenaki from Maine with some skill in English, to talk to the Pilgrims. Samoset had recently arrived in Massachusetts brought from Maine by Captain Thomas Dermer who was sailing along the coast in 1619. On his arrival Samoset noted that what had once been a populous region was now "utterly void" because, he told the Pilgrims, of a terrible sickness that had killed off many of the local people. The Pilgrims were given more details of the missing population after Massasoit arrived with Squanto, one of Captain Hunt's 1614 captives who had been able to return to Massachusetts on Dermer's ship from London. When he returned after five years, Squanto said that he found his village deserted and everyone dead.

As the story was pieced together, the Pilgrims learned that sometime between 1616 and 1617 an unidentified plague had visited the Indians and eventually killed close to 90 percent of the coastal population. Squanto's kidnapping by Hunt in 1614 had inadvertently saved his life. Charles Mann estimates that the Wampanoag confederacy included as many as 20,000 people in 1614 but was reduced to 1,000 by 1619 after the epidemic had run its course. That left Massasoit, the surviving Wampanoag chief, in a dilemma. He had only sixty men left to fight his enemies the Narragansetts, tribes that had not been affected by the disease. His gods, he believed, had abandoned the Wampanoag, and now he was forced to accept the English as allies. Taking advantage of Squanto's English skill, Massasoit offered friendly relations, trade, and assistance in return for loyalty and support in war. The Pilgrims, in turn, were confirmed in their belief that God had cleared the land for them by bringing a pestilence to the Indians, providing additional incentive for them to remain to facilitate the "New England Zion." According to John Winthrop, God had cleared the land to "make room" for them. Such smugness did not bode well for the remnant of the Indian tribes of the area. But in

1620 Massasoit was desperate for assistance, and the Pilgrims saw the benefit of allying with him.

The nature of the epidemic that had led the Indians to accept the presence of the Pilgrims is still a mystery. It was not unusual for a variety of illnesses originating in the Old World to appear among the Native Americans before any direct contact with Europeans. This would not be the first time for such a thing to happen. The disease that had decimated the New England coast peoples may well have started in the more northerly French settlements in Canada. Alfred Crosby in his *Columbian Exchange* notes a commentary in the Jesuit *Relations* of 1616 of an Indian complaint: since the French had arrived "they [the natives in Canada] are dying fast and the population is thinning out." Since trading with the Europeans, Indians lamented that they "have been more reduced by disease." Whatever the disease was in Canada could easily have spread south during warfare or as a result of trade. Or the disease may have been present on one of the European ships, either French or English, that had appeared along the coast in 1616. A captured Frenchman may well have been sick at the time.

But what was the disease? There are few eyewitness accounts of the epidemic in New England; to all it was an unfamiliar plague that had ended as mysteriously as it had begun. Some observers described skin marks or pox on those who lived. The Gorges expedition in Maine at the beginning of the epidemic in late 1616 were told that sufferers began with a headache as a major symptom followed by scabs and a yellow coloring of the skin. The latter commentary has led some scholars to the idea that it might have been hepatitis, but that has been recently discounted. Nor was it yellow fever because the weather was too cold for the *aegpti* mosquito to survive the winters, and there is no mention of ships from Africa, the source of the disease. Measles, in turn, would not have caused such a high mortality, although it may have accompanied the more virulent disease. Nor did crowd diseases that require dense populations in close quarters (like the bubonic plague or typhus) fit the conditions of Native life. The most convincing analysis of the situation comes from Timothy L. Bratton. After considering all of the possibilities based on the timing, the extensive mortality, and the nature of the symptoms, Bratton concluded that it was most likely smallpox, that scourge of the Indian population since 1518 when it first appeared in the West Indies.

Smallpox can be caused by any of nine types of the variola virus, with symptoms that range from merely flu-like aches to the most lethal type: runny scabs that cover the entire body including the soles of the feet and palms of the hands and could lead to massive stripping of the epidermis.

Blindness was often the result for those who survived the worst type. The fatality rate could vary between 7 percent (in London in the seventeenth century) to 15 percent (Boston in 1721) and 30 percent (Scotland in 1787). Elizabeth Fenn estimates that the fatality rate among Natives was much higher, closer to 50 percent and the rate of infection more than 80 percent. A disproportionate number of the very young and the very old died from the disease. In addition to age, survival also depended on nutritional status or pregnancy. Possibly 75 percent of pregnant women aborted. During the winter Indians often suffered from lack of food and that may have contributed to the high death rate during the cold months of 1617 and 1618 when sustenance was especially scarce.

Smallpox is a disease that can sustain itself over long periods of time within a community and just as easily spread to neighboring groups as a result of social contact or during warfare. It is easily communicated from person to person from droplets in the air, from the urine of an infected person, or from the fluid from unhealed skin lesions. In addition, the virus can live outside the human body for weeks on clothing or other inanimate objects that harbor the scabs. A long incubation period means that the infected person can mingle with the well for ten to fourteen days before knowing that he or she is sick. The first symptoms are like the flu—headache, fever, backache, nausea, and a general malaise. After four days sores usually appear in the mouth, throat, and nasal passages and then on the surface of the skin, including the face forearms, neck, and back, causing excruciating pain. Sometimes the pustules run together or turn inward, hemorrhaging under the skin, which, according to Timothy Bratton, may have given the impression of yellowish skin. A secondary bacterial infection is also possible. Death is usually after ten to sixteen days of suffering but can sometimes occur before the rash appears. The sick person, however, remains contagious until the last scabs falls off, sometimes a month after the first appearance. It is quite possible that Natives carrying gifts in blankets or other containers also carried the disease with them as they visited friendly tribes. The long incubation period and ease of communication thus fit the conditions of the Wampanoags in 1616. The extraordinarily high fatality rate of 90 percent is a different problem that requires explanation.

Because smallpox was a new disease in the Western Hemisphere, no one in America had any acquired immunity from a previous bout. The same circumstances applied to a host of diseases that were taking a devastating toll on Indian life: measles, typhus, typhoid fever, diphtheria, influenza, plague, whooping cough, and chicken pox, among others. Such diseases began in the Old World through the exchange of microorganisms between humans and domesticated animals. Smallpox, for instance, is thought to have evolved from a cattle or horse virus or one that affects camels. Bovine rinderpest became human measles in the same way that avian influenza became human influenza. What was missing from the Native American environment were the "crowd" diseases from microorganisms that needed animal hosts when not circulating among humans. Whatever herd disease immunities Indians may have had before the migration across the Bering Strait from Asia to Alaska (about 15,000 years ago) were lost when the cold killed off many of the germs, infected people died off, and the microorganisms no longer had hosts to maintain them. Such organisms died quickly outside the human body. Eurasians and Africans continued to live in close proximity to livestock and to exchange infections with the animals. But Native Americans had close contact with few animals and did not herd livestock. The New World had no cows, horses, or camels, and very few other domestic animals.

Old World people had adjusted to these diseases both socially and biologically to moderate the effects. There was always a proportion of the population, especially the adults, that had some immunity during an epidemic and could care for the sick. People had learned ways of protecting themselves against spreading the contagion through isolation and quarantines. Centuries of experience with smallpox had taught Old World societies that only those who had suffered a previous bout of that illness were safe from the contagion. Smallpox was a common affliction in populated areas in Europe and the British Isles; nearly all urban children caught it and were either soon dead or immune. American Indians had none of those advantages. Because they were a "virgin population" in the case of many bacteriological and viral diseases, adults were as likely as children to become sick. Their medicine provided no protection and may have made matters worse through practices that spread the disease. There appeared to be no concept of contagion in Indian culture. The healers and the shaman often played out their rituals in the presence of many people in the community who were then exposed to the disease and could carry it back to their own families.

Native medicine, like that of the seventeenth-century Englishmen, was closely identified with religion. Sickness was ascribed to offended or malevolent spirits that had to be appeased. The function of the shaman was to divine who was causing the trouble and either propitiate the spirit or find a friendly spirit to intervene. Thus the medicine man, in the presence of the community, used a variety of paraphernalia along with incantations, dances, the sprinkling of substances, and bloodletting to remove the poison introduced by those spirits. Spiritual healing was supplemented with herbal concoctions, many of which were eventually borrowed by the Europeans: sassafras, ginseng, ipecac, and snakeroot entered the pharmacopeias and became important herbal exports to Europe. European observers thought many of the treatments were effective even though they condemned the spiritual elements as witchcraft. For fractures Indians made splints, used moss and other materials to stop bleeding, and treated rheumatic problems with sweat baths followed by cold-water plunges, massage, and aromatic fumigation. There was little attempt at surgery except when used as torture on prisoners. However effective the Native medical practices were for traditional ailments, they could be harmful when used for European diseases.

There are innumerable conditions that can influence the way a body reacts to a disease and determine how dangerous it could be. Inadequate nursing care, poor nutrition, inappropriate healing customs, mutation of the virus, previous contact with the disease, or genetic factors can all play a role in an epidemic and influence the mortality rate. Native healing practices that sometimes called for a sweat bath followed by a plunge in cold water was dangerous for those with smallpox. Many times entire families were laid low together. When a large number of people became sick at the same time, there were too few of the uninfected to care for them. Nor were there enough adults to tend to the gardens or cook the food for either the sick or the young, contributing to the nutritional deficiencies. Alfred Cosby points out that a disproportionately large percentage of Native Americans aged fifteen to forty died during that first century of contact leaving children neglected and food and water procurement precarious, all of which contributed to the deadly results. When faced with such a catastrophe, apparently healthy Indians often ran away from the tribe in panic and unknowingly carried the virus to others, thus spreading the disease far and wide. Moreover, such diseases often became more virulent when transmitted by a family member (rather than by an unrelated person) and many in the tribes were closely related. All such conditions probably prevailed in New England between 1616 and 1619. One indication of how new the disease of smallpox was to the Americas was in its very virulence. A disease new to a population may mutate, a process known as genetic shift, and will usually be more dangerous and have more painful symptoms in that primary form. In time it will become less virulent. If it kills off all its hosts, it will not be able to survive; thus it becomes a milder disease to keep the virus alive.

Smallpox had been around in Europe for many centuries. It has an even older history in the East: there is evidence in Egyptian mummies from 1200 BCE, and it devastated the Roman army in 164 CE. It is suspected that the virus became more virulent in the sixteenth and seventeenth centuries in Europe and that the American Indians were infected with a more dangerous mutation than had been usual in the past. Nonetheless, the fatality rate and the symptoms among New World peoples was worse than experienced elsewhere. The mortality surpassed the deaths from the plague when it was a new disease in Europe in the fourteenth century.

For reasons that have recently come to light regarding the genetic makeup of Native Americans, we now suspect that they were innately more susceptible to contagious diseases like smallpox and measles than were Europeans and Africans. Charles Mann points out that Indians come from a small gene pool and, because of isolation from communicable disease, lacked most of the special molecules inside human cells that make it possible to recognize and attack dangerous viruses. European immune systems, on the other hand, with a more diverse genetic background, have a greater ability to identify and therefore attack harmful invaders. Long contact with such viruses and bacteria shaped immune systems to find and counter many contagious diseases, ultimately leading to genetic changes that were handed down in the DNA of offspring. Even unexposed Europeans, those who had been isolated from contact with smallpox, were more likely to ward off the worst symptoms and had a better chance of survival than Native Americans. In fact, Native Americans do not lack such molecules but have fewer of them inherited from their relatively disease-free ancestors.

The original gene pool of Native Americans was small from the beginning. Successive waves of migrants from Asia came from related peoples in the Old World—almost all were of the "O" blood type with few variations in the mitochondrial DNA, a quality inherited matrilineally and often used to trace genealogy. A small group of later migrants from Asia were of the "A" blood type, but they did not move far beyond central Canada. However, there is no B or AB blood type among any of the early American Indians. Moreover, in physical characteristics, Indians are fairly uniform from the northern part of North America to the tip of South America: black hair, brown eyes, high cheek bones, with small variations in skin tone and body shape. There is nothing resembling the genetic differences seen in the Old World from the fair-skinned, blond, blue-eyed northerners to the black skin of sub-Saharan Africans with dark eyes and dark hair; and variations in body type from the diminutive pigmies to the more than the six-footers in central Africa. The lack of genetic variation among American Indians was sometimes beneficial. For instance, Indians lack the genes of Old World people that predispose them to cystic fibrosis, asthma, or some kinds of diabetes, but it also meant that they lacked the genetic qualities that provided immunity to certain communicable diseases. Thus, contact with Europeans was a disaster waiting to happen.

Nor all historians agree with Charles Mann that genetic factors explain what happened to the Native American population. They do not deny the presence of smallpox, measles, or the variety of respiratory ailments in a population that had had no contact with those diseases, but some scholars put a greater emphasis on environmental factors. David Jones, for instance, insists that the cause was a lack of adaptive immunity and not from genetic characteristics. He argues that the emphasis on genetics as the major cause of depopulation removes the responsibility from human behavior and "deflects attention away from moral and political questions." Instead, Jones focuses on a combination of social, cultural, and environmental factors, more than the immune factors, to explain the devastation. For example, when everyone in a tribe fell sick at the same time, there was no one to comfort or take care of them. Many diseases appearing at the same time also took its toll. Smallpox victims become vulnerable to respiratory problems as well as measles. Measles in turn leaves its victims open to other diseases such as tuberculosis. Malnutrition also increases susceptibility to infection, and Jones notes the archeological evidence of malnutrition among American Indians before 1492, especially in Mexico and the Andes. In New England, colonization introduced a host of damaging "ecological changes" that destroyed the Indian economy: deforestation, livestock overrunning Indian crops, insect blights, the presence of rats, and erosion. But most of all the mental and physical stress of displacement, warfare, drought, overwork, slavery, and economic chaos increased vulnerability to disease. In this latter argument Jones draws heavily on Crosby's discussion in a subsequent article on "Virgin Soil Epidemics," which stresses the environmental factors and the psychological impact that undermined the ties of kin and tribe, and led to demoralization to the point of self-destructive behavior.

In another argument against Mann's thesis, Paul Kelton focuses on the enslavement of the Indians and the vast network of trade that spread new diseases. The weakened immune systems that made the native peoples vulnerable to these new diseases was due, he says, to deteriorating living conditions and a "synergy of germs and slave raids" that carried the disease throughout the Indian world. It was made worse by settlement practices and the poor sanitation that came with it. Kelton denies that Indians suffered any genetic anomaly and places the onus of population loss on the behavior of the Europeans, arguing that the Natives had experience with countless infectious diseases long before European incursions; that contact with wildlife exposed them to rabies from bites and possibly anthrax from infected animals eaten or handled. Eating raw or undercooked meat could convey trichinosis and brucellosis, although Kelton admits fatalities were rare;

Indians took precautions by bathing, cooking food, and treating of wounds. Indians tended to leave wounds uncovered after washing them with herbal concoctions. The wounded were usually isolated, which kept infection to a minimum. But the potential for food poisoning from botulism and gangrene from wounds was always there. Indians also suffered from Chagas disease, which is spread by blood-sucking bugs, leishmaniasis spread by a sandfly, and Lyme disease from ticks (such infections cannot be transmitted to others, though). Kelton also posits that common pathogens like staphylococci and streptococci existed in America long before Columbus, and therefore blood poisoning and dysentery were problems. A newer study by Douglas Ubelaker confirms many of Kelton's suppositions about the existence of a large number of Native American diseases.

Nonetheless, such arguments do not give sufficient attention to the diseases that reached the Indians before Europeans appeared in those communities, causing enormous population loss that lead to disorganization and demoralization, which in turn made it easier for the Europeans of whatever nationality to cause further damage. There is another twist to the genetic factor. Mann points out that most immune systems are skewed to defend against either parasites or microorganisms but not both, and that such propensities are inborn. Because of the kind of diseases they experienced in the New World, Natives probably had some innate protection against worms and nematodes while Europeans systems were better able to target microorganisms. In both cases their genetic makeup shaped those immunities or the lack of such. Certainly the Indians suffered from many ailments, some of which were unique to the New World, but their vulnerability to the new diseases was still extraordinary.

What amazed the Europeans on first contact was that the Indians appeared to be so healthy and many of their healing ways seem to work. They were certainly taller than the Europeans, their skins unmarked by previous disease. John Brickell, drawing on other eyewitness reports remarked that the Indians of the Carolinas were inclined to be tall and very straight. "They never bend forwards or stoop in the shoulders" except when aged. He thought they had "extraordinary good Teeth" although yellowed from smoking tobacco. Many years later William Bartram, commenting on the Cherokees, said they were the largest race of men he had every seen with "bright complexions." John Smith in 1614 found the New England coast "inhabited with a goodly, strong and well proportioned people." The most common complaints were related to digestion because of the habit of alternating fasting and feasting, and rheumatic discomforts from constant exposure.

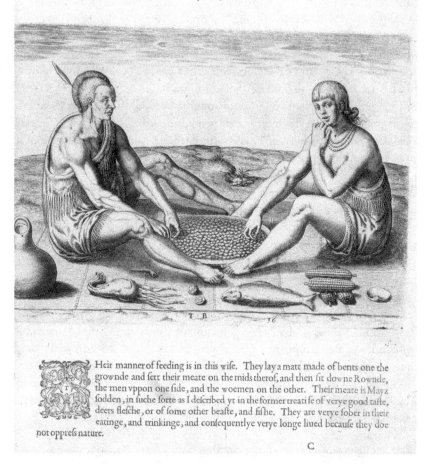

Their ſitting at meate.   XVI.

Heir manner of feeding is in this wiſe. They lay a matt made of bents one the grownde and ſett their meate on the mids therof, and then ſit downe Rownde, the men vppon one ſide, and the woemen on the other. Their meate is Mayz ſodden, in ſuche ſorte as I deſcribed yt in the former treatiſe of verye good taſte, deers fleſche, or of ſome other beaſte, and fiſhe. They are verye ſober in their eatinge, and trinkinge, and conſequentlye verye longe liued becauſe they doe not oppreſs nature.

C

This engraving "Their sitting at meate" by Theodore De Bry, 1590, based on a watercolor by the artist John White depicts Virginia Indians at a meal. They are described as "verye sober in their eatinge, and drinkinge, and consequently verye logne lived."

The experience of New England Indians was typical of what had happened elsewhere in America but on a smaller scale than that of the Spanish "conquests." The first recorded epidemic of smallpox broke out in the Caribbean island of Santo Domingo in 1518–19 and killed somewhere between one-third and one-half of the Indians there. Enslavement and malnutrition explain part of that horror, but it does not explain what happened subsequently in Mexico and the Inca Empire. Perhaps someone in Cortez's expedition to Mexico in 1519 carried the virus to the mainland, where it reached the Aztec center before the main expedition arrived. At first the Aztecs were able to drive the Spaniards back, but the epidemic raged for sixty days, and at that point Cortez attacked again and laid siege to Tenochtitlán, the capital, until it finally capitulated.

The disease raced through Central America carried by Indians in their vast trade network, went through the Isthmus of Panama, and down the west coast of South America to reach the Inca Empire in Peru before Pizarro arrived in 1532. Mann quotes a recently discovered comment by a Spanish soldier, Ciéza de León, who reported that "a great plague of smallpox" had broken out in Inca land in 1524 or 1525 and killed 200,000 people. The number, of course, is only anecdotal; the actual mortality is probably much higher, and later estimates assume that in the course of three years about one-half of the population was gone. Regardless of the actual number, Ciéza's collection of information from the Incas tells us that the pestilence was there *before* the arrival of the Spaniards. The epidemic also killed Huayna, the Inca leader and father of Atahualpa, an absolute monarch, his family, and his court, creating a hiatus in the leadership that led to a series of civil wars on the eve of Pizarro's arrival. With no legitimate claimant to the throne, Pizarro played one faction against another, captured one side's leader, Atahualpa, and had him killed (after taking a fortune in gold and silver) while the other swore allegiance to the Spanish throne intending to turn on Pizarro when he had regained some supporters. That never happened and Pizarro, with his 168 men and 62 horses, was able to take over the Inca Empire that covered most of the western edge of South America. It was disease and factionalism—problems that predated the arrival of the Spaniards—that made this conquest possible.

The mystery of missing Indians in the central part of the United States may provide additional evidence for the power of infectious diseases on a genetically vulnerable population and the importance of animals in that exchange. Hernando De Soto landed on the western coast of Florida in 1539 with instructions from the king of Spain to find more gold. Over the next four years he wandered north from Florida along the eastern side of the

Appalachians where he came across evidence of death from an unidentified disease within recently emptied villages. Once he crossed the mountains to the west, the situation changed. He passed through Tennessee and traveled south along the Mississippi River valley, finding only thriving communities and no sign of epidemic damage. De Soto mapped about fifty settlements along the lower Mississippi River, all well populated with highly urbanized societies. There was no evidence of smallpox or measles. According to Mann, De Soto and his men were thoroughly obnoxious individuals who managed to wreck "most everything [they] touched." De Soto's force raped, tortured, enslaved, stole, and killed wherever they went. Nonetheless, the expedition's devastation did not destroy the cultures they found west of the mountains. The Indians continued to thrive and were able to protect themselves from the worst depredations. And yet, about forty years later when the next groups of Europeans appeared with the French explorer La Salle, the hordes of people had disappeared, forests had grown up, and bison roamed freely where Indians had built ceremonial platforms and public plazas. Archeologists estimate the population of one very urbanized group, the Chaddo living along the Texas-Arkansas border, was around 200,000 people early in the sixteenth century, but when LaSalle arrived in 1682 the population had fallen to 8,500, and by the eighteenth century had shrunk to 1,400. Other societies, it appears, had been completely obliterated.

What happened? Mann attributes the destruction of these Indian societies to the pigs brought by the Spaniards. Such animals were part of their food supply and usually traveled with the explorers. Pigs carry a variety of diseases (such as anthrax, brucellosis, tuberculosis, and trichinosis) that can be passed to other animals such as the native deer and wild turkeys, which then can mutate to infect people. Such a scene may well have happened with the local animals maintaining a reservoir of pathogens waiting to be passed to people. De Soto's wanton pillaging had little effect on the population, though. It was long after he left that the deaths began and the diseases appeared. It was not smallpox but some other new infections or series of different infections carried by animals to which the Native Americans had no immunity or knowledge of how to care for the sick. The result was no different from the epidemics of smallpox that raged through Mexico, Peru, and eastern Massachusetts.

Although smallpox was the major factor in the death of most Native Americans throughout the Western Hemisphere in the century following Columbus's ventures, other diseases complicated the picture and contributed to the mortality. Within a hundred years of the appearance of the Spanish, successive infections may have reduced the native population by at least 90 percent.

COLUMBIAN EXCHANGE >> 23

Soon after the enslavement of Africans in America, malaria and yellow fever brought from that continent was added to the list. In fact, the Indians became a reserve of pestilence as they traveled from place to place. The initial ravages of smallpox were followed by a host of new bacterial and viral diseases brought by the Europeans, from respiratory ailments to measles and typhoid for which, again, the Natives had no immunity. William McNeill notes that influenza pandemic (one stretching across the continents) took many lives in America during the winter of 1558/59 and spread as far as Japan. It is possible that Sir Francis Drake brought typhus or some other contagious fever to the Caribbean and Florida in 1585 on his way to Roanoke in North Carolina and introduced those North American natives to the new infections.

The "lost" colony of Roanoke began in 1585 with 107 people. More than one hundred men, women, and children arrived the following year, but by 1590 all had disappeared. There was no sign of disease in the encampment to account for the loss, and the disappearance remains a mystery. Reports from the settlers in 1586 tell of some diseases that visited the Indians shortly after the English arrived. The Indians, unfamiliar with such infections blamed the English for shooting them with invisible arrows that caused them to get sick and die. It is possible that in 1585 Drake's fleet along the southeast coast brought typhus or typhoid or possibly malaria to the land, and the infections reached Roanoke before the English settled there. Or the smallpox in the Spanish missions in Florida led to the spread of that disease to the north. To the Indians it appeared that the diseases came from the Roanoke settlers themselves. The problems were so unfamiliar that the Indians admitted that they did not know how to treat them.

How lethal were these diseases? The most common estimate of the result of this contact between Europeans and Native Americans is that 95 percent of the Indian population died within the first one hundred years of the Spanish explorations and settlement. As other Europeans penetrated into the more northerly sections of America, the decline continued from a combination of disease, warfare, overwork, starvation, and demoralization. How many people did that encompass? The estimates of the pre-Columbian population vary widely depending on the methods used to determine the numbers. Herbert Klein provides the most recent synthesis of those studies. A rough but conservative estimate for the Andes area of South America is somewhere between five and ten million people; in Mesoamerica (Mexico and Central America) possibly ten to twenty million, and in North America about two million, of whom about one-half million lived along the Atlantic coast, a similar number along the Pacific coast, and the rest within the central sections. In another study John Daniels notes that the population numbers for North America vary from one to eighteen million people. The larger the number, the greater the assumed loss of population and therefore the more devastating the effect of contact with Europeans. A lower number could suggest a less severe impact. No matter the exact number, all agree that contact with Europeans was destructive whether the disease arrived before a particular settlement or afterwards, and was later complicated by opportunistic diseases and the resulting demoralization.

At the same time, the Spaniards seemed to be invincible; few came down with the diseases that killed Native Americans. The Spaniards claimed a superior medicine from their doctors, but in fact it had more to do with existing immunities and well-supplied coffers. The English experience was different; unlike the Spaniards, the king did not personally support the early settlers. Left to their own devices, the early English colonists did not allow for adequate food at the beginning. They suffered from a variety of nutritional ailments during the early years of settlement. In Jamestown, the first permanent English settlement in 1607, the mortality rate during the first three years was as high as that of the Indians. Of the original 144 who left England, 104 landed in May 1607. Because of the lack of food, that number was reduced by one-half within months. By the following year only 38 were alive. Over the next thirteen years, Wyndham Blanton counted 7,549 people entering the colony, but at the end of 1624 only 1,095 remained. There was no sign of either smallpox or measles among the group because, like the Spaniards, most had had those diseases as children in the old country. And too, with the scarcity of women, there were very few children to maintain the population. The English suffered from winter diseases such as pneumonia, pleurisy, or influenza exacerbated by malnutrition. The Pilgrims experienced a similar deprivation, but that lasted only a year, and by the end of the first harvest in late 1621 there was adequate food and a surprisingly healthy environment with rapid population growth. The presence of children born in Massachusetts prepared the way for the early smallpox epidemics among the next group of New England settlers, the Puritans in Boston. An epidemic began with those children in Boston in 1648/49 and spread to the Indians and other English settlements in the more rural areas. When smallpox appeared in Virginia during the last quarter of the century, the trade network spread the disease down into the Carolinas leading to what Kelton calls an "epidemiological nightmare," in southeastern United States, which repeated the experience of Spanish–Indian contact of the previous century.

No discussion of health conditions in America can avoid a reference to syphilis. It was a new disease, or a mutated form of an old disease that appeared in Italy a year after Columbus returned from his first voyage. The timing has led commentators to connect it with America and to assume that the new disease was part of the Columbian Exchange. There is very little evidence either archeological or documentary to prove that it was an Native American disease. Most of the evidence—the ghastly symptoms and high fatality in particular—points to a new disease, which is most virulent when it first appears and then is moderated as the pathogen mutates to sustain itself. Lesions found on bones in America are suspect, but they could have been from other diseases. Charles Mann points out that it is possible that people with syphilis in Europe before 1493 may have been diagnosed wrongly with Hansen's disease (leprosy). In 1490 Pope Innocent III abolished all the leprosaria in Europe and thus released the sick into the population. Did some of those people actually have syphilis, which then spread into the larger population? The timing of the pope's action is as intriguing as that of America as the source of the disease.

Those who study the history of epidemics note that the *treponema pallidum,* the wormlike bacterium that causes syphilis, is related to three other diseases that have a longer history. As yaws from Africa, it infects cuts on the skin and leaves long-lasting sores; as bejel in the Middle East, it causes cold sore lesions around and in the mouth; as pinta, it is a mild skin infection in Meso America. Only syphilis of the *treponema* is passed on with sexual contact and can have deadly results infecting bones and brains years after first acquired. It is notable that an antibody created by any one of these diseases conveys immunity to the others, and they were often treated with the same therapies. One historian of diseases, Mirko Grnek, traces a form of the germ to ancient antiquity and says it is more related to yaws than to the other forms. John Tennent's medical handbook, popular in eighteenth-century America and England, assumed that yaws and syphilis were different forms of the same disease and suggested the same remedies for both. If a mutation of yaws, syphilis becomes another Old World infection visited on the Indians; if a New World pathogen, syphilis is the Indian answer to smallpox. The debate continues, especially for those who want some retribution for the Indians for the devastation wrought by the Europeans. Proof will await more scientific evidence.

Throughout the period and long afterwards, there was nothing that medicine could do to help those who got sick and no way to prevent the death rate. Although the English rejoiced in the deaths of the Indians, the Spaniards were horrified. They were losing their workers to forces they did not understand. It led then to the introduction of slave labor from Africa to replace the dying Indians, another consequence of the Columbian Exchange that began in 1492. The Africans who shared many of the disease immunities with Europeans had a better chance of survival, but they also brought new diseases that were less familiar to their northern neighbors—malaria and yellow fever. The African resistance to these pathogens further encouraged the growth of the slave trade. Thus the Americas became a melting pot of infections at a time when no medicine could cure. In time, the population in America—whether of European or African descent—became isolated from Old World infections and began to repeat, on a smaller scale, the earlier experience of the Indians. They became healthier and taller than their Old World ancestors, freed from the endemic diseases that stalked those in Europe and Africa. But when ships arrived with those diseases, those born in America became vulnerable. As a result sporadic epidemics raged anew among the descendants of Old World people and continued among the Indians who had remained untouched by earlier incursions. As people tried to protect themselves from those diseases, older preventive measures proved to be ineffective in America, and newer ideas ran into opposition from a medical profession unable to respond and unwilling to change.

2

Epidemics

In early May 1721, the ship *Seahorse* readied its crew to leave Boston harbor. Captain Wentworth Paxson, a Boston resident, had successfully offloaded his cargo and prepared to set sail again. He was delayed: a man on board showed the telltale signs of smallpox. The sick man was removed from the ship and taken to a house where a red flag flew warning of a deadly disease. No one besides doctors or nurses were permitted to enter the house; a guard was posted to enforce the ban. The ship lay at anchor until the doctors were sure that there were no more cases, but they were disappointed. By the end of May at least six more from the *Seahorse* were sick. They too were isolated in the house near the shore, a makeshift lazaretto or "pest house" as it was known. Cotton Mather, local minister, noted in his diary that "The grievous calamity of the smallpox has now entered the town."

The *Seahorse* had been inspected when it first arrived on April 22 and had been declared free of epidemic disease. Only then were crew and passengers permitted to disembark or the cargo unloaded. Quarantine hospitals (lazarettos) were common in seaports, ready to isolate the sick and warn others away from what was considered a contagious disease. The action taken in Boston harbor in 1721 was not uncommon nor was the fear that smallpox aroused. It was not only the Indians who dreaded the signs of the pox. Almost all of the adults in Boston knew that they could suffer the painful and disfiguring results and the likelihood of death if they contracted the disease. Few had acquired immunity.

Those who were able left Boston, then with a population of 11,000, to distance themselves from this plague, knowing full well that anyone who had not had the disease earlier was vulnerable. The last epidemic of smallpox in Boston had been in 1702, and children born since had no protection against the disease. There was no means of curing the disease then. Nor is there a cure today, which is why eliminating the disease in the twentieth century became so important. Prevention was essential, but such measures were not always successful. Once smallpox appeared, it was rapidly communicated to others, seaport cities being the most vulnerable. Arriving ships were often held away from land until inspected to make sure no one on board had the disease.

For centuries smallpox appeared as one of the many endemic disease in Europe, but it became more virulent in the early sixteenth century. It took a deadly toll of its victims, a fearful situation that continued into the eighteenth century and spread havoc among the Native Americans for two centuries. Over time Europeans had observed that mortality among children, except for infants, was not as great as that for adults and that their symptoms were not as devastating even when it was at its most virulent. Scholars note that the lowest fatality rates among Europeans were those between the ages of five and fourteen: as adults those who had survived the outbreak seemed to be immune to the disease. In England prudent parents made sure that their children had early contact with smallpox in the hopes that a milder form would confer that protective immunity In colonial America where people lived in rather isolated communities, seldom coming in contact with the dreaded disease, smallpox always appeared as an epidemic taking the lives of all, regardless of age or social class.

Boston, like many American communities of the time, suffered sporadically from smallpox epidemics with few opportunities to expose children to the disease, and so in 1721 a good part of the Boston population was vulnerable. Deaths could run as high as 20 percent of the population. Although mortality was usually less in America among the British settlers than in England, the disease was no less frightening in its intensity. When possible, people fled from the town, a habit that could spread the disease into the countryside, in a behavior pattern that mimicked the Indians response.

The 1721 epidemic in Boston, however, did not follow the path of previous epidemics. It marked the beginning of a new era in medicine brought on not by a physician but a member of the public, a minister in the Congregational Church, Cotton Mather, whose diary marked the progress of the 1721 epidemic. An idea had captured his imagination that would forever change the way communities reacted to the threat from smallpox. He had studied medicine as a youth with plans to become a doctor and continued his interest in health problems even after he decided to follow his father's path into the ministry. Mather developed an unusual theory, for the time, about the cause of disease. He was among a select few who examined excretions from the body through the microscope and saw something he assumed to be living matter swimming in those liquids. The few Europeans who saw those excretions in the past century had speculated that such "animicular" matter might be the cause of the disease, but they had had no influence on the medical profession. Traditional theory held that disease was caused by bad air, a miasma that upset the balance of humors rather than by living material that incubated in the body. Any living matter that appeared, according to that theory, was an accident, a result of spontaneous generation. Mather, on the other hand, was convinced that the "little animals" that existed in the pus from smallpox victims had something to do with causing the contagion.

An inveterate medical observer and voracious reader of medical treatises, Mather wrote down his theories and observations. His collection of thoughts on health, some culled from his diary begun in the 1720s, was titled the *Angel of Bethesda* and which was not published until 1972. Here he suggested that something more specific than a miasma was a causal factor in smallpox and possibly other diseases. He went further and also suggested that the eggs from that "animicular" matter could invade the body through the pores or the mouth. This was a revolutionary idea and scoffed at by the professionals until the acceptance of the idea of the germ theory of disease a century and a half later.

Mather thought there was some evidence for his idea about a specific cause in the experiences of people across the Atlantic. His African slave, Onesimus. had told him about an operation, "that," wrote Mather, "no Person Ever died of the Smallpox . . . that had courage to use it." Onesimus had been injected with the pus from a smallpox victim and then acquired a mild form of the disease that conferred lifetime immunity. He showed Mather the scar on his arm from just such an inoculation and said it was a common practice among his people in Africa. Later, a few years before the 1721 epidemic, Mather read about a similar procedure used by people in Turkey described by Dr. Emanuel Timonius in a letter to the London Royal Philosophical

Society and published in the major scientific journal of the day, the *Philosophical Transaction*. Timonius had argued that the procedure did protect against the worst aspects of the disease. The 1716 report reminded Mather of what he had learned from his "Guramantee-Servant." He then wrote to the Royal Society to confirm Timonius's observations that the procedure did definitely confer immunity and that once inoculated the patient would suffer only a mild form of the disease. Shortly afterward another experience with inoculation was reported to the Royal Society by a Jacob Pylarius of similar folk practice he too had observed in the East.

Such was the tradition of many people in the Far East, Africa, and Middle East where smallpox had first appeared centuries ago and where the effective preventive measures had been devised and used. No one knew why, nor does anyone today understand exactly how it worked, but by giving someone a milder case of smallpox through an injection of the pus from a sick person, fewer people died than from catching the disease the "natural" way, although the inoculated were still capable of spreading the disease. The British medical profession was ignorant of this "folk" practice until reported in writing by Timonius, Mather, and Pylarius between 1716 and 1718. Mather, the colonial American clergyman, was one of the few from the Americas to make a major contribution to an understanding of disease and to promote the procedure for battling smallpox. Like many clergy and the general public of his time, Mather believed in witches and witchcraft. He agreed with other religious leaders that disease was caused by sin and could be cured by prayer and forgiveness, but he also believed that science could and should come to the aid of faith. Spiritual matters did not hinder his belief in the value of science because Cotton Mather blended science and theology. Those experiments with inoculation were proof that science could help.

To take advantage of these discoveries, Mather proposed calling a meeting of doctors in Boston to discuss this practice called inoculation (or variolation) in the event that smallpox should appear in the town again. Fully aware of the dangers, he was anxious to take steps to prevent the spread of the disease. After noting the appearance of smallpox in Boston in 1721 (the "grievous calamity"), he assembled the doctors at a meeting but ran into immediate opposition to the idea of such an unnatural procedure. It was, after all, practiced by heathen peoples and was unknown to European medicine. According to Dr. William Douglass, a major leader of the opposition and one of Boston's few university-educated physicians, inoculation fit no known theory of disease. Moreover, it was immoral to give someone a disease, ignoring the fact that for generations children had been deliberately exposed. The idea of injecting someone with a deadly disease

A Portrait of Cotton Mather, Puritan minister and 1721 promoter of a smallpox inoculation procedure that he learned from his African slave, Onesimus. (Courtesy of the National Library of Medicine)

was rejected by the medical profession in Boston, except for one doctor, Zabdiel Boylston, trained by his father and other doctors as an apprentice. Unlike Douglass, he had no academic credentials so was less restrained by academic theories. Boylston took a more experimental approach to medicine, willing to put aside all theories and try the procedure by offering to put Mather's suggestion to the test.

On June 26, 1721, Dr. Boylston proceeded to inoculate three people—his six-year-old son, one of his slaves, Jack, and Jack's two-year-old son. The rest of Boylston's family had left Boston in the exodus the previous month. According to Mather, the public reaction to Boyston's experiment was shock and fear, a wild "clamour," he called it. The people of Boston, he complained in his diary, "rave, they rail, they blaspheme, they talk not only like Idiots, but also like Fanaticks." Mather's hyperbole about public hysteria was probably just that, and he may have been reacting to the behavior of the political and medical leaders. A month later when the physicians, local political leaders, and private citizens met again to reconsider the procedure, they heard only a report of some fanciful examples of dangerous complications from inoculation that supposedly took place in France and Spain more than twenty years ago. Boylston entreated the group to observe *his* patients as a more useful sample; by that time he had inoculated seven more people, and all were doing well. His advice was ignored, and the eminent group declared that "Inoculation . . . was likely to prove of dangerous consequences." The opposition, led by William Douglass, a "vain, narrow and stubborn man" as described by one medical historian, began a vendetta to discredit both Mather and Boylston. Douglass reminded his followers that Mather had been associated with the witchcraft scare in 1692, and Boylston he described as a quack, lacking professional training. Douglass was correct in his assessment of the danger: such an operation *could* spread the disease, but many in the public were more than willing to take a chance.

In the absence of any law regarding medical practice, there was no way to restrain a doctor from trying whatever surgery he believed useful. Boylston continued to inoculate his patients, including one of Mather's sons. A part of the lay public, seeing the inoculated alive and healthy in the streets, appealed to Boylston for help. In spite of opposition and warnings that inoculation could spread the disease and could also cause death, his practice grew. By the end of the epidemic he had inoculated 247 people, only six of whom died, probably from causes other than smallpox. Those inoculated were in truth able to communicate the disease in its worst form to others; patients often ignored warnings to isolate themselves until completely well. Boylston may have inadvertently spread the disease by inoculating people who felt well enough to continue their sociable life.

The smallpox epidemic in Boston continued to rise in severity, reaching a peak by October 1721. Entire families became sick at the same time; many shops had to close because so few people dared to venture outdoors. Public meetings stopped except for church services when families submitted requests for prayers for their ailing relatives (and probably inadvertently spreading the disease). By the end of the epidemic, early in 1722, it was estimated that possibly 6,000 had been infected (in a town of 11,000) of whom 844 had died: that is one in six deaths or about 14 percent of those who contracted the disease. The record for Boylston's patients was far superior: only 2 percent of those inoculated died. Nonetheless, the local medicos continued to oppose inoculation, and the epidemic ended with a temporary truce in the war of words between the Douglass and Boylston-Mather factions.

Douglass's prestige as a physician was threatened by those questioning his authority; he especially resented being upstaged by a layman. Part of his objection to the procedure may well have been due to that resentment. He was the only university-trained physician in Boston at the time and had no reason to respect the ideas of those he did not consider his peers. His European education and training, he assumed, put his medical knowledge far above any one else. His opposition in some ways was also a reflection of his lack of confidence in his position in this relatively new and unformed society and an urge to establish his hegemony as medical professional. Years later, when Dr. Alexander Hamilton of Annapolis, with credentials similar to Douglass's, visited Boston. He found the Boston physician to be

a man of good learning but mischievously given to criticism . . . [he is] only a cynicall mortall, so full of his own learning that any other man's is not current with him . . . loath to allow learning, merit, or a character to any body. . . .[He is] of the clinical class of physicians and laughs att all theory and practice founded upon it, looking upon empiricism or bare experience as the only firm bases upon which practice ought to be founded.

This had been Douglass's criticism of Boylston and the other "empirics" during the inoculation controversy. By 1744 Douglass, whose disagreeable personality quirks had not altered, had softened toward the less learned doctors in the community. They were now his own students and disciples. He was now also sufficiently confident of his social status to accept what was becoming an American way of medicine, a decided anti-intellectual strain that emphasized individual experience rather than accepted academic theory.

Concurrent with these events in Massachusetts were similar experiences in England. Lady Mary Wortley Montague, the wife of the British ambassador to Turkey, had returned to London in time to face the 1721 smallpox epidemic there. Her son had been inoculated while in Turkey, and she asked her doctor to perform the operation on her daughter. Supported by the naturalist Sir Hans Sloan, the published letters to the Royal Philosophical Society, and the surgeon Charles Maitland, she convinced the royal family to follow suit. With such distinguished supporters of the preventive measures, it quickly became an acceptable medical practice. Further recognition of the procedure came when the Royal Society of London elected Zabdiel Boylston a Fellow of the Society in 1726 for his daring role in introducing inoculation in America. Nonetheless, few people in the British Isles required such protection. With a larger immune population, epidemics were less severe than in the colonies. But when the threat of an epidemic arose as it did in 1746 and 1752, "inoculation," according to Genevieve Miller was, "taken up at once."

The question of inoculation came up again in Boston when smallpox reappeared in 1730. By that time Douglass had accepted that Boylston and Mather were not completely wrong. He admitted that there was an advantage to inoculation but continued to warn of the potential danger to the rest of the community. "Smallpox," he wrote, "received by inoculation, is not so fatal, and the Symptoms frequently more mild, than in the accidental contagion," but he advised to apply it with "discretion" and to manage the "Distemper" with proper care. Such management required an elaborate procedure using traditional therapies of cathartics, purging, diet, and rest as preparation before inoculating. The preparation was similar to the remedies used to treat smallpox itself. There was still a public health issue, and Douglas was right in his warning about the dangers of contagion. Little was done to overcome the problem of spreading the disease.

Mather's method slowly attracted interest in other colonies. In New York, Cadwallader Colden recommended the new procedure in 1725, and during an epidemic six years later a few doctors did attempt inoculation. But in 1747 a particularly virulent episode in Massachusetts was blamed on the inoculated, and the procedure was forbidden to prevent the further spread of disease in that colony. In Maryland, inoculation ran into little opposition and was encouraged by the leading physicians who in 1750 established a hospital to isolate those being inoculated. During a very severe epidemic in South Carolina in 1738 (one that devastated the Indians in the colony), Charleston had prohibited inoculation within the city. But in his account of the epidemic, Dr. James Kirkpatrick demonstrated again that those he had inoculated in Charleston *before* the prohibition fared better in surviving than others. He successfully changed the public opinion in South Carolina with the publication of his statistics in 1743.

Benjamin Franklin, who had initially opposed the procedure, changed his mind in 1736 after his son died of smallpox, and he urged other parents to consider the procedure to save the lives of their children. In spite of Franklin's support, in Philadelphia most doctors obstinately refused to accept the procedure. As in Boston earlier, the medical establishment led by John Kearsley opposed the use of the inoculation because it could not be supported by the prevailing theories of disease and also because its major proponent had only recently arrived in Philadelphia to take up a medical practice. That was Adam Thomson, who had been trained in Edinburgh, where the idea of specific remedies for different diseases had become fashionable. Thomson in turn was defended by Dr. Alexander Hamilton, his Edinburgh classmate now living in Maryland, in a pamphlet that argued in favor of experimentation and innovation. Hamilton's pamphlet stands out as an important early explication and justification of the procedure. It was widely read and added to a growing enthusiasm for inoculation among both the public and most doctors.

It was hard for old-school professionals like Douglass and Kearsley, fearful of their loss of prestige from upstart competition, to accept a procedure identified with a folk practice, especially one associated with non-Christian people. Such customs, they thought, were heathenish, uncivilized, untried, and therefore suspect. The practical effects—that few of those inoculated died whereas those contracting the disease the "natural" way had a high mortality rate—had too little influence on a profession that demanded a proof of use that was more impressionistic than numerical. Statistical analysis was in its infancy and foreign to the thinking of the medical professional. Numbers then were still inconsequential in understanding the cause or cure of disease, although Mather, Boyston, and Douglass did try to use arithmetic to support their conclusions, Mather taking the first steps and Douglass following his lead. Douglass had reluctantly conceded to Mather and Boylston but, unwilling to completely give in to them, continued to argue against their numbers in later years.

Despite the Philadelphia controversy between Kearsley and Thomson in 1750–51, in the following years there were few objections to inoculation in the colonies. Throughout the 1760s and afterwards more and more reports appeared in local newspapers and pamphlets attesting to the success with inoculation. Not everyone, however, had access to the protection against smallpox. Inoculation was beyond the means of the poor, who were left to suffer the disease in its worst manifestations. Some doctors tried to handle the problem by offering free inoculation. That group included Dr. Robert Tootell in Maryland who offered to inoculate the indigent at no cost. In Boston in 1764 many physicians made a similar offer, and the city allowed the establishment of temporary hospitals for that purpose. The doctors lacked sufficient public support to have ongoing inoculation hospitals

The opposite situation prevailed in Virginia. Norfolk residents rioted in 1768 because a doctor was freely inoculating people without isolating them. A mob burned down the doctor's house and subsequently and effectively petitioned the House of Burgesses to prohibit the practice. Such popular opposition came from those who could not afford either the cost of inoculation or the time away from work for the extensive preparation. And they feared the consequences from their affluent neighbors who could communicate the disease while undergoing the procedure. When the public was at odds with the medical establishment, they showed their displeasure by resisting or forcing action. The effectiveness of inoculation, the meager regulations to protect the public, and the role of the medical profession would be tested, as were many other pressing issues, during the Revolution.

Smallpox, of course was not the only dreaded disease in early America. Yellow fever occurred sporadically until 1805. Typhoid, tuberculosis, influenza, and a host of other infectious diseases were a constant presence. But the most ubiquitous of epidemic diseases in the colonial era was malaria, especially for newcomers, both black and white. The so-called "seasoning" process in the colonies really meant suffering through a bout of malaria and surviving. In the seventeenth century, malaria was a threat even in Massachusetts. But by the beginning of the eighteenth century, it was a problem only south of New York and most prevalent in the South Carolina Low Country. Seldom fatal, recurrent bouts of malaria often weakened the victim so that he became susceptible to more fatal illnesses. Malaria was most likely the major cause of the low birthrate (it caused miscarriages), short lifespan, and poor health in the Chesapeake Bay area.

It was not known at the time that malaria was caused by a mosquito-born parasite, which first infects the liver and then enters the bloodstream. The action of the white blood cells to kill the parasite sets off a reaction that results in the typical symptoms: intervals of sharp chills and high fever accompanied by headaches and fatigue. There are several species of the parasite that can cause a range of virulence. It was usually the mild form of the parasite (*Plasmodium vivax*) that plagued the colonies, but a more dangerous strain (*falciparum*) could kill and was especially dangerous for those under the age of five. Unlike smallpox, previous exposure to the malaria parasite did not provide full protection against a recurrence. After an initial attack of the more deadly *Plasmodium falciparum*, some immunity was acquired, but victims (if they survived) could be reinfected several times before full immunity became possible. In the *vivax* form, death was less likely, but the parasite remained dormant in the liver and could cause a relapse months or years later. Because the milder *vivax* plagued the colonies most often, relapses were always possible, even when isolated from the mosquito.

Many Africans arrived in the colonies with a genetic immunity to various types of malaria. An African woman who had had the *falciparum* type could transfer her immunity to her children, but they could not pass it on to the next generation. Additionally about 90 percent of West Africans carry the "Duffy antigen" in their genes that makes them resistant to the *vivax* form. Some 70 percent of African Americans have inherited that antigen. Unlike the sickle-cell trait (found in Africans as well as some people from the Mediterranean area) that also confers some immunity to malaria, the Duffy antigen has no adverse side effects. Sickle cells can predispose individuals to pneumococcal infections and other problems. Not all people of African descent carried those protective genetic factors and, as with those of European descent, only repeated infection in the most malaria-ridden areas provided future protection. Those repeated infections were just as debilitating for both groups. But excessive work, deficient diet, and unhealthy living conditions of the slaves contributed to more sickness and discomfort, and left them susceptible to other diseases that were rampant at the time

There was no Cotton Mather to analyze the source of the disease or suggest some new theory about this "intermittent fever," and nothing at the time was known of insect vectors. It became obvious, though, that malaria was most prevalent in the summer and fall, and in low-lying swampy areas. Quarantine measures did not work, so the usual means of prevention were useless. Common sense dictated that those who could should go to higher ground during the season and many in South Carolina did, which, of course, left the slaves and the poorer whites, who could not migrate, constantly subject to debilitating attacks of malaria.

As with other diseases throughout Europe and America, doctors followed a regime of depletion, bleeding, and purging to remove the infected matter; infusions made from the bark of various trees reduced the fever. Dogwood bark had become a favorite antidote. It relieved the symptoms but was ineffective against the parasite. During the seventeenth century, the Spanish in South America discovered that the bark of the cinchona tree not only eased the symptoms of the disease but also apparently helped to cure malaria. This bark, known as "Jesuit's bark," contains a quinine alkaloid and proved effective in killing the parasite. The remedy, like the inoculation for smallpox, did not fit any of the known theories about disease, but its obvious value made quinine an acceptable antidote and a useful addition to the apothecary's medicine cabinet.

Such was the personal experience of Dr. Alexander Hamilton in Annapolis in his experience with malaria—not as a doctor but as a patient. He had arrived in Maryland in late 1738 and by the next summer was laid low with what was described as an "intermittent fever." In a letter to his brother in Edinburgh he reported that he "now had had my seasoning in the country." For two weeks he had experienced

> a very Severe Sickness, Such as I never felt in my Life before . . . the most violent fevers that can be Imagined, being deprived utterly of my Senses and Speech during the continuance of them. [The sweats were] as thick almost as boild starch that Stuck in the pores, and weakened me more than anything else."

During the intermissions of the fever he became so weak that he could not hold up his head but recovered due to his brother's advice (another doctor in Maryland), "who removed the distemper," he announced, "by administrating the Jesuits bark." Nonetheless, Hamilton did not fully recover. During the following summers, he suffered repeated bouts of malaria, complaining "that the remains of that Seasoning Sickness" stuck close to him and caused a host of other debilitating conditions. It took him four years to completely recover.

Cinchona bark usually did alleviate the worst symptoms of malaria, but it was not always effective and not universally applied. As a specific for that one disease, malaria, doctors like John Kearsley in Philadelphia rejected its use because it did not fit into any known theory about the cause or cure of fevers. Other doctors used it indiscriminately for all fevers because, like other barks, it could reduce fever regardless of the cause. When it did not work to cure nonmalarial conditions, doctors abstained from prescribing "the bark" for any disease. There was no standard dosage for the cinchona bark; often too little was given and the poor quality of the material hindered any therapeutic value. At the least it caused no harm. The wise medical person made good use of what was at hand, whether smallpox inoculation or "Jesuit's bark," despite the lack of knowledge about how or why they worked. But not all were wise, and protests against therapies that conflicted with established theory and practice limited the use of what could be helpful.

Although health professionals had access (even if they chose not to use them) to methods of amelioration for both smallpox and malaria, the same cannot be said of other diseases that appeared as epidemics in early America. Measles, which was an endemic children's disease in England, appeared as epidemics in America. With its short incubation period (8 to 12 days), few ships' passengers arrived with the disease in its contagious state because the voyage took three or more months. During the eighteenth century, ships sailed faster and the danger of carrying sick passengers increased with the shortened time. Meanwhile, sparsely populated areas kept children out of contact with carriers, and without contact with measles as children, adults—whether Native American, African, or European—were more vulnerable and thus in danger of more serious complications. The first record of measles in the English colonies was in Boston in 1657 when many adults were still immune. But an epidemic in 1713 brought heavy adult fatalities. By the late 1740s many of the colonies were suffering epidemics of measles, and ten years later another epidemic was widespread among the colonies, which took an especially heavy toll on life in Philadelphia.

Doctors followed the usual regime of bleeding, vomiting, and purging, which probably increased the danger of death. But some laymen left behind recommendations for less drastic measures. Wait Winthrop of Boston advised taking sage and baum tea, to keep warm and to "let nature take its course" without the usual depletion process. Cotton Mather, who lost his wife, a maid, and three children within two weeks from the disease, noted correctly that measles was a "Light Malady" in Europe but was a "calamity" in the colonies. The problem with measles was not necessarily with the disease itself but the deadly complications that often followed. Mather, as usual, was right about the disease as well as the treatment. His advice. like Winthrop's, was for complete rest with the warning that a high fever could follow the conclusion of the rash. This was not a course of treatment popular with doctors because it did not require active treatment. but it indicates that laymen could and did disregard drastic therapies. Douglass and Kearney had good reason to be concerned for their future role as professionals.

Measles epidemics raged regularly in the colonies until, as John Duffy points out in his classic study of epidemics in colonial America, the intervals between outbreaks became shorter and shorter until they "permitted the development of a considerable group of non-immunes." As the disease became self-sustaining within each community (i.e., did not require an outside source of infection), it reverted to its usual children's mild disease with the occasional deadly complication of throat, respiratory, or intestinal infection. Such was the case by the end of the eighteenth century.

If smallpox, malaria, and measles did not kill the colonists, there was also the danger from the winter diseases, often called "pleuristic disorders," which may have been influenza, pneumonia, or pleurisy (inflammation of the lining of the lungs). Colonies, both North and South, suffered from poorly ventilated houses, unsanitary living conditions, and often lack of adequate nutrition in the winter months. Each year brought reports of a variety of unspecified fevers and upper respiratory problems. One of the worst years was in Maryland in 1750 when forty people died in a short period of time in early January. The winter diseases fell hardest on the poor and especially on the black slaves, who ranked highest on the list of fatalities. Many observers noted African Americans' susceptibility to pulmonary infections, but whether it was due to genetic or environmental factors is not clear. It is likely that the immune systems of people from Africa, who had not been exposed to the germs that cause pulmonary diseases in the Old Country, left them especially vulnerable. The sickle-cell trait that provided protection against malaria, may also have contributed to the winter fatalities among the black population. And, of course, the situation was complicated by the poor and cramped living conditions in the slave quarters.

All colonists suffered from dysentery, which ranked second among the debilitating diseases after malaria. Often called a "bloody flux," the symptoms included fever, bloody evacuations in diarrhea, and cramps. Although there were outbreaks everywhere, the mortality was greatest in the Carolinas and is well documented in the correspondence of the missionaries sent by the Church of England. One reported in 1710 that "This Distemper is one of those incident to this climate, and has been fatal to a great many this year." Like most newcomers, the missionaries were more subject to dysentery as well as the other "seasoning" disease, malaria. Farther north, as malaria disappeared, dysentery took its place. One new arrival noted in 1751 that "various kinds of fevers rage fatally & fluxes carry off Numbers." Dysentery has become the "Common Distemper." The usual remedies of bleeding, vomiting, and occasionally a laxative to further purge the body if the diarrhea was not sufficient, offered little release. Cotton Mather, in his usual less extreme regimen, suggested sweating and a vomit. Occasionally doctors added an opiate to relieve pain and for its antidiarrheal effect along with a host of strange and obnoxious ingredients from "Ratts-Dung" to deer's horn and turpentine.

Other diseases that appeared as epidemics such as typhoid fever, yellow fever, diphtheria, and scarlet fever played more minor roles in health in the colonial period. Diphtheria and scarlet fever were restricted largely to children who had escaped smallpox as a major cause of death. Although dangerous, the most virulent form of diphtheria would not appear until the mid-nineteenth century with a much higher mortality rate. Typhoid fever was often confused with dysentery but was distinguished by a constant high fever or a "continuous" or long fever. It appeared sporadically in most of the colonies. However, it was not, according to John Duffy, one of the chief "infectious disorders." Yellow fever would not become a menace until after the Revolution and is discussed in a chapter 6. A host of other unidentified agues and fevers stalked the colonists, most of these illnesses difficult to identify because the descriptions are too general.

Protection against epidemic diseases was minimal in the colonial era. Smallpox inoculation was a saving grace, but not all colonists had access to it or even wanted it. Parents were often afraid if they inoculated one child others in the household would be susceptible to the more virulent form of the disease. Rural areas, protected by isolation, had fewer reasons to resort to that drastic operation. The poor remained unprotected except when a benevolent gesture from a local doctor offered free treatment. But such offers were not consistent, and most communities continued to rely on isolation as the safest method. The continuation of severe epidemics of so many diseases throughout the eighteenth century testifies to the failure of those actions. In fact, none of these diseases could be cured except malaria. In all other cases, medicine could relieve pain; it could not save lives.

The small number of professionally trained physicians who had been educated abroad looked to tradition and approved theory rather than innovation or experimentation. Some, like Douglass in Boston (in his early years) and John Kearsley in Philadelphia, worried more about safeguards and a loss of reputation if they accepted unorthodox procedures. Others, like the apprentice-trained Boylston, because of their ignorance of tradition and academic niceties, depended on trial and error to learn and were willing to attempt new methods even recklessly. The conflict within the medical profession of traditional versus experimental treatments—and that often drew the lay public into the controversy—gradually dissolved the magical aura that had accompanied the physician for so many centuries; it would eventually lead to a loss of faith in their mostly ineffective medicine. Although the controversy over smallpox inoculation was an early sign of that tension between physician and populace, those who challenged orthodox medicine in those early years remained on the sidelines as a small minority—an annoyance, an oddity of the times that could be overcome by the traditional power and prestige of the educated elite. Whatever tension existed in the relationship between doctor and patient in the pre-Revolutionary era was kept under control by the acceptance of the elite status of the university-educated physician. He (and they were always men) was still wrapped in an aura of almost magical esoteric talent, and their medicines were imbued with supposedly powerful antidotes to the ills of mankind. The greater challenge to the authority of the physician in the eighteenth century would come from another direction: a variety of popular medical practices that were spreading among a population that would in time become decidedly less deferential.

3

Tools of the Trade

On October 14, 1743, Dr. William Wooten visited the family of James Cann, a carpenter in Anne Arundel County, Maryland. Mrs. Cann complained of "a long Continued Intermittent Fever." For this condition Dr. Wooten prescribed a "vomit" and gave her eight double doses of the "Bark" with "aromaticks," the latter to cover the bitter taste with a sweet odor. One of their children suffered from an "asthma and peri-pneumonias," an upper respiratory and lung condition that he treated with a "Large pot of Expectorating Electuary;" a sweetened tonic to aid in clearing the mucus. But he also provided a "Blister" for the child—raising a blister by putting heated cups on the skin. Dr. Wooten recommended for the child (gender and age unspecified) a glister (enema) and further cupping to create more pus-filled blisters. Like the vomit for Mrs. Cann, the glister and the blisters were designed to remove some substance from the child's body that supposedly was causing the breathing difficulties. The presence of pus was good; it brought the "morbid" matter to the surface, which could then be removed. When the blister was broken, the resulting pus was drained. These were less drastic procedures than bleeding (venesection), a process not recommended for childhood illnesses.

These treatments were common and would have been familiar to doctors and domestic healers throughout the Western world, based on a theory of illness that had prevailed for 2,500 years. Expounded first by Hippocrates in the fifth century BCE and slightly modified by Roman physician Galen in 130 CE the theorists assumed that disease or any ill health was a result of a morbid state of bodily humors (blood, yellow and black bile, and phlegm). The doctor's role was to restore the balance of those humors by depleting the excess. Recovery meant that the morbid matter had been removed. In the eighteenth century new theories called "nosologies" suggested that the source of the offending matter was possibly in just one of those humors or that lay in the spasms of the vessels. In any case, depletion of some bodily liquid was essential to restore order. Illness then was not a distinct disease; it meant that something was out of balance within the individual and had to be treated accordingly. The new theories had not suggested any major changes in those therapies that provided visible and predictable effects.

The discovery of inoculation for smallpox and the use of quinine for malaria should have led to a questioning of those traditional theories. If one remedy cured or prevented only one disease and did so for all patients, then the problem should not have been interpreted as something within the individual constitution but specific to a particular disease. A more scientific attitude, a more rational view of these two discoveries, might have led toward a search for more specific remedies much as Cotton Mather had proposed and was beginning to influence medical thought in the Old World. That did not happen in the British colonies. Those who could not reconcile the contradiction between the use of specifics and the general states theory of the Greeks rejected the newer procedures in favor of established practice. They focused on removing the excess humors by purging, vomiting, sweating, salivating, bleeding, leeching, or cupping. Others, less influenced by theories, casually ignored the contradiction and combined both therapies. Such was the approach of Dr. Wooten.

His early treatment of Mrs. Cann and the child followed orthodox recommendations. The results were obvious and predictable; whether they had any therapeutic value is another question other than causing more misery. The medication may have alleviated some of the symptoms, but we can never know because neither the diagnosis nor the exact ingredients is known. The expectorant prescribed for the child is not specified; it could have been anything from honey to myrrh or turmeric combined with vinegar, and it may well have relieved the child's immediate symptoms. The following fall Wooten visited again and provided a "phial of asthmatic Elixir for the child."

For Mrs. Cann he also gave a heavy dose of the "Bark," an indication of his use of a specific. The intermittent fever may well have been malaria, and the quinine in the medication therefore useful for that purpose. But there was no laboratory test to establish the cause of her fever or establish a correct dose of quinine. If she revived after his attention, it could just as well have been nature healing as the quality of the medication. But no doubt Wooten took the credit for her cure. Records do not indicate a further follow-up for Mrs. Cann.

Little is known about Dr. William Wooten or his training. His father had emigrated from England early in the century and his family lived in Londontown, near Annapolis. Wooten died in 1744 and left no ledgers or accounts of his practice. He was probably one of the many apprentice-trained doctors that successfully competed with those of formal education and was often scorned as an "empiric" or "quack" for his lack of esoteric knowledge. But his therapies in the case of the Cann family did not differ essentially from traditional medicine or even folk remedies. We know about this particular event because Wooton's widow, Elizabeth, sued James Cann for the cost of that 1743 visit (and several others) when he failed to pay his bill. Other doctors or their heirs had taken similar action. Such court records, which itemize medical bills, provide some insight into the way medicine was practiced during the colonial era, many of them itemizing the various remedies used, and the variety of pills, powders, ointments, opiates, astringents (for diarrhea), diuretics (for edemas), and the specifics of mercury (for venereal disease) and quinine (for fevers) provided as medications.

This approach to illness is similar to that found in the few extant doctor's ledgers in New England. The doctors may have shared the general theory of disease inherited from the Greeks, but they varied in the kinds of procedures or medications prescribed for similar symptoms. Exactly what was prescribed depended on the personal experiences of the practitioners and their particular training, and possibly what their patients could afford. Some preferred to bleed more often using the lancet to pierce the skin, others to purge, to cause a sweat or salivation, but all were focused on depletion of some bodily substance. Bleeding was not as popular as cupping or leeching until later in the century.

Diagnoses were generally based on symptoms as described by the patient. The doctor seldom touched the patient except to take a pulse or check for fever and thus was dependent on how individuals described their pains or discomforts. He would then diagnose a flux as anything from simple diarrhea to dysentery, typhoid, or typhus. A pox was any kind of skin eruption such as smallpox, syphilis (great pox), and sometimes measles. A quinsy was a throat disorder that could be diphtheria or an infection of the esophagus or possibly whooping cough. A pleurisy referred to respiratory or lung diseases such an influenza or pneumonia. If the patient's skin was very hot, then a fever was diagnosed, and the type depended on the intervals between shivers and the rate of the pulse. Thus there were tertian, quartan, and intermittent fevers. A severe fever with many other symptoms was called a "bilious fever", which could have been yellow fever. Historians do not always agree on what particular disease has infected a community because the diagnoses were often too vague for any useful analysis.

In spite of these deficiencies, eighteenth-century medicine had made some progress by rejecting the supernatural as a cause of disease, an idea that had infiltrated medical practice during the Middle Ages. In the centuries following the decline of Roman civilization, under the influence of the Christian church, people thought of disease as a visitation from God for their sins. As late as the seventeenth-century, Puritans prescribed days of fasting and humiliation as cures. Doctors could help to cure, but the priest or minister was of greater value. The eighteenth-century colonist still prayed for recovery but relied more and more often on the comfort of medical intervention to focus on natural causes. Western orthodox medicine (as distinguished from folk healing) had begun a major shift from a spiritual to a rational basis drawing even more on the older Greek humoral theory. Disease, it was now assumed, had only natural causes, did not require the intervention of spiritual counsel, and could be cured by medical therapies regardless of how little evidence the doctors had to prove their effectiveness or safety.

Some of the medicines prescribed were harmless, but many could cause dangerous side effects. Mercury, often prescribed for syphilis, caused hair loss, discolored teeth, and injury to the nervous system. For the pregnant or lactating woman, mercury could cross the placental barrier or be concentrated in breast milk. Laxatives used for purges could leach nutrients and electrolytes from the body. Commonly used calomel (a combination of mercury and chloride) for purgatives was poisonous and is now used an insecticide and fungicide. Dehydration was a real possibility with many of the depletion procedures.

One of the more drastic of the depletion procedures, venesection or bloodletting may have had some advantages. By lowering the availability of iron in the blood, some pathogens lose their ability to grow and multiply, thus aiding the body to throw off the disease. Bleeding also lowers the viscosity of blood and may possibly reduce blood pressure. These are extreme methods of bringing about such changes and could also easily lead to death. If nothing else, bleeding to the point of fainting will force the patient to rest and let the body heal. Nonetheless it is hard to see how removing blood helped those with smallpox, yellow fever, pneumonia, stomach disorders, or discomfort during pregnancy—all conditions for which it was practiced.

Clinical trials, statistics, and laboratory investigations had little to do with medicine. Libraries, according to Charles Rosenberg, backed up by "a structure of formal ideas," were the relevant sources of information on health and disease for the highly respected physician. Physicians easily ignored the microscope as a source of information. Living creatures seen through the lens came about, they assumed, through spontaneous combustion and thus were irrelevant to the cause of poor health. Such "animicular" matters were possibly a result but not a cause of disease. Even though the clinical thermometer was also available (although in a very primitive form), doctors preferred to rely on their hands and eyes in determining the extent of fever, at least until the middle of the nineteenth century. Neither science nor technology had any application to medicine in the eighteenth century. Medicine was thought to be an art dependent on the skill of the doctor.

The most potent medicine in the medical bag was not in the procedures used or in the medications prescribed. It was in the nature of the doctor himself, the belief that he was right. The real power in any healer's arsenal of cures was in the aura of authority and omniscience. That ability had less to do with the prescribed potions and procedures than the power of suggestion: the placebo effect. Patients endowed their medical practitioners with enormous authority; they believed in their power to cure. Few patients had reason to question the power that was based on centuries of belief about the nature of disease and the means of curing human ailments. The dramatic results of the prescribed therapies gave visible proof of the doctor's magical ability to bring about change to the body, changes that were thought to be necessary to restore the balance of the humors and thus to effect a cure. Science could offer no alternatives to such beliefs until the latter part of the nineteenth century. There was, therefore, little reason at the time to question the medical assumptions of the healer, whether educated or folk. Physicians, in particular, continued to follow the bizarre prescriptions (including cow and horse dung, and assorted other excrements as poultices and sometimes mixed into medications taken by mouth) listed in the accepted pharmacopoeias.

No matter how many people failed to thrive under the ministrations of the physician, there was no blame laid on his therapies. The doctor was considered successful if he seemingly cured one person, and only a few testimonials were necessary to attest to such skill. In the eyes of the public, failure did not count; only minimal success pointed to the value of medicine. As today a certain number of people recover from the most life-threatening conditions or go into remission without medical intervention, many health problems resolve themselves even if nothing is done. So too in the old days people survived despite the most inappropriate therapies. That a few patients did recover was taken as proof of the power of the healer to cure.

Hidden among the strange medications used at the time were some remedies that may have had therapeutic value. Quinine and smallpox inoculation probably saved many lives and alleviated some discomforts when used correctly. In addition, opium, in a variety of forms, had an ancient history and was widely used for pain and a sedative, as were other narcotics and hallucinogens like mandrake, henbane, and hellebore. With ergot, most people knew it was possible to hasten births but it was also used as an abortificiant, which, in the language of the day, was expected to "stop the obstruction of the menses." For a "dropsy," an accumulation of fluid in the body that may have been due to weak heart action, doctors resorted to fox glove, a folk-remedy plant that contains digitalis. And, of course, the ipecac, jalab, calomel, and other such laxatives and vomits had the expected result; but whether they actually aided in cures in questionable. In addition, the dosages were not standardized and varied with each practitioner. They were often diluted or mixed with other ingredients that modified any possible therapeutic value. The quality of those plants also varied, depending on soil and growing conditions. The erratic results from those medications contributed to the idea that diseases were peculiar to individuals; each individual required different medications or combinations and depended on the physician's special understanding of illness. There were wide variations in therapies—some practitioners preferring one type of medication or procedure and others relying on a different approach. The lack of standards would eventually help to undermine confidence in all orthodox medicine.

The physician held a special place in the social hierarchy of medical practitioners. He (and physicians were always men) was at the top, as an educated member of the elite, and therefore assumed the deference accorded to his class. His decisions were compelling. When England was planting her colonies in the New World, academically trained doctors were scarce, and those

Every Man His Own Doctor; or The Poor Planter's Physician. Cover of a facsimile of John Tennent's 1734 American edition of his manual for the "plain and safe means for persons to cure themselves" to avoid the expense of paying a doctor. The remedies include the conventional bleeding, laxatives, and vomits using local herbs. (Courtesy of the Colonial Williamsburg Foundation)

Every Man his own *Doctor:*

O R,

The Poor Planter's Physician.

Prescribing

Plain and Easy Means for Persons to cure themselves of all, or most of the Distempers, incident to this Climate, and with very little Charge, the Medicines being chiefly of the Growth and Production of this Country.

———————— ———— ———— But many Shapes
Of DEATH, and many are the Ways that lead
To his grim Cave, all dismal, yet to Sense
More terrible at th'Entrance, than within.
Some, as thou saw'st, by violent Stroke shall dye,
By Fire, Flood, Famine, by *Intemperance* more
In Meats and Drinks, which on the Earth shall bring
Diseases dire, and Doctors still more baneful.
             Last Edition of *Paradise lost*, Book XI.

The Third EDITION, with Additions.

Printed and Sold by WIL. PARKS, at his Printing-Offices in *Williamsburg*, and *Annapolis*. 1736.

with such credentials were much in demand. It is possible that their social status and the public confidence in their skills grew in proportion to their scarcity. Dr. Alexander Hamilton (see chap. 2) was a Scotsman with a rarely seen medical degree from the University of Edinburgh. A well-mannered gentleman from a highly respected genteel family but with few financial resources, he became physician to the political and social elite in the Maryland colony soon after his arrival in 1737. To cap his achievements he married a daughter of one of the richest men in the colony, successfully entered the political realm, and became a leading figure in social and cultural life when he founded the famous Tuesday Club of Annapolis in 1745. This organization was primarily for those interested in literary, musical, and other such cultural concerns, not readily found in colonial America. His social position and education might have had more to do with his success as a physician than any scientific training or medical skill, but he probably did less harm than those who had not had the benefit of his training in anatomy and the newer medical theories.

Those like Dr. Hamilton educated either in Holland or Scotland had the advantage of a new eclectic perspective that recognized the healing power of nature and tended to avoid depletion procedures as much as possible. Many physicians also came to the conclusion that there were specific diseases with distinct causes and specific remedies. The success of inoculation and the cinchona bark added to the belief in specific diseases that was spreading through the faculty of those major medical institutions in Europe. Since the university-educated were trained to keep careful clinical notes of their observations, this became a start toward a more scientific medicine. Unfortunately, there were too few in the colonies who were familiar with those developments, and by the end of the century such ideas would be overtaken by newer humoral theories that led to more extreme measures.

While traveling through the colonies in 1744, Dr. Hamilton met several people who were eager to inform him of deficiencies in medical knowledge. One traveler he met on Long Island, New York, ranted against doctors (along with lawyers and the clergy), who "tricked the rest of mankind out of the best part of their substance and made them pay well for doing nothing." In upstate New York, he heard another complaint about doctors; the experience that the complainer spoke about had taught him "to shun them as one would imposters and cheats." He asked Dr. Hamilton to "Find me a doctor among the best of you, that can mend a man's body half so well as a joiner can help a crazy table or stool."

Roy Porter wrote about similar critical comments from disgruntled patients in England, a sentiment that was echoed in a popular do-it-yourself medical handbook compiled by the English physician John Tennent.

So many poor people, Tennent noted, avoided doctors because they "think the remedy near as bad as the Disease. . . . [Doctors are] so exorbitant in their Fees, whether they kill or cure, that the poor Patient had rather trust to his Constitution, than run the Risque of beggaring his Family." Tennent thus recommended the "cheapest and easiest ways of getting well again" with medications drawn from local plants administered by the layperson. Tennent's commentary and the popularity of his book, which went through several editions in America, are indicative of the tension between the domestic and profession spheres of practice and confirms Dr. Hamilton's impression of the unpopularity of doctors among the less affluent who preferred their own traditional medical remedies.

Every Man His Own Doctor was only one of many such self-help books written by both doctors and laymen. Lamar Murphy, who has made an exhaustive study of those self-help works, suggests that the writers of medical manuals encouraged rather than challenged domestic medical practice, noting that the esoterica of orthodox medicine was not a monopoly of the professional. Among the more popular in the eighteenth century was the seventeenth-century work by Nicholas Culpepper, *The English Physician*; George Cheyne's *Essay on Health and Long Life*, first published in 1724 and followed by at least six English editions by 1745; John Wesley's *Primitive Physician* of 1747, which transmitted both folk traditions and that of learned authorities; and Scottish physician William Buchan's 1769 *Domestic Medicine*, written to introduce the folk to the established medical practices in order to undermine reliance on older superstitious beliefs.

There was an outpouring of such publications in the first half of the eighteenth century. The presence of these titles in American libraries attests to the widespread knowledge of orthodox medical procedures in the colonial mind and of the tenuous hold doctors had on the practice of medicine. In addition, local newspapers and the popular London *Gentleman's Magazine* published many remedies that were intended for lay administration. At least in the pre-Revolutionary era, doctors approved of the layperson acquiring medical knowledge as part of their partnership in the curing process. The patient's knowledge of medicine supposedly supported the doctor's treatment and his authority. But, however, there were exceptions.

Landon Carter of South Carolina, an affluent layperson well read in medical literature, called on doctors only when his own remedies failed to work. Carter complained of the "harsh medicines" recommended for his daughter and stepped over the line of propriety when he directly questioned the physician's treatment advice for her. Instead of humbly accepting the professional's opinion, Carter challenged his authority. Such impertinence was unusual but was not necessarily a threat in the context of the eighteenth-century acceptance of the medical man's therapies. Only when large numbers of people began to challenge orthodox medical practice in much the same way that Carter did, would such behavior imperil the physician's position and authority. What Carter did not challenge was the traditional theory of illness, nor did anyone else, except for Cotton Mather, suggest that there could be another explanation for illness and disease other than an imbalance of humors. As long as humoral theory prevailed among the populace, the physician's therapies maintained a hold on colonial America.

Alongside the acknowledged physician, whether apprentice trained or university educated, were a host of medical practitioners that formed a shadow health system made up of midwives, herbalists, and cunning people from Britain, African obeahs or conjurers, the local minister, and the ordinary housewife who kept her recipes for her family's ills. This group regularly treated more people than did the traditional physician. They were less expensive—often free of cost, carried knowledge of treatments that more often than not worked for minor ills, and used less drastic remedies. Unlike the physicians they seldom left records, legal or otherwise, and their routines are harder to discern. References to these healers and midwives are often hidden within their own diaries or in those of their patients, or as witnesses to events noted in a legal report (but not as major protagonists in court cases), in plantation records, in elusive recipe books kept by their families, in the oral folklore of a particular ethnic group, or in the presence of self-help medical manuals. In some cases their treatments came to light a century later when some enterprising scientist decided to test the oral record of a particular remedy, such as aspirin and digitalis, and brought those practices to the professional's attention.

Most historians, regardless of their approach to medical history, agree that this informal health system was probably much more important in the day-to-day lives of colonial peoples in early America than the medical establishment. As mentioned earlier, university-trained physicians were rare and expensive; even the apprentice-trained empirics were costly. And too, it is obvious that few people wanted to subject themselves to the unpleasant and painful therapies of orthodox medical practitioners. Most people dealt with their illnesses with home recipes, drawing on an outside person only when those lay remedies refused to work. In many rural areas there were no trained medical personnel available, and locals had no choice but to fall back on folk remedies, stick to their "kitchen physick," call on the local minister, or consult with a local herb doctor. Thus the health of most early Americans was in the hands of family and neighbors with the least formal training or knowledge of the workings of the body. The lay treatments, however, like those of the trained physician, were based on traditions and theories that bore little relationship to the causes of their maladies and still depended on a variety of depletion procedures. Tradition (and the ubiquitous placebo effect) gave confidence to continue with whatever remedies the family had followed in the past.

The boundaries between professional and lay healers were not clearly defined before the end of the nineteenth century. During the colonial era in particular, people, even of the upper class, were expected to diagnose and treat a host of illnesses without a doctor. Landon Carter was not alone. Eliza Lucas Pinckney's commonplace book, begun in 1756, included a collection of recipes for both food and medicine, many of which were copied and amended to reflect newer information by her daughter Harriet Horry in the typical "kitchen physic" manner. They generally followed the practice of mainstream medicine, much of it taken from the medical manuals. They also included what Kay Moss calls "a few curious remedies," such as the cure for yaws that included brass and steel filings, brimstone (sulfur), gun powder, and black pepper ground up and added to "fowle dung" and some local flowers put into a broth and used as an ointment. Other commonplace books, many of which were kept by women, also followed orthodox practice using angelica for poison, antimony as an emetic, and arsenic for cancer and fever, calomel as a purgative, and Indian sassafras tea for many ailments. Garlic was widely used as a remedy for all kinds of diseases from chest complaints to palsy, fever, dropsy, and colic, and these remedies, too, were often copied from the available self-help medical manuals

Alongside the orthodox medications were a host of carryovers from folklore reflecting magical practices from the distant past. There is a long tradition of curative charms among German and Irish folk, many of which continued into twentieth-century Appalachia. Sometimes old English lore was influenced by Indian mystical practices. One adaptation of an Indian cure for a child's hernia required one-and a-half-inch of the penis of a deer "culled in the old of the moon" and boiled in milk. The child was to drink the concoction three mornings running (between cock crow and daylight) while abstaining from other foods. Like many other folk cures, this remedy included a boiled liquid and an obnoxious material ingested according to some mystical rite. The penis of various animals was assumed to have curative value in both societies. Such a remedy was in line with other sympathetic magical practices such as stopping a nose bleed by having a few drops of blood fall on a knife (to cut the bleeding), or curing asthma by "measuring"—cut a stick the length of a child and place it up the chimney.

As the child outgrew the size of the stick, so too he or she would outgrow the asthma. Such superstitious beliefs did not die out in the eighteenth century but persisted over the next centuries, no doubt continuing to undermine the role of the professional even after modern medicine broke with humoral theory.

One counterweight to the superstitious layman, and probably the most learned of the lay practitioners, was the clergyman who ministered to the rural areas. They were well read, had medical books in their libraries, and often wrote about health and medical treatments. Cotton Mather was not the only cleric to deal with diseases. The Reverend Jabez Fitch prepared a statistical account in the 1730s of a "throat distemper" (probably diphtheria) he observed in New Hampshire. John Wesley's *Primitive Physician* went through seven American editions between 1747 and 1829 and warned against excessive bloodletting and strong drugs. Ebenezer Parkman, a minister in Westborough, Massachusetts, kept a diary between 1724 and 1782 recording the many times he assisted at the sick beds of his parishioners. In Maryland Thomas Bacon depended on his large library of medical books, works on anatomy, midwifery, surgery, children's diseases, pharmacology, and diseases, and included the "Entire Works "of Dr. Thomas Sydenham, a noted seventeenth-century advocate of clinical medicine and natural healing. To supplement his books, Bacon had an extensive set of medical instruments and utensils for the preparation of medications all listed in his inventory. The German settlers in Pennsylvania had their own ministerial sources for medical care. Heinrich Melchoir Muhlenberg is the best known of such providers, as he too was called on to care for the sick using drugs as much as faith to comfort.

Those clerics provided a public service, promising the least damage to the health of their parishioners or competition for professional medical personnel. Like the do-it-yourself medical books and the kitchen physic, the minister-medico reinforced orthodox medical practice and theory. Like the "kitchen physic," they often suggested less drastic measures than expected of the physician. By offering low-cost or free medical advice that caused the least pain and discomfort, the clergy were playing a part in undermining faith in the necessity for the professional doctor. As Americans relied more and more on their own devices and that of the amateurs in the community, they had fewer reasons to call on the high-cost physician, and that made it much easier to reject the professional completely in the future when social conditions undermined the authority of such an elite body.

Indian remedies easily entered into the local medical lore of the various European groups who settled in America, supplementing and sometimes replacing the Old World drugs. Based on the belief that the Native Americans, who had lived in this land for so long and had appeared so healthy and tall at first contact, must have acquired knowledge about local herbs, the colonists borrowed and adapted remedies from the tribes in the area. Sassafras, ipecac, tobacco, and ginseng were native plants that were adapted by white practitioners. In addition, exchange of remedies was made easier because both Natives and Europeans believed in the doctrine of signature—that the shape of a plant gave a hint of its curative powers. Because European lore already accepted hairlike herbs for baldness and wormlike ones for worms, there was no difficulty in accepting the Indian remedy of snakeroot for snakebites. Indians too readily adapted European medications, but the choice could be purely accidental, relying on what they considered mystical signs to indicate usefulness. None of this exchange was coercive. Indians were not forced to accept European cures, nor did Indians have reason to resent the colonists' practices. In time the exchange of drugs and the similarity of practices also make it difficult to determine who first used a particular remedy or how it was altered.

Those practicing medicine in America—whether Indian shamans, English folk herbalists, or traditional European surgeons, apothecaries, and physicians—all employed similar techniques although their explanations for treatment varied. They all aimed to remove the offending substance from the body and to relieve symptoms with some kind of medication. Indian drugs, for instance, like those of the European pharmacopeias, included purgatives, emetics, sudorifics to induce sweating, or expectorants for phlegm. One early observer, John Lawson, noted among the North Carolina Indians, that the medicine man cut the skin of a sick man in several places. He then sucked out the blood that he put into a vessel and buried to eliminate the offending spirit. The depletion procedure echoed the practices of the European therapy to remove a substance from the body but here, the remedy was attended with more mystical rites. The Natives also relied heavily on the sweat bath, which was created by pouring water on hot rocks in a closed area and was ubiquitous among American tribes.

Native Americans may have used therapies similar to that of Europeans, but they ascribed their illnesses to an offended or malevolent spirit. According to John Duffy, the function of the medicine man was to "divine which spirit was causing the trouble and either propitiate that spirit or secure the intervention of a friendly spirit." Thus the medicine man/shaman drew on a variety of incantations, dances, amulets, and other sacred objects combined with the usage of herbs sprinkled or blown on the person. Native Americans had found herbs to use as expectorants or diuretics whether they had any real therapeutic value or not. but some of their procedures may have actually worked as cures. They had found plants to lower blood pressure, used other roots to clot blood, and attempted to heal wounds with, as Lawson noted, "rotten grains of corn" mixed with the tail feathers of a rooster.

Natives in general used a wide range of botanicals, but most tribes relied on only a few of those possibilities and often in different ways, some employing the bark and others the leaves of the same plant for similar complaints. For flux (diarrhea) the Alabama Indians boiled the bark of the pine whereas the Creeks boiled the roots of the wild plum. Ginseng was used an as all-purpose tonic by most Indians, but the Huron and Abenaki used it specifically for dysentery. The Pawnee used the smooth sumac with its widely recognized astringent qualities as a remedy for dysmenorrhea and flux. The Omaha used the same concoction but only in cases of bleeding after childbirth. Nonetheless, these herbs were usually diluted with large quantities of water, which had an emetic effect and quite likely nullified what may have been effective therapies. The power of the medicine man, like that of the physician, with the aura of competence, ability to heal, and spiritual privilege, continued in spite of any deficiencies.

Neither Indian medicines nor popular do-it-yourself measures directly threatened the professional physician in the re-Revolutionary America, although they did indicate what a limited hold the professional had over the practice of medicine and the ease with which people could dispense with orthodox treatments. One group, however, conflicted directly with those treatments from the beginning: African Americans, the enslaved population. Unlike the larger population, slaves ostensibly had very little control over the treatment of their bodies and few choices in the kind of medical care they received. Poor whites, at least in the early period before almshouses, could choose from among the various herb doctors, ministers, kitchen physic, ethnic leanings, folklore, or even a regular physician, but a slave could not. Once a disease or physical ailment came to the attention of the master, the slaves were forced to submit to either the ministrations of the white plantation owner or to a regular doctor's depletion therapy or surgery regardless of the slave's desire or need. To some extent those depletion procedures were deadly for poorly nourished and overworked slave. Jefferson recognized that problem and recommended never to "bleed a negro." The problem was that poor ventilation in their homes, contaminated water, damp earthen floors, infrequent baths, and unwashed clothes added to skin and intestinal ailments as well as respiratory illnesses. Both plantation owners and physicians blamed the slaves for their poor health, ignoring or at the best unaware that poor nutrition, inadequate clothing, and unsanitary living and working conditions were major factors leading to ringworm, dysentery, tuberculosis, influenza, typhoid fever, and a host of other diseases and chronic conditions within the slave community.

To treat those conditions, slaves were given the usual doses of calomel, ipecac, and blister powders from the medicine cabinet of the plantation. When all else failed, the physician was called to use his more drastic therapies. Slaves with high market values (i.e., healthier and stronger workers) received more intensive medical care than the least valuable slaves. Mercifully, the elderly were neglected and left to their own devices. Nonetheless, slaves tried whenever possible to ignore the ministrations of a physician. The harsh purgatives and the unwanted surgery became symbols of white control. They saw the doctor as a collaborator with the slave owner to maintain control over their bodies and minds. It was not unusual for the doctor to use purgatives as torture to force the slave to work. This suspicion of the physician as a threat to life and limb was reinforced later on in the nineteenth century by forced surgeries and experiments on unwilling slave bodies discussed in chapter 7. But even in the pre-Revolutionary years, slaves resisted white medicine by not taking the prescribed medications or refusing to admit to an ailment. Slave owners would complain that slaves neglected to tell about their physical ills; the slaves covertly questioned the authority of the physician and denied them the deference expected from a patient. Thus, struggles over their illnesses were a part of the larger efforts to resist the management of slave owners and their proxies, the physicians.

Within the slave communities there was a complex system of black herbalism, which was used to deal with ailments undercover and away from the notice of the masters. Like immigrants from Europe, slaves preferred their own homegrown remedies; many carried over from African traditions and often combined with local knowledge borrowed from Indians. Only when slaves became incapacitated and unable to work did the plantation owner order treatment, which was then resisted whenever possible. Dr. Alexander Garden of South Carolina and John Brickell in North Carolina noted that slaves were well versed in the medicinal powers of plants. In 1752 Garden even suspected that slaves used their own herbal antidotes to "render the use of Medicines entirely ineffectual even when given by the ablest practitioners in the province." Because of their extensive knowledge of plants, there was a widespread fear that slaves were using poisons to harm themselves and others with their herbal preparations. The power of slave remedies was a direct threat to the authority of both doctors and masters. In response Virginia passed a law in 1748 making medicine the strict providence of planters.

The law was unenforceable because slaves continued to treat themselves discretely, defying management of their bodies by slave owners.

African slaves and their descendants also distrusted European medicine because it lacked any notion of spiritual power. Like American Indians, blacks viewed illness as a spiritual problem, one possibly caused by a conjurer's spell or because the individual had violated community norms. Cures required mystical rites as well as herbal concoctions, both supplied by those skilled in overcoming the evil spiritual power. Archeological digs have uncovered charms and magical symbols among the debris of slave quarters, from polygonal objects shaped from glass and wood to a raccoon penis bone recovered from George Washington's plantation, which may have been a fertility symbol, and blue glass beads to ward off the evil eye that caused disease. The "boundary between conjuring and folk medicine," within the eighteenth-century slave communities, says Phillip Morgan, "was porous." By combining the mystical with the herbal, slaves considered their own methods of treating disease, both physical and mental, as superior to that of the whites and certainly more emotionally and spiritually satisfying.

The white community occasionally recognized this special quality of African medicine. In 1729 Virginia freed a "very old" slave, James Pawpaw, so that he would reveal his "many wonderful cures." He was offered a pension of £20 to continue his work and find "other secrets of expelling poisons and cure of other diseases." In North Carolina the General Assembly allotted £100 to "Caesar" for his various cures, including that of the "bite of a mad dog." Slave women were also in demand as midwives, nurses, and doctors throughout the plantation areas, sometimes with the slaveowner's consent but many times without. There were various reports of African doctors practicing in town in the Chesapeake and many instances of enslaved women serving the daily health needs of the slave quarters without the slaveowners' permission. Whether accepted or ignored as healers, slaves continued to doctor themselves whenever possible.

The understanding of disease and ill health had made little progress since Galen's time, despite variations on the humoral theory. Whether university-educated physician, apprentice-trained, folk healer, shaman, or obeah, the medical man or woman was most successful when they conveyed a sense of their ability to heal. Their lotions, potions, and pills were often more magical influence than effective medicine. Little divided the folk healer from the physician except for formal education, but that formal education and the scarcity of trained physicians were crucial in the doctor's continuing attraction. They may have been unable to cure, but they could inspire a great deal of confidence. Whatever tensions existed between the professional physician and the rest of the populace were muted and controlled by the deferential quality of colonial American society. Not even Landon Carter, Cotton Mather, or Eliza Lucas Pinckney could completely dismiss the doctor. When that deference was undermined by more democratic ideals, what had been taken as mere impertinence on the part of the laymen to oppose harsh and hurtful remedies would become a real threat to medicine as a profession.

4

Abundance

When the teen-aged Eliza Lucas in South Carolina described her environment to her brother, Lucas, at school in England in 1742, she extolled the very fertile soil that easily produced even European fruits and grains. "The Country," she continued,

> abounds with wild fowl, Venison and fish. Beef, veal and motton are here in much greater perfection than in the Islands [West Indies], tho' not equal to that in England; but their pork exceeds any I ever tasted any where. The Turkeys [are] extreamly fine, especially the wild, and indeed all their poultry is exceeding good; and peaches, Nectrons and melons of all sorts extreamly fine and in profusion, and their Oranges exceed any I ever tasted in the West Indies or from Spain or Portugal.

What young Eliza noted about her colony was echoed in the various diaries, letters, and other commentaries written throughout the eighteenth century. Andrew Barnaby in his *Travels Through the Middle Settlements in the*

Years 1759–1760 remarked on the "incredible quantities of fish" in the rivers and Chesapeake Bay especially sheepshead, rockfish, drums, perch, herring, oysters, crabs, sturgeon, and shad. The forests provided rabbits, turkeys, pheasants, woodcocks, partridges, and delicious soruses (a species of bird), ducks, squirrels, opossums, raccoons, foxes, beavers, and deer, most of which he experienced at the table. Barnaby commented on the grapes, strawberries, hickory nuts, mulberries, chestnuts, and several other fruits and nuts that grew wild. Like Eliza Lucas, he noted that European fruits did well in America, especially the peaches, which "grow in such plenty as to serve to feed the hogs in the autumn of the year."

The availability of food was a major factor in the extraordinary growth of the American population during its early years, a development that was not related to medicine and occurred in spite of epidemics and occasional wars. The abundance and variety of food was a notable part of the American experience, a special quality that distinguished Americans from Old World residents, whether European or African, and the most important factor in explaining the robust (for the time) health of the population. Such abundance did not mean that early Americans had a balanced diet in modern terms—their food contained a great deal of salt and sugar and not enough vitamins. Excessive amount of salt and sugar necessary to preserve food probably contributed to rapid tooth decay and circulatory problems, the salt additionally altering the nutritional value of meats. But the sheer quantity and variety of edibles provided a much more nutritious diet than had been available to Old World inhabitants.

The typical English husbandman (poor peasant) or yeoman lived almost exclusively on bread and cheese, the bread made of rye and wheat and often stretched with peas or beans. They could taste some beef, mutton, or pork mainly at public feasts. "Everywhere," says Carl Bridenbaugh, "rural inhabitants lived close to the subsistence level, and the fear of famine possessed them all." In America, on the other hand, almost everyone ate well and could indulge in meat that had been available only to the elite of Europe. The abundance that was the traditional privilege of the rich percolated down to ordinary people, the poorest, and the enslaved. Diet was limited not by availability so much as by custom and ethnic traditions. Those food habits, in turn, adapted to the abundance so that regardless of the limitation of ethnic inclinations or seasonal variations, the available variety and contact with new traditions reshaped and expanded the food habits of the population.

For instance, a typical meal eaten by the indentured servant-tutor John Harrower, in 1774 Piedmont Virginia, reflects the variety and the heavy reliance on meat and grains that came to characterize the American diet. He began with a breakfast of "Coffie or Jaculate [chocolate], and warm loaf bread of the best floor, we have also at Table warm loaf bread of Indian corn." For dinner (the midday meal) he sometimes ate "smoack'd bacon or what we call pork ham [which] is a standing dish either warm or cold." When the weather was warm they had "greens with it, and when cold we have sparrow grass [asparagus]." At other times they ate "roast pigg, Lamb, Ducks, or chickens, green pease or any thing else they fancy." Unlike Harrrower, Andrew Barnaby noted that the Tidewater Virginians continued the "ancient [elite] custom" of eating meat at breakfast. In addition to their tea and coffee, they breakfasted on roasted fowls, ham, venison, and other game. A few years later, Jean Brillat Savarin visiting Hartford, Connecticut, was served a simpler meal of corned beef, stewed goose, and leg of mutton along with "vegetables of every description." He drank cider with the meal and tea afterwards with the ladies.

This bounty noted by eighteen-century observers was a far cry from the starvation times of the first settlements. Neither the settlers in Virginia in 1609 nor those in Plymouth, Massachusetts (1620), were prepared for the hardship of a wilderness existence. The Virginians, suspicious and contemptuous of the successful Native Americans, antagonized the most important aid to their survival by stealing from them and destroying their crops. Unable to produce enough agricultural products in a short time by themselves and unfamiliar with methods of hunting wild game or fishing, they suffered from nutritional diseases and starvation for years. It is possible that the Jamestown Virginia settlers were also beset by an additional problem of salt poisoning from drinking the brackish water of the river, a problem that was not solved until they imitated the Indians and moved farther upriver and away from Chesapeake Bay.

The subsequent colonies in both Massachusetts (the Puritans beginning in 1630) and Maryland (1634) learned from those earlier experiences. None suffered the famines of their predecessors nor did the next settlers in Pennsylvania, the Carolinas, or Georgia. The areas of New York and New Jersey were already functioning colonies under the auspices of other European powers, and the other New England settlements were outgrowths of the Massachusetts colonies. None of these colonists reported difficulties in acquiring sustenance. Food was in abundance, and in a very short time it became possible to say that no one went hungry in America. There is no recorded evidence of famine such as was common in the Old World. As a result the New World population grew rapidly but unevenly.

The pattern of population increase varied from region to region. In New England, with its balanced sex ratio, natural increase brought rapid growth.

¶ The kindes.

OF Turkie cornes there be diuers sorts, notwithstanding of one stocke or kindred, consisting of sundry coloured graines, wherein the difference is easie to be discerned, and for the better explanation of the same, I haue set forth to your view certaine eares of different colours, in their full and perfect ripenesse, and such as they shew themselues to be when their skinne or filme doth open it selfe in the time of gathering.

The forme of the eares of Turky Wheat.

3 Frumenti Indici spica.
Turkie wheat in the huske, as also naked or bare.

¶ The temperature and vertues.

Turkywheat doth nourish far lesse than either wheat, rie, barley, or otes. The bread which is made thereof is meanly white, without bran: it is hard and dry as Bisket is, and hath in it no clamminesse at all; for which cause it is of hard digestion, and yeeldeth to the body little or no nourishment; it slowly descendeth, and bindeth the belly, as that doth which is made of Mill or Panick. We haue as yet no certaine proofe or experience concerning the vertues of this kinde of Corne; although the barbarous Indians, which know no better, are constrained to make a vertue of necessitie, and thinke it a good food: whereas we may easily iudge, that it nourisheth but little, and is of hard and euill digestion, a more conuenient food for swine than for men.

Figure 1. Woodcut of ears of corn and reproduction of original text. From J. Gerarde, *The Herball or Generall Historie of Plantes* (2d ed.; London: Islip, Norton, and Whitakers, 1633).

Indian corn or maize was so new to Europeans eyes that this early history of plants traced the origin to the Near East in Turkey. From J. Gerard, *The Herball or Generall Historie of Plantes*, 1633. (From the author's collection)

The population grew more slowly in the South where a greater incidence of infectious diseases kept life expectancy lower, and the lack of women held down the birthrate. Doctors, of course, could do little to stem the tide of infections, and their therapies may have contributed to the death rate. The middle colonies had a more even sex ratio than in the South, but because men still outnumbered women, the birthrate was lower than in New England. From New York south to Maryland the colonies depended on a substantial immigration from various parts of Europe and Africa. By the middle of the eighteenth century, however, there was no doubt that the population in all the American colonies was growing through natural increase. Medical care or knowledge about health had little to do with that growth (except possibly in the case of inoculation against smallpox, but that protected only a small number of people).

Benjamin Franklin, who was interested in statistics and compiled numbers from the few population counts available, concluded in the 1750s that the American population, unlike that of Europe, was capable of increasing every twenty or twenty-five years. Franklin reasoned that the availability of land increased economic opportunities and thus encouraged the early marriage that resulted in a higher birthrate. He attributed part of the increase to the Puritan values of thrift and hard work. Other Americans picked up on his ideas, and both Ezra Stiles and Edward Wigglesworth reaffirmed Franklin's estimates with special attention to the relationship of population to the means of subsistence. Thomas Malthus in his study of population in 1798 used the American experience as an example of how fast a community could grow under optimum conditions, meaning an abundance of food and the absence of war and pestilence that were traditional population controls. He put a great deal of emphasis on the relationship of food resources to demographic growth. Most modern historians of demography have tended to ignore nutritional issues, concentrating instead on the number of immigrants, the prevalence or absence of disease, or the presence of women and their fertility in order to explain population change. The fact that female fertility and resistance to disease depended on food and nutrition was seldom taken into consideration.

With Alfred Crosby's study of the *Columbian Exchange* in 1972, the significance of food—its variety and quality and the contribution of the New World's agricultural bounty—took on new meaning. After examining the growth of world population after Columbus's voyages, Crosby concluded that this increase was the result of a change in the quantity and quality of food available. And it was not just the increase but also the introduction of new foods unique to the New World, many of which had greater nutritional value or were more productive than similar Old World foods. This was especially so in the case of Indian maize or corn; its caloric yield per acre was greater than wheat or other European grains. In addition, the method of cultivation was easier than wheat with its shorter growing season and survival under a variety of climatic conditions. Maize also has a higher proportion of sugar and fat than wheat, and is a possible source of protein when eaten with beans or treated with an alkali to free the amino acid, tryptophan, that the human body converts to niacin. Daphne Roe's study of the vitamin-deficient disease pellagra points out that Indians, who did not suffer from pellagra, ate little meat and always treated corn with wood ash (lye) to release the essential amino acid. Maize had spread over Europe and Africa by the seventeenth century and helped to raise the nutritional standards everywhere, which improved the chances for population growth even in the Old World. So ubiquitous was maize in the colonial diet that it was seldom mentioned in the cookbooks of the time and appears only in offhand comments by individuals. John Brickell commented on the diet in North Carolina of the 1730s and noted that in addition to the many meats both "Wild and Tame," many vegetables, butter, cheese, and rice, they ate "Indian corn, . . . which they concoct like a Hasty-Pudding."

Maize may have been the most important of new foods throughout the world, but there were many others that also became diet staples. The potato, like corn, produced more food per land than other starches. The white potato that originated in the highlands of Peru and Chile spread from Spain to Italy, France, and finally to Ireland, and was brought back to the New World by the Spanish when it was introduced to North America in the seventeenth century. The sweet potato, native to North America, with its high quality of vitamins C and A, contributed a great deal to the British colonial diet. America also contributed the tomato, crabapples, plums, walnuts, chestnuts, and a variety of berries including cranberries, along with many new types of beans: snap, kidney, pole, navy, and pinto. There were peanuts from South America and cacao (chocolate) from Mexico. In addition to the flora of the New World, there were many new fauna that quickly entered into the world's foodstuffs. The turkey is the best known, but there were also many varieties of wildfowl and an abundance of deer and bison.

When the Europeans brought their own seeds and animals to America, they found a land with few natural predators. European animals such as cattle, sheep, goats, chickens, and pigs could thrive, although the local wolves kept the sheep population down. Imported horses, oxen, donkeys, and mules provided the muscle power to help cultivate the food and provide transportation. The European horse, in fact, changed the Native American way of life and in many places made him a hunter instead of a farmer. The English also

imported fruit trees as well as their favorite vegetables such as lettuce, rad-
ishes, and cabbages. With the Africans came a variety of greens, rice, and
new ways of preparing corn. The mixture of foodstuffs increased the possible
variety in the diet, but it also meant that if one crop did not succeed, there
was always another form of agricultural produce that would survive in spite
of too much rain, drought, cold, heat, or threats of plant disease. When the
wheat crop succumbed to blight in New England, the farmers turned to rye
and corn for their bread. The bounty of agricultural and animal products
provided sufficient protein and calories to support the most rapid natural
population growth known up to that time.

Seventeenth-century Massachusetts has the distinction of being home to
the longest-lived individuals. A large proportion of people in the Massachusetts towns lived into their seventies. In an early pathbreaking study, Philip
Greven analyzed the family structure in seventeenth-century Andover, Massachusetts, and found that the first generation of men born in the town (not
immigrants) lived to an average age of 71.8 years and the second generation for 65.2 years. John Demos found similar life expectancies in the early
Plymouth colony. Infants had an extraordinary chance to survive. Probably
eight out of ten children born in colonial New England could expect to live
beyond the age of twenty. In most places of the world including the southern
colonies, one-half of children born died before reaching maturity. Although
the life expectancy in New England as a region declined in the eighteenth
century, it was far better than could be expected in the British Isles.

Maryland is one of the few southern colonies to attract scholars to demographic problems. One study concludes that life expectancy in the seventeenth century was forty-three years for men. Women died at an earlier age
because of the dangers from childbirth, but if they survived to age forty-five,
they outlived the men. In another study of one county in southern Maryland,
the authors estimate that if a native-born man reached the age of twenty, he
could expect to live another 24.5 to 27.2 years (thus 44 to almost 48 years
of life). Immigrants, who were not "seasoned" to the local diseases, could
expect to live only 20.3 to 24.2 years longer after the age of twenty. As late as
the 1770s average life expectancy at birth throughout the colonies was about
forty years. In contrast, in England at the time it was only thirty-seven years
and in France it was less at twenty-eight years.

The relative absence of disease because of isolated communities goes a
long way to explain this longevity, but it does not explain another intriguing
American quality. Americans, regardless of their ancestry, were among the
tallest people in the world and continued to be so until only very recently.
Because there is a correlation between nutritional status and stature, the

improvement in food consumption, particularly that of protein, has this very visible and measurable result. Poorly nourished children are more susceptible to infection, and infection in turn reduces the body's ability to absorb the nutrients in food and therefore the chances of growing. The infant's health also depends on the nutritional condition of the mother. There is abundant evidence of this change in height from muster roles during the Revolution and from bone length in skeletal remains found by archeologists.

The average height of American men during the Revolution was about 5' 7". Their European counterparts were several inches shorter. Robert Fogel in his many studies of slavery estimates that men of African descent were also taller than their contemporaries in Africa. Even though the estimates of African American height come mostly from the muster roles during the American Civil War, it is still a startling fact considering that the health on the plantations may have declined in the nineteenth century. The only factor that could explain the height factor is the quality and quantity of protein and vitamins in the diet. Americans obviously consumed more protein and more nutritious food than those in the Old World from the eighteenth century through the nineteenth centuries, adding to their resistance to disease.

Historically, the food thought to have the greatest nutritional value was that which was most filling. Thus meat and cereals were favored. For people of European descent, vegetables were assumed to have little nutritional value but were useful for sauces and condiments to provide a contrast in the sensations on the tongue, a relish. Taste often entered into the evaluation of food and its relation to health. Foods with a hot or sweet taste, it was thought, cleansed and nourished the body. Sugar, then, was the perfect food. It became the universal panacea for all ailments and became a major ingredient in many of the pills and concoctions of the time. Cold tastes that came from rough, sour, or harsh tasting foods, it was thought, cooled the body. Food was not just sustenance for life; it was also medicine and was often treated as such in recipe books of the time. Thin soup (especially the ubiquitous chicken soup), as well as bread, milk, and wine were standard for the sick and infirm. Wine played a special role in the preparation of drugs. It was as common in the recipes in cookbooks used by housewives as they were for those in the pharmacopeias consulted by physicians.

Ideas about food, unlike views of medical treatments, did not create many conflicts between the general public and the medical profession or within the profession itself until late in the eighteenth century. In accord with medical theory of the time, food helped to balance the humors in the body. Doctors often recommended specific diets for different maladies depending on how they interpreted the needs of the body. All foods were classified as hot or cold, moist or dry, or a combination of hot-moist, hot-dry, cold-moist or cold-dry. Depending on the physical problem, food could be used to make up a deficiency in the humors. For the lack of bile, the recommendation from both doctors and self-help manuals would be to add foods that were considered hot and dry such as garlic, onions, leeks, mustard, or pepper. "Slimy" meats such as new cheese, fish, lamb, offal, and cucumbers produced phlegm with their assumed cold moisture. Among those foods considered cold and dry were beef, goat, hare, boar, salt flesh, all legumes, brown bread, old cheese, and the like. Salty, bitter, and sharply spiced foods dried the phlegm. In her analysis of the medical literature Kay Moss concluded that medical books "dwelt heavily on theories of proper diet." They rejected highly seasoned and salty foods as unwholesome. The problem with such advice literature is that in the absence of refrigeration, it was necessary to pickle, smoke, or salt foods to preserve them for later use.

The wealthier and more educated population took a great deal of interest in eating well. The variety of foodstuffs possible on the New World table is reflected in Charles Carroll's orders to his suppliers and his comments on what he could acquire either locally or from his own garden. Carroll was one of the wealthiest men in Maryland and freely enjoyed the benefits of his income. He ordered claret from Ireland with a note that his household consumed ten hogsheads of this red wine a year. From a Barbados merchant he ordered sugar and rum. An English supplier sent raisins, Cheshire cheese (50 pounds), and a variety of seasonings (some for food, some for medicine) collected from around the world: pimento, mace, cloves, nutmeg, ginger, black pepper, chocolate, vanilla, tea, and almonds. His Annapolis plantation itself supplied the basic foods of pork, lamb, wheat, oats, corn, carrots, rye, and potatoes (both sweet and white). He had fruit trees for pears, peaches, grapes, apples, and cherries, of which the fruit was fermented into wine or cider. Beef tongue was secured from a local "Dutch" butcher. Much of the local economy was not noted but he probably consumed some of the wild game mentioned by Barnaby.

At the same time, there was a growing sense that an excess of food and nourishment was a vice. Several commentaries found in *The Records of the Tuesday Club of Annapolis, Maryland* on the variety of foods served during their meetings stressed that their eating habits were quite abstemious. This meant, in the most modern fashion, that they ate a little less than was common for meals. On November 6, 1750, the host served a roast and boiled meat plus pies, custards, and "delicate tarts and deserts." The following January the meal also consisted of two meat dishes, some "Garden stuff," and a variety of deserts. On January 9, 1753, the minutes noted that they had "a large haunt of venison for the first time" in the club. A special committee meeting on February 19, 1754, consumed only a turkey with oyster sauce, apple pie, plum pudding, and cranberry tarts, washed down with a "good Hermitage." Drinks were not always specified but generally included a variety of imported wines and beer. The Tuesday Club spent time satirizing their luxurious method of eating and drinking, while enjoying the plenty. As usual the members made fun of the moralists of the time, those who condemned the excesses of the table along with the other excesses of the aristocracy. Gluttony had always been the privilege of the rich; the poor traditionally subsisted on a limited diet of monotonous and less nourishing foods. Now that more food was available to ordinary mortals, moralists saw reason to condemn the practice of variety and abundance at the table. Benjamin Franklin had recommended that one eat for necessity and not for pleasure. The gentlemen of Annapolis found that idea a source of amusement.

The more sedentary lifestyle among the wealthy certainly called for a more restricted diet, and doctors began to recommend limiting the amount and number of foods consumed at any one time and to restrict consumption of alcohol. Benjamin Rush preferred one hearty meal a day with only one plain dish because, he argued much like Benjamin Franklin, that too much food made men slothful, sleepy, and therefore unable to work. There is little evidence that people heeded such advice except for a few elite men, like William Byrd, who found pleasure in depriving himself. Because of this abundance, food in America had lost its role in distinguishing the elite from the masses. It was the quality of material goods that separated the poor from the elite. The cutlery, the linen, and the quality of the plates signified refinement, not so much the food on those plates. High meat consumption and full stomachs had become the American way. By the closing years of the eighteenth century, Americans could rejoice in their ability to feed themselves and feel more secure about the state of their health. It was that abundance and the superior nutritional intake that made for healthy long-lived Americans. To their benefit, their cookbooks, following the new French fashion, also warned against overcooking either meat or vegetables.

Unlike the elites, the ordinary working farmhand (and most Americans lived in rural areas) needed a diet heavy in calories and protein with a good infusion of fats. A man typically needed between 3,500 and 4,000 calories a day to maintain a full days work. When the founders of the Georgia colony sent their first settlers to America in 1735, they provided for a daily intake of 3,600 calories during the passage to America. Continental army rations during the American Revolution varied from 2,600 to 5,400 calories a day, although in practice the military seldom actually reached those numbers.

These estimates give some indication of what was expected, though. Because of the hard physical labor of those early Americans, many more calories were necessary than is recommended for the generally sedentary life style of the twenty-first century.

The eating habits of slaves and poor whites are more difficult to determine. There is no doubt that poor people did not eat as well as the more affluent. Poverty was a fact of life throughout American history but affected only a small number of people before the Revolution. Public charity was available to keep the poor from starving, but even that did not mean an adequate diet. There is no evidence, however, that there was widespread starvation among the poor or enslaved.

Historians assumed that the diet of slaves was inadequate because plantation records listed only a partial and monotonous diet of corn and pork. But more recent studies, especially those based on archeological records, have revised that opinion. Alan Kulikoff, in his studies of tobacco plantations, concludes that masters provided a subsistence diet and, "though food was plentiful, slave diets were not well balanced," a comment that could apply to most early Americans. Philip Morgan, looking at slave life in both the tobacco and rice areas (Chesapeake and the Carolinas) assumed that because the mainland slaves were taller than the Caribbean slaves and the native born were taller than immigrants, the diet was adequate. "It is inconceivable," he notes, "that the mainland slave population could have increased so rapidly" if the food intake had been so poor. He points out that Virginia slaves were taller than those in South Carolina, indicating that food intake was less adequate in the Low Country than in the Chesapeake area. Charles Carroll noted that his field slaves did not "live as well as" the "House Negroes." They were not as well fed, but he thought they survived as well as any other "Plantation Negroes." On George Washington's plantation, slaves were allotted food amounting to around 2,800 calories a day, mostly in the form of pork and corn, but they were able to supplement that diet with food provided by themselves. If slaves were allotted anywhere near these amounts, then, they did have sufficient calories to maintain life and to reproduce.

But caloric intake is not by itself a sufficient diet; the quality of food and the variety to provide necessary vitamins and minerals are as important. Archeological findings in the slave quarters indicate that they had access to a more nutritious and varied diet beyond the usual corn and pork. Remains of cattle, chicken, and turkey have been found as well as wild species of raccoon, turtles, deer, squirrel, duck, and rabbit. Seeds from pumpkins, watermelons, beans, peanuts, various fruits as well as corn and peas, and other vegetables also indicate a more varied diet than given in written records. Slaves hunted for wild animals and fished, and in most places had their own garden plots, and they raised poultry. John Brickell, traveling through North Carolina in the 1730s, remarked on the preference of "Indians and Negroes" for raccoons and opossums, the latter meat he described as "generally fat, white, and well tasted." Slaves grew for themselves a variety of leafy plants, which had been a mainstay of the traditional African diet, as well as squash and root vegetables including the most important tuber, the sweet potato, high in vitamins C and A. In this early period, people of African descent may well have consumed a more nutritious diet than those of British parentage who often disdained vegetables as a mere relish.

Much of this abundance was seasonal, and in between harvests and when they could not store enough to tide them over for the winter, slaves suffered from lack of food. It was not a deliberate denial of food since everyone probably suffered from nutritional deficiencies during winter. Food deprivation was rarely used to enforce discipline because such deprivation could undermine the worker's ability to perform. On the other hand, additional rations of meat were often used as rewards. At times, when neither their own gardens nor the allotted rations filled their bellies, slaves stole food or poached game. Such theft was also a means of resisting the system, an expression of frustration at the lack of freedom to choose what to eat or when to eat. There were times when the very presence of the abundance on the farm and on the master's table probably encouraged slaves to want more for themselves. They saw the masters eating what they wanted, when they wanted it, and the slaves too wanted that freedom to choose. The theft of food then, like the refusal to obey the physicians' therapies was a means of resisting the system and another way of getting back at the masters for depriving them of their freedom.

Food preference played an important role in the nutritional component of all diets including that of the slaves. Maize, which was first introduced in Africa by the Portuguese, was a major ingredient in African cooking long before slavery began in the English colonies. When George Washington offered wheat as a substitute, his slaves balked. Many other native American plants had already entered into the African diet; they were already consuming American chili peppers, peanuts, and sweet potatoes. The basic cooked food in West African countries was a porridge made from a cereal, root, or starchy fruit accompanied by a sauce made of small pieces of meat or fish, palm oil, leaves of plants, and hot peppers. The one-pot cooking practice was carried over to America, and slaves continued to consume similar stews heavy on vegetables but with greater amounts of meat than before.

Slave ships in turn provided the food most familiar to Africans depending on their home area. The ships carried yams, limes, pepper, palm or sesame oil, peanuts, beans, and corn, supplemented by European foods of dried beans, wheat, and barley. Peanuts were a particular specialty but did not enter the white diet until shortly before the Revolution. Like maize, peanuts had been adopted by Africans and brought back on the slave ships. They were a major subsistence staple of African American garden plots. The ships from rice-growing areas of Africa laid on rice in the stores. Rice had been cultivated in West Africa along the Atlantic coast for millennia, and planters in South Carolina consciously looked for slaves from those areas who knew how to produce rice. One of the possible reasons for the more deficient nutrition in the Low Country was because rice, which had a lower caloric and fat value then maize, was the staple of the slave diet there.

Although no area was completely self-sufficient in producing food—importation and intercolonial exchange of goods provided the commodities they could not produce such as tea, rum, salt, sugar, wheat or Charles Carroll's beef tongue—colonial women cooked, preserved, and stored what their families grew or hunted or gathered locally. Nonetheless, in every colony the settlers tried to reproduce the eating habits of their home countries. All eating and cooking habits to some extent reflected the ethnic traditions of food and drink brought by immigrants to America, modified by local conditions. Those immigrant food habits and agricultural practices, whether white or black combined with that of Native Americans, shaped the culinary traditions of each region. The more northern colonies with their lower immigration rate remained British in their eating habits. There was only a smattering of borrowing from the Indians such as combining corn with rye to make bread. Southerners were more imaginative and tolerant in their approach to food, more willing to borrow from the Indians and the larger population of Africans. Southern stews thickened with okra, and the leafy tops of vegetables like collards and turnips became distinguishing southern foods. The African origins of such food practices are usually forgotten. The water left over from those greens was often consumed by the slaves in a custom taken from the Indians and called "pot likker." Corn, so long a staple of the African diet, became more significant in southern cooking than elsewhere. In South Carolina, African rice often substituted for the corn and was combined with local beans. In the middle colonies, food habits reflected the cooking of the British Isles, Germany, and Holland with a little less influence from the Indians. Maize was added to the sausages, replacing traditional European grains to create a scrapple—a corn-based pudding with meat "scraps." Meats were preserved by salting; when salt was not available, they were smoked or dried in the Indian way or pickled with vinegar in the European manner. The American table, whether free or slave, was a fusion of local produce and ethnic habits. Visitors may have been critical of the strange combination of foods eaten by Americans, but they also marveled at the variety and quantity available.

There was less variety in the available beverages. Few people drank water. The rivers were often muddy and filled with the filth of human and animal waste. Unless boiled for tea or medicines, or mixed with alcohol, the result could be deadly. For most people, tea was too expensive and milk was difficult to store. Distilled and fermented drinks were viewed as nourishment, and all kinds of fruits were used to produce wine or brandy. Probably the most popular drink was apple cider, which was easy to produce in the home. A better quality was imported from England for the more affluent. Beer was also a domestic product, but both the quality and the alcoholic content were low. Until the larger German immigration of the 1840s brought new skills in the production of beer, it was a drink that remained on the sidelines. Rum, on the other hand, was easily available from Barbados and became more abundant when distilleries appeared in Boston, Providence, New Haven, and Philadelphia. As a result of the increased production of rum, the price dropped after the 1730s and consumption increased proportionately. Rum continued to be the most popular distilled beverage until the Revolution when trade with the British West Indies cut off the supply of sugar and molasses. Thereafter, corn whiskey (today's Bourbon) took its place. That whiskey came from farms producing large grain surpluses, grain that could not conveniently be transported to the markets because of its bulk. Once the corn was transformed into a liquid, it was easier to move by wagon to more densely populated areas. Demand was greatest in the taverns, inns, and later in the nineteenth century, in restaurants.

Alcohol was pervasive in American society from its very beginning in the seventeenth century. Although the tavern or public house was the major locale for alcohol consumption for groups, the home was where most people drank. And they drank at all meals—breakfast, dinner, the afternoon break, and the evening meal. Whenever food was served, so too was alcohol. Slaves, day laborers, and militiamen expected to receive their ration of drink. Moderate drinking was acceptable to even the most abstemious. Overindulgence, on the other hand, was frowned on, and the upper classes tried vainly to reduce the sale of alcohol to slaves, common people, and seamen by restricting the use of taverns. In spite of sporadic attempts to prevent public drunkenness, the consumption of alcohol for all classes continued to increase throughout the eighteenth and into the nineteenth century. While the water supplies were polluted, such excesses may well have contributed to better health.

The abundance and variety of food in pre-Revolutionary years goes a long way to explain why, for at least two centuries, Americans were generally healthier and taller than people in the Old World, and experienced a faster natural increase. Such experiences gave birth to the idea of American exceptionalism, that they were different from and possibly superior to the Old World. As America grew in population and expanded in size, as it became more urbanized in the early nineteenth century, health conditions began to deteriorate. Poor food habits and heavy whiskey drinking were among the factors contributing to that decline; the increasing poverty and poor health added to the problem. But as the Revolution began, Americans knew only about that earlier world with minimal poverty and a generally healthy, well-fed, and relatively disease-free population when compared with their counterparts in Europe. They also discovered that there were disadvantages to their healthy life style.

5

Wartime

For failure to pay his debts, Ezekiel Brown of Concord, Massachusetts, was sentenced to jail in March 1773. In an unusual circumstance Brown's creditors kept him there for years. Most debtors, according to Robert Gross, who describes Brown's ordeal, remained imprisoned for only a few months, but his creditors suspected that he would abscond. Brown was seemingly caught up in the conflict between the British government and the mainland colonies that would result in the Revolutionary War. Boston was firmly in the hands of the British military, and Brown's creditors were decidedly Tory in their leanings. They had no intention of setting him free. Brown was an enterprising sort and spent his time in jail reading about medicine, preparing for a new career as a doctor. He had no mentor but because most men were self-educated in the field, there was no reason to assume that his solitary book learning would be a disadvantage in a place with few well-educated physicians.

As Brown languished in jail, the first battle at Lexington and Concord took place in April 1775. George Washington was appointed by the Second

Continental Congress to take command of the newly created Continental forces that were maintaining a siege of Boston. In July Washington took
charge of the various militia from Connecticut, Rhode Island, and New
Hampshire that had come to aid the Massachusetts military, and as a result
the patriots under Washington's command kept the British holed up in Boston for an entire year. When the British finally gave up and the Continental
forces marched into the city in March 1776, Ezekiel Brown's tormenters fled
with them, and he was released from jail. He immediately joined the army
with the usual short-term enlistment. In recognition of his knowledge of
medicine he was appointed a surgeon's mate. Brown served for six months
and then returned to his wife and children. With four children and only a
few acres of land in far-off Maine and no visible prospects, he responded to
a new call for long-term army enlistments early in 1777. He was considered
trained enough—even though he had had only six months as an apprentice—and was granted a commission as a regimental surgeon. In this Brown
was not unusual. A mere smattering of knowledge and hands-on experience
were the only requirements for the lower levels of the medical service during
the American Revolution.

Most of the regimental surgeons—a term denoting a military status and
not level of education or skill—took care of the wounded and sick from their
own geographic area and were accountable only to their own line officers.
They were never examined for medical competency, and there were no standards set for the medical service. Very few of the medical men who ampu-
tated limbs, dosed patients with the usual vile concoctions, and diagnosed
illness for the military, whether regimental or Continental, had had much
formal training. As a group they were no better trained and certainly were
no better read than Ezekiel Brown. The regimental surgeons, however, were
described as a disgrace to the profession as ignorant, dishonest, and incompetent and were scorned by those elite men chosen to head the Continental
army medical department. On the other hand as Mary Gillett notes in her
history of the army medical department, soldiers often felt more secure in
the regimental hospitals with surgeons they knew rather than in the more
distant Continental hospitals even if the doctors there professed to be more
competent. In fact, those regimental hospitals may have been less hazardous
to their health because of their smaller size. Doctoring was not an esoteric
science as experiences during the war indicated, and soldiers had little to fear
from the half trained.

An elite education in medicine was no guarantee of skill nor any indication of ability to handle illness. An academic degree or experience in lectures
attended at a university was a sign of gentlemanly status, one that entitled

men to appointments to important government positions. At the beginning of the Revolution there were only a handful of men with academic training in the colonies who could claim such appointments. Of the estimated 3,500 medical practitioners in 1775, about 400 held degrees mostly from foreign universities, but not all in were in medicine. Some, like Gustavus Brown in southern Maryland, William Hunter in Newport, Rhode Island, and John Kearsley in Philadelphia, established medical dynasties, training generations of apprentices who in turn trained other apprentices, some of whom went on to more advanced training. A handful of others offered private lectures in an attempt to improve the knowledge of anatomy within their profession. Most American "doctors" learned the trade from others who also had learned medicine as apprentices. Whitfield Bell, one of the leading medical historians, noted, "most men never saw an anatomical chart." Their knowledge of the human body was severely limited, but they were familiar with the standard pharmacopeias and most often had learned how to amputate a limb. Ezekiel Brown missed the five- to six-year apprenticeships of most doctors, but he was well read and managed to deport himself satisfactorily for three years.

There were two small medical schools in the colonies before the Revolution: Philadelphia established one in 1765 and New York in 1767, and both closed during the war. The medical school in Philadelphia was established under the most inauspicious circumstances for the Revolution and revealed the kind of petty rivalries that would haunt the medical war effort. The impetus for the school came from John Morgan and William Shippen (both American-born) who, while they were studying in Edinburgh, Scotland, decided that the colonial world needed its own means of training doctors following the Scottish model. They wanted to limit the practice of medicine to men like themselves—educated gentlemen with specialized training. Morgan hurried back to Philadelphia and presented the idea to the college as his own, denying Shippen any credit. Morgan was then appointed the first professor of theory and practice of medicine. When he returned to America, Shippen was furious and never forgave his former friend for the betrayal. Morgan piled insult on more insult when he organized a medical society and again snubbed Shippen. Meanwhile, Shippen was appointed professor of anatomy in the new school, but the two men maintained a less than cordial relationship hidden behind the façade of polite manners. When the time came to organize a medical service during the war, that same animosity threatened the process.

In 1775, as the first battles took place, local regimental surgeons were the only source of medical care available. When Congress created its own organized medical service and the Hospital Department was headed by the elite of the medical profession, it immediately set off a storm of controversy. The regimental surgeons refused to give up their positions and demanded a share of the supplies appropriated by Congress. The Director Generals appointed by Congress declared that they had no authority to share those supplies and indeed made little attempt to do so. The rivalry between the regimental surgeons and the men at the top of the medical hierarchy resulted in "waste and anarchy both in the distribution of medical supplies and the handling of the sick and wounded," according to Phillip Cash, who wrote of the early years of the war. Fourteen armies—one Continental and thirteen state militias—without a central command to care for the sick and wounded did not make for an efficient system, nor did the situation improve with time. The quarrels between the Continental and regimental surgeons intensified during the war and added to the waste of resources.

The good health enjoyed by most American on the eve of the war left them with some major disadvantages. They had known relative isolation from most infectious diseases. Like the Native Americans at the moment of contact with Europeans, most colonials in the British empire did not have immunities to diseases that had become endemic in Europe, particularly smallpox and measles. Their dispersed lifestyles kept them free of typhus, typhoid, or malaria. Their habits on the farms did not prepare them for life in crowded military camps, which required a very different set of sanitation behaviors. The spirit of independence did not prepare them for the discipline necessary in the military. Shaping this unruly, disease-free, independent population into a functioning army, capable of protecting themselves against illness, proved to be a daunting task made all the more so because many soldiers lacked any concern for personal cleanliness. For the elite, neatness and personal hygiene were values associated with the virtue and integrity of gentlemen, but for the majority of Americans, especially of the poorer sort, such values were foreign. As the war moved beyond its first year, most of the soldiers were recruited from the landless, wage-earning, or transient populations who had more important interests than keeping their bodies or clothing clean. Food and drink were priorities, not soap. As an army they were brave men, said General Washington, but "an exceedingly dirty and nasty people."

The treatment of bodily ills followed the usual prescription of bleeding and purging although it varied with individual physicians. One theory regarding dysentery was that the breath of the infected spread the disease, and it was to be treated with a mild purge followed by a dose of opium. For respiratory ailments, the usual treatment was bleeding and blistering. Mercury was a popular remedy used for inflammatory diseases such as pleurisy, pneumonia, rheumatic problems as well as typhus, yellow fever, dysentery, smallpox, tuberculosis, dropsy, and, of course, syphilis. Wine was often used to stimulate the appetite or as a sedative. Mary Gillette notes that one of the few effective remedies for a skin condition such as scabies was that of sulfur, a remedy that was still used in the twentieth century. On the other hand, Dr. Thacher, one of the "better" surgeons, treated a rattlesnake bite with repeated doses of olive oil until a full quart had been ingested, and then Thacher rubbed the affected leg with mercurial ointment. Somehow the patient survived. John Duffy comments that: "The knowledge that his physicians were doing everything possible to save him may have supplied the necessary psychological lift to enable the soldier to survive the snake bite and the therapy." Dr. William Eastes of Massachusetts treated a patient with liberal bloodletting when he was shot through the lungs. He too survived and probably for the same reason. The lack of medical supplies, especially drugs like mercury and ipecac, probably helped to save some lives. On the other hand the difficulty in procuring blankets for the wounded, opium for their pain, cinchona bark for malaria, and sulfur for scabies contributed to the misery of those felled by disease or wounds.

The low state of medicine in America was all too obvious at the opening round of battles in the Revolution. The actions taken by Congress to handle health problem reflect both a casual attitude toward a medical profession that lacked real prestige and a general ignorance about how to protect health. Neither the military nor the civilian leadership in America had any concept of the health problems that would be faced by a country at war, and Congress often ignored the complaints of the doctors regarding supplies and medicine. The lack of military experience, even though some, like George Washington and Dr. John Morgan, had participated with the British during the earlier French and Indian War (1754–63), was most obvious in the slow response to immediate problems and the apparent indifference to the suffering of the wounded and sick men. During one of the opening campaigns in the fall of 1775, in preparation for an attack on Canada, the Continental army did not include any physicians. Some state units even failed to bring a minimal requirement of regimental surgeons.

This situation was complicated by the problems in the command structure. Corruption, incompetence, disorganization, personal animosities among medical personnel, professional rivalries, and disease all played important roles in the condition of patriot soldiers during the American Revolution. A new army, lack of discipline within the ranks, and a dearth of experienced officers combined with the general ignorance about disease to severely undermine the patriot cause. Smallpox, dysentery, malaria, malnutrition, and a shot of "fevers" swept through the Continental army and state militias, taking a greater toll of lives than that suffered by the wounded who succumbed to infections. Rough estimates give about 10,000 deaths each year, of which only 10 percent were due to battle wounds, out of an army that included fewer than 50,000 troops. The number varied considerably because the regular Continental army had enlistments from one year to the "duration" of the war; the state militias had terms from only a few days to a few months. James Thacher, who participated in the war as a physician, estimated that there were a total of 70,000 deaths between 1775 and 1781, the year when most battles ended. The British fared only slightly better, with the advantage of many wartime experiences and previous encounters with disease until the theater of war moved south where they faced unfamiliar bouts of malaria that devastated the military.

Before George Washington arrived to take command in the summer of 1775, the battle of Bunker Hill (Breed's Hill) demonstrated the necessity for some coordination of medical services. There was no organized corps of stretcher-bearers to evacuate the wounded and no chief physician to direct medical personnel. Thirty-two percent of the American forces were lost to deaths, wounds, and capture during that battle. Soon after he arrived Washington sent an urgent request to Congress to provide for a medical service, but even he underestimated the medical needs of the military. He took his army from Trenton to Princeton in January 1777 without a single surgeon and did not inform the existing medical officers of his move.

Congress did establish a "Hospital" to be administered by a Director General and Chief Physician in 1775 and appointed the Boston doctor Benjamin Church to that position. Following what he thought to be his authority, Church immediately stepped on local toes when he ordered the abandonment of regimental hospitals in favor of the General Hospital. This was not what we think of today as one place but was a collection of miscellaneous buildings, including private homes and abandoned buildings, that were used to house the sick and wounded. Church attempted to bring all the wounded and sick under his command in these various quarters. The regimental surgeons were insulted by this infringement on their authority, and the complaints poured into Congress. As Congress began to investigate the problem, Church, in a scandal that included his mistress, a coded letter, and a British officer, was found to be in "treasonable correspondence" with the British. He was dismissed from the service in October 1775. His few months as Director General and Chief Physician were a foreshadowing of the problems to come. He faced severe shortages of all kinds of supplies: food and drink, blankets, drugs, and medical instruments. The conflict with the regimental surgeons would not be resolved, and the problem was intensified by the petty rivalries and jealousies that had permeated the Philadelphia medical profession even before the war.

In October, Church was replaced by Dr. John Morgan because he was one of the few physicians with previous military experience and was an acknowledged leader of the profession as the founder of the Philadelphia Medical College. He was also, as one of his contemporaries, Dr. Barnabas Biney, described him, "the most implacable, revengeful man under the Heavens." His was not the kind of personality fit to resolve the conflicts in the medical service, but he was also faced with an overwhelming task as Church had left no records of patients in the hospital, and there was an inadequate supply of medicines or bandages, blankets, or surgical instruments. When Morgan managed to collect a smattering of supplies by appealing to local communities, he refused to share that largesse with the regimental surgeons who were in desperate need. In an attempt to improve the caliber of regimental surgeons and establish an effective system of sick returns, he merely antagonized those surgeons even more.

Meanwhile, the sick and wounded often lay on the ground without straw or blankets to cover them, which contributed to additional suffering from colds, fevers, chills, pneumonia, and arthritis. There were not enough tents or wooden barracks in those makeshift hospitals; shelter was at a premium; men lay in overcrowded and unhealthy conditions. As one sick soldier, Joseph Plumb Martin, described his predicament: "I had the canopy of heaven for my hospital and the ground for my hammock." Martin reported that during his illness he was given nothing to eat or drink and was too sick to get up and find food; only an empathetic mate came to his assistance. There were no nurses or other attendants to treat those sickened by conditions in the camp. Dr. Morgan, however, attempted to personally visit with and tend to the sick and wounded.

The complaints about Morgan's handling of his multiple tasks poured into Congress from those he had offended over the years. Criticism came from Dr. Samuel Stringer, who had competed with Morgan for supplies for the Northern Department (areas upstate in New York) and who had fought with him over the authority to choose surgeons. Congress had further divided the medical service into two areas by assigning William Shippen to handle the hospitals west of the Hudson, leaving Morgan in control to the east in an area that included Boston and New York City. The lack of a unified command encouraged additional backbiting and complaints. Congress, annoyed by the continual friction, dismissed Morgan as director in January 1777 and appointed his old Philadelphia enemy, William Shippen, in his place.

Portrait of Dr. John Cochran, the most competent of the Director Generals and Chief Physician of military hospitals during the Revolutionary War. (Courtesy of the National Library of Medicine)

Nothing could have antagonized Morgan more than to see Shippen replace him, and he spent the next six years attacking the new director and his supporters for ineptitude, both real and imagined. With the help of Benjamin Rush, Morgan was able to bring charges against Shippen for waste in the Hospital Department, misuse of funds, and neglect of his duties. Shippen, who had had no previous military experience and knew nothing about camp life, never bothered to visit the hospitals and learn firsthand of the problems; Shippen, unlike Morgan, did not personally try to care for the patients and so was easy to attack for his indifference. A court martial acquitted Shippen of all charges of misconduct, but offended by the charges, he resigned in a huff in January 1781. His deputy, Dr. John Cochran, was appointed in his place.

Cochran proved to be the least combative and the most competent of all the directors; he finally brought some order to the handling of records and the distribution of supplies. The medical service, however, continued to be plagued by shortages now exacerbated by an inflationary currency, which plagued the country during the closing years of the war. No major military actions were taken after the British surrendered at Yorktown in October 1781 while negotiations over a peace treaty slowly progressed (it was signed in 1783). The pressure on the medical service was greatly reduced during Cochran's term because the sick and wounded were allowed to go home on furlough. Those who remained suffered through another cold winter in early 1782 without sufficient supplies and with inattentive doctors. Joseph Martin, the "Ordinary Soldier" who participated during most of the war, reported on the problems in a Trenton, New Jersey, hospital. The men had come down with some kind of fever; they again lacked sufficient food, drink, or medical attention since the military surgeons had been furloughed. Of the twenty men who fell sick in the Trenton hospital, eight died between January and March 1782, but Martin himself recovered because a local doctor volunteered to help him.

The acute problems regarding the health of the troops were not just in the hospitals but also among the healthy. For those in the camps, living conditions were deplorable. The lack of supplies, clothing, and food combined with poor sanitation in the camps severely undermined the health of the troops. Uneaten food was left to rot where the men slept. No provision was made to cart away the residue. Few officers in the American armies recognized the importance of camp hygiene or attempted to enforce orders for cleanliness or rest. Even the men themselves were indifferent to the need to separate their food preparation from where they deposited bodily wastes. Not until 1779, as a result of the influence of Baron Von Steuben, did Congress accept the idea that the preservation of health was the responsibility of command.

Von Steuben, with his experience in the Prussian army, had been hired as a drill master. He convinced Congress that it was necessary to have latrines located three hundred feet from the tent lines and to be moved every four days in winter, and more often in summer. Earlier suggestions from Benjamin Rush and other doctors for such sanitary provisions had been ignored, but Von Steuben had more influence than the medical personnel.

George Washington, meanwhile, had sent out general orders for the men to wash their hands two or three times a day and to change their shirts and stockings every two or three days in order to keep their bodies free of a "disagreeable smell" and to prevent skin diseases. Such orders were generally ignored. The situation was made worse when Washington, in an effort to stop the overindulgence in liquor brought into camp by prostitutes, banned women from the camp. It was a futile act because the women continued to tag along but in insufficient numbers to have any effect. Most of the camp followers were wives and servants—especially among the officers—but others were refugees fleeing British-controlled territory and fearful of being raped. Some were women who had become destitute while their husbands were serving in the military and became dependent on the largesse of the military.

It was taken for granted by military men of the time that the presence of women in the army camps was necessary for neatness and cleanliness. The men depended on their wives and other camp followers to do the washing and provide the incentive to be neat. Without the presence of women, the men seldom changed their clothes. Because there was no common mess with a cook, each man was also responsible for preparing his own ration of food, which, when he did receive it, was distributed in the raw state. Few men knew how to cook or how to handle the food; thus camp followers had traditionally provided those services. One of the reasons the American army appeared to be so bedraggled and unkempt was because so few women were attached to the military. All observers noted that there were fewer women among the Americans than was usual in the British camps. Washington never set a quota for women or the children who usually came with the women for each division. The records of the actual numbers are scanty. From one set of incomplete returns Joan Gundersen estimates that the camp at New Windsor, New York, held 10,380 officers and men plus 405 women and 302 children.

Female nurses were much in demand, but again, there were always too few of them. While Morgan was director, he ordered that nurses be hired for the hospital in New York at a salary of twenty-four cents a day and that additional women be employed as washerwomen to clean the bedding "from time to time." Until then, soldiers had been assigned to nursing, but they proved to be ineffective and lackadaisical at the tasks—either unwilling or unable to prepare food. Morgan wanted to provide one matron and ten female nurses for every one hundred wounded and sick soldiers, a goal impossible to achieve. Women balked at the low pay, and there were never enough of them to provide the needed nursing in the hospitals for those without wives or other consorts. Occasionally slave women were hired to work as nurses in the Virginia and South Carolina hospitals. In the usual manner of slave hiring, their masters were to receive their wages. By 1781 the salary of the women providing services in the hospitals had been raised to one-half that of the men. Matrons who supervised the nurses and washerwomen received fifty cents a day. As an additional incentive, the nurses were supposed to receive a food ration equal to that of the men. When Cochran prepared his returns of his hospital staff, he recognized the individual women by including them by name.

The ration for food and drink for all in the camps was generous in accordance with the standards of the day. There was sufficient meat and vegetables, bread and milk, some liquor, butter and rice, and the all-essential vinegar to cleanse both the water ration and their environment. Also included was a small amount of soap for washing clothes. Women camp followers usually received a one-half ration and their children one-quarter. The military was never able to secure the entire ration for the men or women and their children, so most of the time they went hungry and thirsty, contributing to the increasing ailments of what had once been a healthy population. Women suffered and died along with the men during the bad winters when supplies were nonexistent and shelter unavailable.

In his hospital returns, Cochran recorded the number of women under his care between May 1781 and December 1782. Each month a range between forty and fifty-six women and children are included among the sick, mostly in the northern hospitals. There were no returns for the southern hospitals for part of that time. In one return for November 1782 when the southern hospitals were included, the numbers were broken down to include twenty-five women and twenty-nine children in two hospitals: Albany, New York, and Hanover, Virginia, out of a total of 1,048 people. The following month there were forty women and children listed for a Virginia hospital and none in the north out of a total of 767 receiving care that month. Also included in that last return was the illness of six nurses in two other hospitals. But the total number of women in the camps was not registered, only those sick or wounded.

Probably some 20,000 women played a variety of roles during the Revolutionary War. In addition to their activities as camp followers and nurses, they also participated as soldiers either impersonating men or replacing their fallen husbands. Joan Gundersen provides details of many women who served, not as camp followers but as fighters. Margaret Corbin and Anna Maria Lane enlisted in the army as women and wore men's clothes during their services. At the age of twenty-two and pregnant, Mary Hays of Carlisle, Pennsylvania, joined her husband's unit in 1778. Wearing a skirt, she remained with the unit until the end of the war. At the battle of Monmouth, a musket ball went through her skirt without wounding her, an incident that probably gave rise to the Molly Pitcher legend of a woman supplying aid to soldiers at the risk of her life. Neither Corbin nor Lane attempted to disguise their gender as did Debora Sampson, the best known of those who served in the Continental army.

Deborah Sampson put on men's clothes, bound her breasts in a bandage, and joined the army as a man in 1782. At 5' 7" she was as tall as the average man, and her lack of beard did not set her off from many of the teenaged boys who also served. She took the name of Robert Shirliff (or Shurtlef or other variants of the spelling). Wounded in the thigh during the war, she managed to avoid the ministrations of a doctor and thus continued to hide her gender. She apparently operated on herself by cleansing the wound with rum and extracted the musket ball with her knife and a needle. She successful eluded any possibility of being discovered until a bout with fever when she was unconscious. A doctor, attempting to determine if she was alive, removed the binding around her breasts and discovered her secret. The dissembling did not harm her cause; she received an honorable discharge from the service in 1783 and eventually a pension from the army. The following year she married Benjamin Gannet and with him had two children. After her death he successfully argued to continue to receive her pension as her spouse. That Sampson was so successful in hiding her gender and treating her own wounds is an indication of the fluid nature of medical care. The general public was as capable of handling most conditions as those supposedly trained in medicine. They drew on the same theories and used similar techniques. The folk and the professional shared a common knowledge of surgery and treatments.

Part of that common knowledge was the reliance on inoculation to prevent the worst aspects of smallpox. Although a number of Americans had benefited from inoculation before the war, the majority had not. Most people lived in isolated farm areas where the dangers from the disease were minimal, and they saw no reason to consider inoculating themselves. Slaves on the southern plantations were seldom inoculated, and the poor everywhere could not afford the time or money necessary for the procedure. But those very people who had avoided inoculation became the ones most susceptible to the disease once the population began to move around to join the military or became refugees, when cities were besieged, or when armies appeared in new areas. The movement of people meant the bringing in and contact with unfamiliar microbes. Smallpox, because of its deadly and disfiguring consequences, was the most feared and the most likely to attract attention and force preventive action. The disease was central in three episodes at the beginning of the war from the fall of 1775 through 1776: (1) the attack on Quebec, (2) the siege of Boston, and (3) Lord Dunmore's appeal to slaves in Virginia.

The first invasion of Canada in the fall of 1775 failed because of a smallpox epidemic, which began in Quebec and spread to the Continental army and the local Indian tribes. As the army retreated from Canada, more than four hundred American soldiers were captured by the British, many of whom died from the disease. New Englanders and those from the southern colonies fared the worst. Those from the middle colonies had had more encounters with smallpox in the previous years and were thus less vulnerable. The devastation of the army because of smallpox brought not only the retreat from Canada and the loss of a major campaign but also the loss of most of the army. Dr. Samuel Stringer, director of the Northern Department reported that nearly one-half the retreating army was sick mostly with smallpox. He could not enforce isolation of the sick, and attempts to forbid self-inoculation failed. The disease spread even farther because many were inoculating themselves without taking any precautions. The arrival of fresh troops in New York that winter and spring brought in a new, vulnerable population. By the summer of 1776 General John Sullivan wrote to George Washington: "There are some regiments all down with the smallpox—not a single man fit for duty," while Benedict Arnold, commanding another part of the northern army, reported that half his forces were sick with the disease.

Meanwhile, Washington faced another smallpox epidemic in Massachusetts. During the 1775 siege of Boston, the disease raged in the city. The British prepared for the problem by inoculating the few in their own forces who had not had the disease. Civil authorities banned the procedure for the rest of the population, but secret self-inoculations kept the epidemic going. Washington decided not to inoculate his army, which was massed outside of the Boston, because it could so easily spread to put a large part of the men and women out of commission. Most of the men had only short-term enlistments, so Washington had a constant set of fresh troops. He fell back on the older method of prevention by isolating the sick and forbidding those from

Boston who escaped the British to come near his army encampments. When the British abandoned Boston, Washington allowed only those who had had smallpox or had been inoculated to enter the city. In July the authorities lifted the ban, and by the end of the year 5,000 people had been inoculated resulting in only 28 deaths. The immediate threat was over but Washington knew that it was only a reprieve. The returning soldiers from the Canadian expedition brought smallpox back to their homes in Pennsylvania and Connecticut. Native American allies of the British brought the disease to other Indian tribes around the Great Lakes areas, and civilians in New York suffered repeated episodes during the British occupation of 1777.

The greatest vulnerability to smallpox, however, was in the South. The last major epidemic in that area was in the 1760s with minor flare-ups in 1768 among the Indians from South Carolina northward and in Williamsburg, Virginia. In the absence of any threat of an epidemic, there was less reason to encourage inoculation; thus most of the population was not immune at the beginning of the war. Virginia had banned the procedure after the anti-inoculation riot of 1768; residents had to go elsewhere to protect themselves. In 1770, for instance, Mary Ambler took her two children to Baltimore to be inoculated by Dr. Stephenson. Her diary reports on the lengthy and expensive process. The doctor arrived at the boarding house where they were staying and inoculated them on a Monday with instructions to purge them regularly. Two weeks later they showed no signs of the pox, and Stephenson inoculated them again. They spent the time walking around town waiting for the inoculation to take. Finally they showed signs of the disease. The two children had high fevers for several days before the pox marks appeared; a week later they were up and about but continued the purges for weeks afterwards. The Amblers then returned to Virginia confident in their protection from the disease. Most of the population, however, had no such security.

Virginia was the first southern state to face a severe epidemic during the war. In November 1775, Lord Dunmore, the governor of Virginia, declared that all servants and Negroes were to be free if they joined the British troops. About 40 percent of the Virginia population was black, and somewhere between eight hundred and a thousand men and women were able to join the British forces. Dunmore himself had left the statehouse in Williamsburg and brought the runaways onto his ships that cruised the Chesapeake during the winter of 1775/76. In January smallpox appeared on one ship. As newcomers appeared on board they almost immediately succumbed to the disease. By June 1776 only 150 of the original group was left on Dunmore's ships. The fleet landed at various points and deserters carried the pox to other areas in Virginia and Maryland, infecting the general public and the patriot troops. More runaway slaves boarded the ships and also contracted the disease. By early 1777 men returning from the northern colonies brought a new source of infection to Virginia adding to the growing mortality from disease.

These three experiences with smallpox between 1775 and 1776 convinced George Washington of the necessity to protect his army through inoculation in spite of the cost and complicated regimen. After the American forces were driven out of New York in 1776 and their relative victories in New Jersey that winter, Washington decided the time was right to systematically inoculate the entire army. He was encouraged when Congress permitted more long-term enlistments in the Continental army after 1777. Washington ordered William Shippen, the new director of the medical services, to begin inoculation of the army in February of that year and before any new major offensive in the spring. It was to be done in secret to avoid any public panic or to give the British an excuse to attack while the army was at its weakest. Inoculation hospitals were set up in Alexandria and Fairfax, Virginia, Georgetown, Maryland, Morristown, New Jersey, Boston, and several cities in Pennsylvania and New York. In the process thousands of soldiers received inoculation at no cost to themselves and under supervision by the spring of 1777. The following winter at Valley Forge, Washington discovered that many men had escaped the previous order to be inoculated. Another three or four thousand went through the treatment. Then he decided to centralize the process and ordered all new non-immunized recruits to be sent to Valley Forge for inoculation before being dispersed to their units with "Women of the Army" tending the patients. Only a handful of men were inoculated in other northern hospitals. By 1779 smallpox was no longer a problem for the military. It was a uniquely successful public health measure in early American history.

The lessons of the military were not carried over to the rest of the country. Smallpox continued to devastate the civilian population and the American Indians. Charleston, South Carolina, was defended by irregular troops who had not been inoculated, and smallpox raged through the city the winter of 1779/80. Americans captured by the British were penned up in ships or other unsheltered enclosures and suffered from a variety of maladies including smallpox. The exodus of slaves from plantations in the Carolinas and Georgia to the British side and which brought a vast array of talents as boatmen, nurses, cooks, washerwomen, construction and road workers also brought more non-immune people together. The British in Savannah attracted some 5,000 slaves to their side between 1778 and 1779, about one-third of the slave population in Georgia. With no immunity, many of those former slaves died from smallpox as well as other diseases of camp life. The British did little to help the sick or provide inoculation, and the pestilence continued to spread to Native Americans even when they were only on the periphery of the battle scenes.

Other diseases ravaged the patriot forces. Inadequate diets and insufficient clothing and shelter contributed to susceptibility to all kinds of illnesses. As smallpox faded, dysentery and typhus (camp fever) took its place. In one return from a military hospital in South Carolina for March 1780, there were 302 admissions that included 12 gunshot wounds, 66 continual fever (typhoid or typhus), 60 intermittent fever (malaria), 44 rheumatism, 34 ulcers, and 20 venereal disease. As Baynes-Jones observes in his history of the medical service, efforts to prevent disease and preserve health were centered in the command structure and not in the Medical Department where it should have been. The failures, he claims, were due to ignorance, lack of interest, carelessness, and lack of discipline.

The wounded and sick during the American Revolution suffered the consequences of an inept, inexperienced, and insensitive but ambitious group of medical service administrators. The tensions between the regimental surgeons and the heads of the medical department, conflicts between the needs of the soldiers and the suppliers of materials for their comfort, lack of agreement between the goals of the military physicians and the civilian population, and animosities within the military medical department were never resolved and left military medicine almost where it had started. The doctors may have learned something about the management of a military hospital system, though, and surgeons probably added to their skills when dealing with injuries, but the knowledge gained did not translate into an effective medical service even though three secretaries of war between 1783 and 1812 were physicians (Henry Dearborn, James McHenry, and William Eustis) and the number of men in the army increased. Both Eustis and McHenry served as doctors during the Revolutionary War and had personal experience with the health problems in wartime, an experience that did not carry over to their new posts.

Little was learned about protecting the health of soldiers during the war. Nor did it promote cooperation between the people in government and the medical personnel. In effect, the experience of wartime pointed to the tension between those two areas of life in the new nation. The most elite physicians could not command sufficient respect from Congress to respond to their pleas for more attention to the health of the soldiers. Congress, it is true, was under difficult constraints for money to conduct the war, and health conditions were low on their priority list. On the other hand, Congress did understand the importance of smallpox inoculation because the procedure and its ramifications were well documented and had become part of common knowledge. Significantly the recommendation to inoculate came from the military, not the medical service. Congress could not respond as easily to the problems of medical organization; it did not understand the importance of basic comforts for men under arms or the dangers from other diseases that plagued the military because of poor hygienic conditions. That lack of concern about health in close quarters would be reflected in later years in the indifference of government to public health problems in urban areas, a topic discussed in chapter 10.

6

New Nation

September 11, 1793. Philadelphia, the temporary capital of the United States, had suffered for weeks from (in the parlance of the day) a bilious malignant fever. The victims had black grainy vomits, nosebleeds, and headaches. Their skin and eye whites turned yellow. In a matter of days, sometimes hours, death followed the first symptoms. Most of the early cases were clustered near the dock where, Elizabeth Drinker noted in her diary for August 16, disintegrating coffee beans, recently unloaded from a ship, had emitted a strong stench that added to the smells of the usual rotting foods. Clearly that was the source of infection. Both public opinion and the medical profession understood that strong smells explained the presence of a deadly miasma. But what was the disease? In late August, Dr. Benjamin Rush, one of the most respected physicians in town, diagnosed the malady as the dreaded yellow fever. At first he urged people to leave the city.

The Philadelphia medical community could not agree on the cause of the disease—one camp argued that a miasma at the dock caused the humoral imbalance that led to the disease, another argued that the fever was

>> 95

Benjamin Rush was one of the most respected physicians in the early Republic. He diagnosed yellow fever in Philadelphia in 1793 and proceeded to dose his patients with mercury and excessive bleeding, tragically claiming success in fighting the disease. (Engraving by Edwin from the painting by Thomas Sully 1816. Courtesy of the Library Company of Philadelphia)

communicated through person to person contact and was a "contagion." The source of the infection probably was most likely at the waterfront, but it was the presence of people with yellow fever traveling from the West Indies and the mosquitoes that came with them that started the epidemic. That summer several vessels filled with refugees from the island of Santo Domingo had arrived at the Philadelphia port. A slave-led rebellion on the western, French-speaking side of the island in 1791 (Haiti today), inspired indirectly by the 1789 Revolution in France, frightened many whites into abandoning their sugar plantations. They looked for refuge in likely American cities and thus their arrival in Philadelphia. Quarantine was very lax between epidemics, and little note was taken of the sick on board in the waters near the city.

Yellow fever was always present on the island of Santo Domingo as in most of the West Indies, and it often created havoc in the southern states. Many people in warmer climates were immune because they either survived a course of the disease or were the children of women who had been sick. The mother's antibodies can cross the placenta, giving the infant temporary immunity and the possibility of a milder case later on as a child. Like malaria, mosquitoes communicate yellow fever. The insect vector is harmless until it feeds on the blood of someone with the disease and then feeds on the body of another person. A bite from that mosquito would then infect a human being. The last time yellow fever had appeared in the Philadelphia area was in 1761, and after more than thirty years free of the disease few people carried the necessary antibodies. Unsanitary conditions in the town, stagnant water in the streets, and rotting garbage provided the breeding grounds for the mosquitoes. The disease slowly spread beyond the confines of the dock area as people moved about and mosquitoes proliferated throughout the city.

By early August doctors were dismayed by the death rate. They bled and purged, but the sick died anyway. The toll in lives kept rising from a few each day at the beginning of August to more than twenty a day by the end of the month. On September 8, forty-two deaths were reported. Most governmental officials as well as the upper, more affluent classes left town. Philadelphia was not only the capital of the state of Pennsylvania, it was also the temporary capital of the United States. The members of the state legislature left first followed by the governor. President George Washington and most of his cabinet had abandoned the city by September 10 when Rush declared that the "disorder was now past the Art of man or medicine to cure." When Washington went to Mount Vernon, he left Henry Knox, the secretary of war, in charge of the federal government, but even he thought it wise to leave after a few days. Most of the officials in the city government also fled, leaving only the mayor, Mathew Clarkson, and a handful of Guardians of the Poor to handle the crisis. By the middle of September there was no one left to clean the streets. Gone were the councilmen, judges, clerks, chimney sweeps, and night watchmen. The federal government, including customs agents, just "evaporated." Many doctors left town along with church leaders and other socially prominent citizens.

Benjamin Rush and a handful of other doctors remained to care for their patients. But no remedies seemed to work and no traditional preventive measures seemed to be effective. Doctors too succumbed and died. In desperation Rush began to experiment on his patients using more drastic methods than ever tried before. From mild purging he shifted to what were considered dangerous doses of mercury and jalap, a powerful purgative from the *Ipomoea purga* plant. And he increased the amount of blood drawn. The new system, he argued, more effectively drew off the "putrid and excess matter." The extreme bloodletting removed what Rush called the "inflammatory stimulus." He acted on the theory that all disease resulted in a "spasm" of the blood vessels that could be relieved by bleeding. The presence of blood in the intestines found after autopsy proved to him that there had been too much blood in the bodies of sick individuals. In fact, yellow fever often resulted in intestinal bleeding, thus the black vomit noticed as one of the symptoms of the disease. His patients were already losing quantities of blood internally, and Rush's extreme methods hastened their deaths. Autopsies on patients who had suffered through Rush's extreme methods also revealed excessive destruction of the lining of the stomachs and intestines more so than with less heroic therapies.

Nonetheless, Rush claimed a huge success. He proudly announced that he saved ninety-nine patients out of a hundred with his new therapy but later revised his estimate down to a more realistic four out of five. "My medicine," he boasted to his wife, "has got the name of an *inoculating powder*, for it certainly and as universally deprives the yellow fever of its mortality, as inoculation does the smallpox." William Cobbett attacked him for this overly optimistic claim, noting that Rush kept no records to prove his success. But if one took the record of mortality in his household where four out of the six who were sick died, then, Cobbett concluded, such a sample indicated that sixty-six out of one hundred did not survive that drastic remedy. How often these extreme methods were used is also questionable. Many doctors, who professed to follow Rush's lead, did not actually use the drastic doses of mercury or bleed as much as recommended. Rush was furious at those who did not follow through completely.

Cobbett was not the only one to question Rush's methods and theory. A small coterie of French physicians who treated those of French and Haitian background, as well as the poor relegated to the pest house at Bush Hill, argued for more moderate treatment. At Bush Hill where French doctors held sway, those stricken with the fever had a better chance of survival with only very mild purges than at home or with Rush's therapies. The overseers at Bush Hill kept meticulous records of admission, cures, and deaths indicating that they saved about 50 percent of those treated in the hospital compared with the 25 percent survival with other treatments. Stephen Girard, in charge of the emergency hospital for yellow fever at Bush Hill, hired Dr. Jean Devéze, who had trained in France and had recently arrived from Santo Domingo. Devéze depended on stimulants and wine as well as mild purging when necessary, the opposite course of treatment from that advocated by Rush. Action, he advised, was not always necessary. The French medical establishment taught that the doctor was not to oppose nature. Following that teaching, Devéze thought the doctor's role was best as spectator, to observe carefully before diagnosing and prescribing. He did agree with Rush that yellow fever was not contagious because, he noted, not everyone at Bush Hill, which was at a distance from the riverfront, became sick in spite of constant contact with the sufferers. Devéze was later celebrated in Europe for his successful and humane treatments even though many Americans ignored his successes at the hospital. He was, after all, a foreigner in competition with an American doctor.

The French were not the only ones to complain about the extremes hailed by Rush. Dr. William Currie, Rush's most vocal opponent, insisted that the disease was not a result of a miasma. There was nothing to fear from walking in the streets, he announced: only direct face-to-face contact mattered. For remedy, he recommended tea or barley water with a mild purgative alternated with laudanum (a form of opium), rejecting both mercury and bleeding as too strong. He advised the liberal use of vinegar for bathing and disinfecting bed sheets, Throughout August and September that year people in Philadelphia who could not leave lit fires, rang bells, hung tarred rope around their necks, carried camphor bags, and generally followed traditional folklore about protecting themselves from disease rather than call on the physician's extreme therapies. Household remedies continued to appear in the newspaper, some hailing the "Bark," others vinegar or pennyroyal as "sovereign" remedies. Malaria may well have been present and thus some people may have recovered from their illness when given quinine.

Rush was infuriated by the publicity for these contending remedies. He could not understand why everyone did not see what he believed to be a cure. The *Federal Gazette*, which managed to continue publishing during the crisis, printed angry letters from both sides. Rush accused his opponents of being murderers and of conspiring against him. Other replied with equal fervor. At the same time, what could have been a major boost to public health from Rush's advocacy of sanitation measures to reduce the miasma rising from the stench—cleaning the streets, draining swamps, and bringing in clean water—received less attention as few of the civil leaders were willing to spend money to clean up the city. A final blow to Rush, and probably the community, came when the College of Physicians declared that the disease was a contagion of foreign origin and not due to a miasma. Rush quickly resigned from the College. In spite of the opposition, his reputation among some colleagues and all his patients grateful for his solicitous attention remained high. The controversy may have raised Rush's reputation, but it did not improve the status of the profession.

It was Rush who became the hero of the day in the new nation and was memorialized for his actions during the crisis. The peculiar role of Benjamin Rush in American history cannot be explained on the basis of his remedies, which were often fatal. His reputation was not due to any true healing capability in his drugs but derived from his personality and social status, his gentlemanly manner, his humanitarianism, and the university credentials. Most likely he also attracted patients because he combined the ability to express both compassion for others and an utter confidence in himself and his methods. Yet again, the placebo effect was very much in play in Rush's ability to attract patients and sometimes help them recover. The purging and bleeding brought dramatic evidence that the "putrid" matter was being banished from bodies of the sick satisfying the public that the right action was being taken. The high death rate was not blamed on the therapies. Unfortunately many others continued to follow Rush's extreme methods. He alone may have held back American medicine for at least two generations as doctors began to use more jalap, more mercury, more bloodletting, to prove that they were taking action, citing the celebrated Rush as their mentor.

As the doctors squabbled over remedies and causes, people continued to suffer. On September 24, ninety-six people died in Philadelphia, the average for the month being about seventy a day. The worst day was October 11 when at least 119 people were buried. The weather turned stormy after that day and then cooled, The death rate began to fall, and by the end of October the epidemic was on the wane. On November 14 there were no more admissions to Bush Hill. People began to return to town, and in December, Congress reconvened in Philadelphia. The crisis was over for that year. It had taken the lives of about 10 percent of the population (55,000) of the city. The black population, which had born the burden of caring for the sick at home and burying the dead, lost three hundred of its 2,500 citizens. Previous experience had indicated that those from Africa carried some protection from the disease, and black residents of Philadelphia were called on to nurse and assist the sick. That belief proved to be untrue. Too many generations of African Americans had lived in Philadelphia and had no more immunity than the white folk.

The cause of the disease soon became a political issue. After the organization of the new government in 1789, two major factions began to form—the Federalists who supported a more centralized government, a closer relation with Great Britain for trade, and opposition to the French Revolution; and the Republicans who advocated support for the French, opposed close relations with the former mother country, and called for greater limits on federal power in favor of states rights. Both groups supported the new Constitution, but they were divided on policy—the Federalists advocating a loose interpretation of the Constitution based on the "necessary and proper" clause, and the Republicans (soon to be the Democratic Party) with a strict interpretation of that document. During the 1790s the parties were just beginning to organize their supporters. Leading the Federalists were George Washington, Alexander Hamilton, and John Adams. Thomas Jefferson, Aaron Burr, Benjamin Rush, and their followers formed the opposition. They were not sectional parties but differed on how best to promote the prosperity of the country.

In a perceptive analysis of a developing party system Martin Pernick demonstrates that the epidemic in Philadelphia helped shape the political rhetoric of the two factions. Each side took a position on the contagion versus miasma question. The Federalists blamed the French refugees for causing a contagion. Their call to close trade with the French islands was an attempt to restrict immigration and cut into the French support for the Republican Party. Republicans blamed it on the effluvia from unsanitary docks causing a miasma to rise. Their solution was an expensive cleanup supported by Rush. Business interests found the Federalist solution more acceptable. Hamilton countered Republican calls for sanitation by scornfully repudiating Rush's mercurial therapy, calling it the deadly "Republican" cure. In effect, Pernick concludes that the epidemic attracted "new supporters to the two developing parties, thereby extending and broadening the base of the new party system." So we can see that early on in American history, health issues indeed had political ramifications.

The fever returned to Philadelphia the following year and again in 1796, and then yearly with little or no consensus about treatment. It spread to other cities—Baltimore, Mobile, and New Orleans. New York suffered a series of epidemics until 1806. The disagreements over remedies and causes of yellow fever split all the medical communities and contributed to the further distrust of professional healers. If doctors could not agree on therapies, or even the cause of a disease, how could any of them be trusted? A New York doctor, David Hosack, vehemently objected to Benjamin Rush's methods. He declared that "bloodletting and drastic purging were fruitless." He, like Rush, proposed major sanitary reforms that were rejected. Fisher Ames, a leading Federalist and the son and brother of doctors, decided that he trusted himself more than the physicians. In 1795 he prescribed for his "bilious" disease "some cider, a trotting horse, keep as warm as I can, abstain from excesses of every kind." More significantly, in the aftermath of the epidemic when local governments established the first permanent health boards, only laymen were appointed to serve. The advice of quarrelsome doctors was often rejected. The one exception was in New Orleans, but that did not last. The doctors clashed with the business interests that opposed strict quarantines early in the nineteenth century, and by 1821 physicians no longer sat on the board of health in New Orleans.

Once the threat of yellow fever subsided in 1805, there was no dramatic epidemic to disturb American tranquility for another twenty-five years. Most attempts at quarantine, the establishment of local health boards, and the few sanitary measures that had been instituted lost public support. What was ignored for a long time were the endemic diseases that took more lives than the dramatic epidemics. Death and disability from malaria, typhoid, dysentery, tuberculosis, and infant mortality, to name a few of the ubiquitous conditions, were accepted as the norm, and no public action was taken to alleviate those problems. In a reflection of their declining influence in America, only a handful of doctors saw what the problem was and recommended sanitary solutions, but they were ignored and often vilified.

American medicine had been severely retarded by the Revolution. Many of the best-trained European-oriented physicians left the country after 1776. Charleston lost a considerable number when it banished thirteen physicians during the war, men the local authorities classified as "obnoxious persons." The medical school in Philadelphia closed during the war and was not revived until 1790s. The plans for another New York school were stifled by the war and not revived until long afterward. Harvard's earlier plans to establish a medical program did not come to fruition until 1782. As of 1800 there were only four small medical colleges, and all provided very limited training. Communication with British medical circles continued to be minimal in the early years of the new nation, partly because many Americans showed little interest in Old World medical practices. The flush of nationalistic feeling that followed the Revolution brought disdain for European institutions, including those pertaining to medical science. American doctors continued to follow the usual humoral and miasmatic theories of illness, often refusing to differentiate between diseases and stressing the responses of the individual constitution as basic to therapeutic decisions.

Although peace brought a resumption of contact with European medical circles through correspondence and printed matter, fewer Americans went abroad to study. Not one American graduated from Edinburgh University in 1803. Self-taught physicians relied on domestic medical books as much as the general populace did, drawing heavily on William Buchan's original 1769 *Every Man His Own Doctor* and his later *Domestic Medicine* that concentrated on diseases of women and children. Both books went through hundreds of printings and were easily plagiarized by other writers. Europeans, though, were moving in the direction of less action and a focus on nature's healing power. Greater attention to clinical studies and statistical analyses had led to the identification of specific diseases. An attempt to correlate clinical observation with autopsies was shaping new therapies. The small number of Americans who went to Europe to study medicine in the early nineteenth century and accepted those discoveries could not counter the growing popularity of Benjamin Rush's heroic remedies.

One important European discovery actually did reach the United States: the new method of protection against smallpox, discovered by the British doctor Edward Jenner in the 1790s. He found that inoculation from a related disease, cowpox, provided immunity against the human disease without the danger of either catching the malady or spreading it to others. That discovery inspired fairly rapid imitation. In Massachusetts the highly educated Dr. Benjamin Waterhouse read Jenner's 1799 book describing the procedure, and he managed to get some of the cowpox toxin for his son. Trained in London, Edinburgh, and Leyden, Waterhouse was distrusted by the local medical establishment for his unorthodox ideas and "foreign education." His lack of popularity among the medical establishment of Boston was no doubt due partly to his contempt for American doctors who he thought, "vulgar . . . conforming to the whims and nonsense of old women and silly people." In defiance of his cohorts, he was able to persuade the lay-dominated Boston Board of Health to sponsor a public test of the new procedure, now labeled "vaccination" after the *variole vaccinae* or cowpox, in 1802 and the process rapidly caught on.

Both lay and medical personnel in other parts of the country also read about Jenner's discovery and tried a variety of experiments with the vaccine. Thomas Jefferson in the usual manner of using his slaves as guinea pigs, had two hundred of his and his neighbor's slaves vaccinated. When they showed no ill effects, he injected his whole family. Dr. Calvin Jones also tried the procedure in South Carolina. Their results helped southerners to overcome much of the fear and distrust that had followed inoculation in the past. In New York a group of doctors led by Dr. Valentine Seaman offered free vaccination for the poor, and in Baltimore Dr. James Smith vaccinated those in the almshouse. Northern doctors lacked the access to slaves, and so the poor became the experimental victims.

Smith successfully lobbied the Maryland legislature to establish a vaccine institute to distribute the substance in 1809. He took his idea to Congress and in 1813 was appointed national agent to dispense the "vaccine matter" to any citizen who requested it. The military also took notice. Drawing on their experiences during the Revolution, army surgeons issued orders to vaccinate the entire army just before the outbreak of the next war in May 1812. Unfortunately, no one followed up with studies to test the effectiveness of the vaccine.

Within a few years, the new system of protection against smallpox had replaced inoculation except among the more conservative physicians who clung to the older system. In order to put an end to the older practice, some of the states began to pass laws forbidding inoculation. New York had led the way in 1816, but acceptance did not imply action. Few people bothered to protect themselves, and smallpox epidemics continued sporadically throughout the century. Vaccination itself was not a guaranteed protection. No one realized that the new procedure did not confer lifetime immunity and required successive treatments after a number of years. When one of Dr. Smith's vaccinated patients came down with smallpox in 1821, the procedure was discredited in the eyes of physicians, and the attempt to establish a national agent to distribute the vaccine was attacked as a monopoly. The 1813 federal law making the vaccine available to the public was repealed in 1822, and the federal government withdrew from its interest in public health concerns for another half-century.

And yet the Revolution had ended in an atmosphere of optimism regarding its political system, its intellectual and scientific achievements, and, by association, its medicine. Americans had created a "more perfect" government as stated in the 1789 Constitution, so too they looked forward to a superior system of medicine, one "distinctively *American*" that they claimed owed little to Europeans. New editions of Buchan's book put out by Samuel Powell Griffets in 1795 and Isaac Cathrall in 1797 were "adapted" to American conditions, on the assumption that American diseases were different from those of the Old World. Dr. William Currie of Philadelphia undertook a survey of climate and disease in the United States, believing that the rules of medical practice in other countries could not be the same in the United States and differed as much as their governments did. Convinced that American health conditions were exceptional—and, like their political institutions, superior to Europeans—Benjamin Rush thought his more extreme therapies were especially suited to the stronger, more vigorous American citizens. Such patriotic enthusiasm did little to advance any scientific study of medicine in the United States but did manage to separate Americans from the advances being made across the Atlantic.

National feelings, however, began to encourage the collection of statistics regarding diseases. Probably the most influential work of the kind was Noah Webster's *A Brief History of Epidemics in Pestilential Diseases* (1799). Webster brought together information from a range of diaries, medical studies, journals, and assorted sets of mortality statistics from the ancient to the modern worlds to correlate diseases with environment. His hope was to promote a systematic collection of disease data that would throw light on the cause or causes of such illnesses. His compilation reflected a yearning for intellectual order that paralleled the political order of the new republic. It is significant that this study of disease and the environment was prepared not by a doctor but by a layman, whose greatest concern was standardizing grammar and language.

Post-Revolutionary enthusiasm also motivated the most educated physicians to try to control access to the profession through the establishment of state medical societies and licensing laws. The Massachusetts Medical Society was granted the power to examine all candidates for the practice of "physic." Doctors in Connecticut tried (and failed) in 1786 to achieve licensing power. New York passed a law in 1792 to restrict practice to those with "acceptable" medical training, a standard that was hard to define. In Philadelphia doctors failed to require association with the College of Physicians as a qualification to practice rather than merely a fellowship that conveyed distinction. Other attempts at establishing qualifications to practice through licensing laws proved to be ineffective and unenforceable. Most state laws merely limited the right to use the courts to collect fees with no penalty for the unlicensed. The tradition of self-help prevented any control over who could be a healer, and by the 1830s even those minimal regulations were repealed.

The health problems during the first twenty-five years of the new nation were complicated by two other significant developments. The first was the growth of cities and the rising numbers of poor; the second was the dramatic increase in the geographic size of the country. As the nineteenth century opened, the new class of workers arriving in the cities often teetered on the edge of poverty. The average overall health of the poor was declining by the 1820s because of the inability of workers to earn sufficient income to feed their families. In Baltimore the infant mortality rate among the poor continued to rise. One main cause of death for children was "marasmus," a term used to describe malnourishment and protein deficiency. These new urban families had much less access to fruit, vegetables, and dairy products than even the poorest rural people. Although in general Americans continued to eat more protein than people in other parts of the world, increasing poverty was gradually eroding that advantage. The sanitation problems became worse as the urban poor populations grew; little provision was made for public health, thus increasing the danger from disease. From 1790 to 1830 the number of cities of more than 5,000 people increased from eight to forty-five. The population of New York City grew from 30,000 to 200,000 people, Philadelphia from 40,000 to 160,000.

As the cities grew so did the size of the country as a whole. At the end of the Revolutionary War, the geographic extent doubled. The peace treaty of 1783 moved the western boundary of the United States from the Appalachian Mountains to the Mississippi River. Twenty years later Thomas Jefferson negotiated with the French to buy the Louisiana Territory that extended America's reach beyond the Mississippi to north of Texas in the south and to the Pacific on the northwest. Florida was acquired by treaty in 1819. That left only the southern and middle areas of the country from Texas to California in the hands of the Spanish, lands that would be taken after the Mexican War in 1848. During Jefferson's administrations from 1801 to 1809 Americans began to fill up the vast territory between the mountains and the Mississippi River, establishing towns and scattering farms, moving farther and father away from the old established ways of the East Coast and, significantly, the influence of European medical learning.

Jefferson himself distrusted learned medicine because of its speculative doctrines and heroic practice, although he admired Benjamin Rush and consulted him occasionally. Rush was asked to provide a list of needed medications and a few commonsense rules for good health for the Lewis and Clark expedition in 1803. Nonetheless, no physician was asked to accompany the travelers in the belief that a knowledgeable layman, in this case, Meriwether Lewis, could provide all the medical attention necessary. Jefferson proved to be prescient. The group of thirty-three including the Indian woman Sacagawea and her infant survived the grueling trip.

There was little incentive for the more established doctors to go west into the new territories. They stayed home, and those with fewer credentials moved on beyond the mountains. While one out of fifty physicians along the East Coast had a diploma from a school of medicine, only one out of one hundred did so west of the Appalachian Mountains in 1810. Few of those physicians in the west had any university education. In the Arkansas Territory, Governor John Pope declared in 1831 "that many who have gone through a regular course in medical schools are grossly ignorant of the theory and practice of medicine." The most educated in the backcountry could perhaps lay claim to three years of an apprenticeship and two short (three- or four-month-long) sessions of lectures in a medical school, the second session merely a repeat of the first after an interval of a year. There were no laboratories; there was no dissection experience available, only lectures from other similarly half-educated physicians; there was no longer any requirement for a college or high school diploma. Apprentices were encouraged to read popular medical books, including the self-help manuals, so they would be familiar with domestic medicine. It was important for the novice doctor to know what kind of care his patients were used to in order to "fit in" to the community. In fact, their remedies differed little from folk medications.

The treatment of George Washington's last illness follows that pattern. With a painful throat and difficulty breathing, Washington sent for his overseer, who usually medicated the slaves, to bleed him. The doctor arrived the next day and proceeded with more depletion—a blister on his neck, more bleeding, and a purgative dose of calomel. Two more physicians arrived and took more blood. One doctor argued against further bleeding and recommended a tracheotomy to open the breathing passage, but he was ignored—orthodoxy was too entrenched. Washington's condition worsened rapidly. He might or might not have recovered from the throat infection, but the therapy probably hastened his death. The original bloodletting was part of the domestic medicine of the plantation, a mild version of the orthodox and Washington's own remedy applied by a layperson. The doctors merely added their heroic measures.

The novice physician was always free to expound his own theories and concoct his own remedies from local herbs, easily borrowing from local Indian lore, domestic medicine, or, in the South, African traditions. These novice doctors then took on their own apprentices and perpetuated the highly personal, nonscientific medicine that followed their own proclivities. Often to prove their competency and in an attempt to distinguish themselves from the midwives and herbalists, they specialized in more dramatic therapies, some using Rush's methods of extreme bloodletting and heavy doses of purging compounds. Dr. David Ramsay, dismayed by the state of medicine, noted in 1800 that the "old remedies, bleeding, blistering, mercury, opium, bark and wine, have been carried to a much great extent than formerly, and applied to diseases for which they were seldom, if ever, prescribed fifty years ago." In typical American fashion, he theorized that diseases were "more inflammatory" than in the past requiring "freer evacuation and more energetic prescriptions." Even among the purveyors of domestic medicine, bleeding was being used as a general restorative to treat pleurisy, sore throat, chest pains, broken bones, diarrhea, fainting, and a host of their conditions. Even so, those domestic healers tended to be less aggressive than the physicians who would be called in when all else failed.

The best that can be said about the practice of the backwoods doctors is that there was a fusion of Indian and African lore with both domestic and professional medical practice that may have modified some of the extreme therapeutic measures. So popular were the Indian remedies that Peter Smith published *The Indian Doctor's Dispensary* in 1813 in response to the public demand. Native lore assisted the midwife Anne Bixby of Hardin County, Kentucky, in solving a mystery of the "milk sickness," a disease unfamiliar in the East and often fatal. Abraham Lincoln's mother, Nancy, had died of that in 1818. The cause was a toxin in white snakeroot, a plant eaten by cows when they were left to graze. Bixby consulted with a Shawnee herbalist who told her about the plant used in small doses by the Indians for various problems but that was poisonous in larger doses. The midwife experimented by feeding it to a calf; the animal became sick, and Bixby warned her neighbors to be wary of cows that grazed when the plant was growing. Although known locally, milk sickness was unfamiliar in other areas and continued to be a problem until scientists rediscovered the cause in 1920.

As the nation expanded westward, so too did slavery. The invention of the cotton gin early in the century had encouraged farmers to move to the newly opened southern areas to expand their cotton lands and thus the necessity of the institution of slavery. Although the slave importation trade had ended officially in 1809, the domestic slave trade increased. States in the East no longer required a large slave population. The tobacco industry in Maryland and Virginia had declined, and farmers sold their excess slaves to the new plantations (down the river) in the Louisiana Territory. In 1810 there were only about 40,000 people in the Mississippi and Alabama areas, but within ten years the numbers grew to 200,000 including a black population of 75,000. Those two areas became states in 1817 and 1819 respectively.

White doctors followed the expanding plantation system, anxious to take advantage of the potentially lucrative contracts caring for the increasing number of slaves. To justify their role as necessary to the plantation owner, doctors wholeheartedly supported the slave system; thus, white medicine became yet another symbol of the degradation of black people. Although there is not much information about the treatment of slaves in the popular health manuals, in other publications and letters many doctors discussed and commented on diseases and health problems of those they tended.

Racial theories did not necessarily translate into differential treatment of slaves, but doctors did note differences in health and reactions to diseases. It was obvious that some African Americans had a greater resistance to malaria and possibly yellow fever than did whites. Doctors were aware of the greater incidence of tuberculosis and pneumonia among slaves and that the infant mortality was greater by two to one. No mention was made of the importance of maternal health or of the need to provide more sustenance to babies. Some doctors commented on inadequate housing but always remained silent on the physical and sexual abuse of slaves.

There was general agreement that black people's sicknesses did not differ from whites and that internal workings were the same. A handful of doctors postulated that there were psychological differences between blacks and whites and that issue is discussed in chapter 8, but there is little evidence that anyone thought that there were major differences in physiology or responses to most diseases.. Thus anything learned from tending the slaves could be applied to the white population. Surgical experiments and the testing of drugs on blacks became commonplace, especially in the newly established medical schools in the South. In the few schools were anatomy was taught, black bodies were often used for educational autopsies. What was learned from these experiments was assumed to apply to the rest of the population. Physicians did not hesitate to make use of information from those experiments and apply it to their white clients. What black people learned from those experiences was to avoid white medicine whenever possible.

The African American population thus has its own peculiar conflicting relationship with the medical profession. Slaves were often subjected to forced treatment by doctors when they preferred African herbal therapies combined with mystical rites. The abusive treatment in medical schools and experiments on the plantation added to their fear of doctors. The long tradition of distaste for doctors and resistance to orthodox medicine left a bitter legacy. In a recent study by Marian Gornick regarding disparities in use of health services, the author notes that black recipients of Medicare continue to lag behind whites in their use of even free or reduced-cost services. Gornick admits that little is known about the causes and explanations for the disparities, but I suspect the long history of abuse by doctors under slavery and afterwards in the twentieth century may indeed be one of the factors.

The living conditions in the recently opened midwestern areas created new threatening disease environments. Settlers moving west into Kentucky and Tennessee, southern Ohio, Indiana, and Illinois tended to establish their farms in low-lying river bottoms where the soil was most fertile and there was easy access to river transport for their goods. But those swampy areas were also a breeding ground for mosquitoes, fleas, ticks, rats, and snakes. The healthier high ground was rockier and more densely forested, and therefore less desirable for the farmers. Louisville, Kentucky, built on a series of falls on the banks of the Ohio River, with an early population of 4,000 in 1820 suffered almost continual epidemics of fever. Summer bouts of dysentery and malaria were so debilitating that the victims were then subject to additional physical ailments. Dropsy, jaundice, consumption, measles, mumps, scarlet fever, pneumonia, and typhoid were endemic. Little was done to keep the mosquito population down or provide for basic cleanliness. Conevery Valencius notes that St. Louis, Missouri perched on porous rock eroded by rain created sinkholes that hampered drainage and left sewage to back up thus creating similar sanitary and disease problems. The scarcity of physicians, however, required medicine to be mostly homegrown. People treated themselves with mustard plasters, sassafras, rhubarb, molasses, and herbs, which might relieve the symptoms, but offered no cures. They easily added Indian herbs to their own lists.

Doctors too improvised. They learned from white folk about ergot as a muscle relaxant and useful for abortions. They learned about the foxglove plant (digitalis) for "dropsy" or heart related ailments and about willow bark (aspirin) for pain and inflammation from the local Indians. They adopted the use of castor oil, which had been a staple of black households both slave and free. Household medicine, in turn, borrowed from professional medicine and kept laudanum (opium) for pain and the "bark" for malaria in the home. And as usual, there were sharp tensions between the professionals and the general populace. Those who considered themselves knowledgeable in domestic medicine or folklore often refused therapies recommended by a local doctor, or they might insist on the more drastic treatments such as bleeding when the professional considered it unnecessary. Because there were few agreements on causes or therapies among the professionals or between the physicians and the public, conflicting decisions were not unusual.

Even eating and drinking habits began to deteriorate in the years after the Revolution. Certainly one of the reasons for the regular consumption of hard liquor like whiskey was due to its easy availability and low cost. But it was also the result of a change in the way food was prepared and eaten. Frances Trollope (mother of the more famous novelist Anthony Trollope), visiting in 1828, reported, "the ordinary mode of living is abundant, but not delicate." She criticized the reliance on meat, the "half-baked" bread and the "want of skill in the composition of sauces." Instead of leisurely meals, food was consumed in haste by all classes. A visitor to New York described the new method of eating in restaurants. The table was covered, he said, with "vast number of dishes," where people spent "from five to ten minutes for break- fast, fifteen to twenty for dinner, and ten minutes for super . . . each person as soon as satisfied leaves the table without regard to his neighbors; no social conversation follows."

Because many homes lacked ovens, food was either deep fried in grease or boiled and definitely overcooked, often prepared in dirty and pest-ridden conditions. James Fennimore Cooper condemned practices that he found in the more western parts of the United States in the 1820s. The food he found to be "heavy, coarse, ill-prepared and indigestible." Henry Marie Brack- enridge's 1818 guide for settlers in the west noted that the food in the west included "great quantities of fat pork, seldom any fresh meat, or vegetables." Daniel Drake commenting on health conditions in the 1850s chided people for eating too much meat, a practice he blamed on the newly arrived immi- grants who, "seldom tasted" meat in the old country and therefore wanted "to indemnify themselves for the past privation as soon as they arrive." Other food, especially vegetables, he complained, was "unskillfully cooked, indiscriminately mixed, imperfectly masticated, and rapidly swallowed." All decried the heavy drinking that often accompanied the often-tasteless food. The whiskey may well have provided more taste to the food but was justified on the grounds that it eased the indigestion that accompanied these poor eating habits.

Visitors remarked on the generally filthy living conditions that pre- vailed in the newly settled areas. William Cobbett, the English agricultural reformer who toured America in 1818, described the American farmhouses as "a sort of out-of-door slovenliness." Suellen Hoy in her study of cleanli- ness quotes William Faux, who when visiting Indiana and Illinois described the people as "filthy, bordering on the beastly." Soap was "no where to be seen" in the taverns and everywhere he met people with dirty hands and faces. Bathing was a rarity; the bathtub was unknown in most homes includ- ing that of the middle class. The indoor bathroom or privy was not even a hopeful dream. Most Americans were oblivious to the need for cleanliness. As they moved west, with less pressure from the elite notions of the coast, the filthy living conditions had become the norm. Contributing to the lack of personal hygiene in the backcountry was the rhetoric of the Republican Party that extolled rural life and hard physical work as healthier than urban life. Almanacs reinforced the idea that while towns and cities posed a risk to one's physical and moral conditions, the healthy, rural life was superior, dirty as it was. Such rhetoric supported the popular notion that filth was a sign of plain living and honest toil. Doctors no longer had the public support to overcome these attitudes, and health conditions continued to decline in many of the disease-ridden western areas.

The spirit of nationalism that followed on the Revolution did nothing to advance scientific medicine in the United States. The yellow fever epidemic and the growing popularity of Benjamin Rush merely reinforced traditional remedies. The dearth of doctors in the frontier areas forced people to depend on their own resources and knowledge about health. In practical terms doctors now faced a population more confident in its own remedies than that of the professional. Adding to the tension between the folk and the professional were the diverging attitudes toward cleanliness. Miasmic theory led many doctors to respect cleanliness and to advocate sanitary reforms. Notions regarding the neat and tidy person were abandoned in the move westward, and doctors had too little prestige to change those attitudes. Many people turned away from a medical profession that could not agree on the basics of disease while white medical practice in the expanding South added to the tension between black people and orthodox medicine.

7

Giving Birth

The weather on November 18, 1793, was stormy and cold when Martha Ballard, midwife, set out from her home in Hallowell, Maine, to tend a "Lady in Labour." The rain had turned to snow before the prospective father, Captain Molloy, was able to contact a group of women from the neighborhood, friends of his wife to assist the midwife. Eight hours and five minutes after the women assembled, the midwife noted, "Capt. Molloy's lady delivered a fine daughter." Mrs. Ballard did not comment about any complications, signs of distress, or concern for either the mother or child's health. All went well and in celebration of the event, the father provided the means for "an Elligant supper" that evening. Shortly afterwards the friends went home, but the midwife spent the night and part of the next day tending her patient. It was the forty-eighth time that Martha Ballard had attended a childbirth.

Two days later she checked on Martha Molloy and found her "Tolerable Comfortable" and with a nurse in attendance. It was not necessary to visit the Molloy household again until the young woman was ready to deliver her second child two years later. Such was the experience of childbirth during most of the eighteenth century—a midwife in charge with neighbors, friends, and female relatives assisting in the "social childbirth." Delivery was in a matter of hours with no complications. Mother and child were well with only the expected afterbirth pains and no need for additional medical attention. Within two years, another birth would be the norm and the midwife was again called to attend Martha Molloy. Martha Ballard's diary repeats this story time after time for different women with the occasional reference to false pains, protracted delivery, and very rarely a stillborn or maternal death.

Ballard's experience as a midwife, beginning in the late eighteenth century and spanning twenty-seven years, followed the tradition of childbirth that was common in the early history of British America. As was customary the husband of the woman in labor called the midwife and female relatives and friends to attend the birth. No man was expected or wanted to be in attendance as childbirth was strictly a very social feminine affair. The women came to provide moral and physical support for the mother during the ordeal and to share advice. For the younger women witnesses, it was an education in what to expect when they married and had children. Older women who had been through childbirth could reassure with their very presence. Hovering over the event was the expectation of extreme pain and the ever-present possibility of death.

Historically, such company was there to insure others that the midwife was not responsible in the event of a stillbirth and that no substitute was made of the child in the event of a male heir. Midwives had long been associated with magic and witchcraft, and in earlier years witnesses were questioned about the use of charms and other magical devices that might have been used by the midwife. By Martha Ballard's day, few people were concerned about such practices, but the women continued to come to assist and socialize, expecting reciprocity during their times of "travail." The attending women also took care of the infant, cooked, washed the bloody linens, and cleaned up. Their very presence helped to moderate the fears of childbirth, to convey a message that all was normal. The mother was "brought to bed" in a natural process that ran an expected course.

Native American women followed a somewhat different path toward childbirth. It was definitely not a social event but a private one constrained by traditional rules and rituals about where and how the birthing took place. The women would retire to a small hut or other shelter away from the main living quarters and were also often attended by a midwife. Like the Europeans, it was a strictly feminine occasion; other women kept in touch from a distance with ritually determined food and drink. Cherokee women were confined to the hut for seven days; other tribes might require isolation for

Drawing by Georges Devy of a Pawnee Indian woman in labor squatting against a tree. A midwife who blows smoke between her legs from a pipe assists her. (from Gustave Joseph Witkowsky, *Histoire des Accouchements Chez Tous Les Peuples*, Paris, 1887. Courtesy of the National Library of Medicine)

up to a month, protecting mother and child from infection. For difficult or prolonged births, the shaman—either a man or a woman—was called to perform their chants and curing ceremonies or to supply roots and herbs or to preside over a sweat bath. Rather than interfering in the physical aspects of the birth process, the shaman offered comfort and reassurance through traditional ceremonies.

Unlike the Europeans, Native women never lay down or took to their beds while giving birth. Rather they stood, knelt, or sat. Some studies indicate that they showed little evidence of pain. They were more relaxed and less fearful of the process than were European women. In her study of childbirth practices, Anne Marie Plane suggests that because there were "cultural constraints on their expression of pain," Indian responses were different from European ones. They also differed dramatically in the attitude toward ailing or sickly infants. No attempt was made to keep them alive. American Indians proscribed neither infanticide nor abortion.

White women apparently were not influenced by the Indian practices nor did they learn anything about the handling of pain. Indians, on the other hand, were forced to make some accommodation to European intrusion into their space, especially in New England. The actions of the shamans were prohibited and distant huts abandoned. But minimizing the expression of pain and distinctive food taboos continued to be important aspects of labor among American Indians. The parallel systems of childbirth maintained their distance.

Nonetheless, childbirth was fraught with danger to both mother and child whether the woman was of European, Native American, or African background. There are no reliable numbers to establish the number of stillborns in early America, but a rough estimate of child mortality is that about 40 percent of all deaths in the colonies were children under the age of five. Among Native Americans the number many have been higher where the practices of abortion and infanticide was more common. There is some indication that African American women had a higher miscarriage rate, but there are no reliable figures. White masters suspected that many cases of miscarriage by slave women were artificially induced. Population studies indicate that slave women had fewer children than their white counterparts, but the reasons may have more to do with excessive workloads, inadequate nutrition, or breast-feeding practices that retarded conception than deliberate action. Nonetheless, the means and methods of ending a pregnancy were all part of the herbal lore within the slave community.

There are a few reliable statistics for white women in New England, though. Of the 814 deliveries attended by Mrs. Ballard between 1785 and 1812, fourteen were stillborn (2 percent) and five mothers died after giving birth, thus one death to 198 living mothers. Martha Ballard herself gave birth to nine babies, of which three died. That record compares favorably with some other New England areas where maternal deaths were closer to one in 150 (a rate similar to that in the 1930s in the United States) and stillborn rates for the area were closer to 20 percent compared to Ballard's 5.6 percent. Parish records for her contemporaries in English villages indicate a range of from ten to twenty-nine maternal deaths per thousand births. In some British hospitals of the time the maternal mortality ranged from thirty to two hundred per thousand. All indications are that the death rate in America, especially for the New England area, was much lower than in the old country in the eighteenth century. Because white American women were better fed and therefore healthier they did not suffer from pelvic deformities due to malnutrition. As a consequence they suffered from fewer complications during childbirth than their peers in England or slaves in the South. An experienced midwife like Martha Ballard, who let nature take her course with little interference, expected few difficulties, and in general watched over successful labor.

But not all births were normal, and after protracted labor or when it was thought that the fetus was dead, a doctor might be called. During such unusual situations, the life of the mother was of major concern, not that of the unborn child. The doctor's role was to dismember and extract the fetus from the mother's body using a variety of instruments: the "crotchet," scissors, or blunt hook. Because of their special role in childbirth, doctors carried an aura of death when called to assist the midwife. That began to change in the Western world after the middle of the eighteenth century with the invention of the forceps in 1720, which made it possible for skillful doctors to not only extract the baby without dismemberment but also to shorten labor. American doctors studying in England, Scotland, and France had opportunities to learn the new methods being developed abroad and began to intrude more often in the birthing room. The first male midwife mentioned publicly in the colonies was John Dupuy of New York in 1745. He had been educated in France where French surgeons had clinical experience with women in labor in hospitals. In Philadelphia a few years later, Dr. Adam Thomson, Edinburgh-born and educated, advertised his qualifications in "physic, surgery, and midwifery." James Lloyd returned to Boston after studying with William Smellie and William Hunter in London, the advocates of the "new obstetrics" that stressed knowledge of female anatomy and the use of forceps.

A few forward-looking doctors attempted to introduce midwives to the new methods. William Shippen, another student of William Hunter, returned to Philadelphia in 1762 determined to teach Americans about the careful use of instruments and the newly discovered details of human anatomy. He proposed to give a series of lectures on midwifery with a separate series for women. It is doubtful, though, that many women actually attended the lectures. Few could afford the fees or thought they needed instruction in what they had been doing successfully for so many centuries. But at least one woman did attend. In 1789 Grace Mulligan advertised her skills as a midwife and noted, as an additional credential, that she had been trained by Shippen. In Salem, North Carolina, Dr. Samuel Vierling offered to give instructions free of charge to local women in 1795. Three years later Agnes MacKinlay advertised her skill as a teacher of midwifery because of her training at Glasgow's Lying-In Hospital and her attendance at a series of lectures in Scotland. There is no record of how many women took advantage of those opportunities, but they do indicate some interest within the medical establishment in the eighteenth century about helping midwives improve their skills.

The "man-midwife" provides a visual comment on the differences between the male and female methods of handling childbirth. The obstetrical tools of the man in an unadorned room contrasts with the lack of such instruments of the traditional midwife. The midwife herself stands on a rug in a warmer, more homelike setting. (Courtesy of the National Library of Medicine)

The forceps may have helped men to escape from the reputation of "harbingers of death," but most women still shied away from the male midwife except for the most difficult cases. Midwives continued to cooperate by calling in the male physician when instruments were necessary. By the end of the eighteenth century, in what was becoming the new fashion of childbirth for those who could afford such services, the doctor was invited into the birthing room to be on hand just in case he was needed. In spite of their claims, however, not all physicians were skillful in the use of the forceps nor knowledgeable about normal labor. Thus Martha Ballard had reason to complain about Dr. Ben Page in 1793 and his inept handling of deliveries. He was a young apprentice-trained doctor who theoretically knew something about the birth process but had had little practical experience. Ballard complained that when delivering a dead infant, the "limbs were much dislocated" suggesting that Page's clumsy use of the instruments might have killed the infant. At another delivery, he gave the mother laudanum, an opiate that was used only for false pains and, as a result, delayed the birth. But the next time Ballard and Page joined forces, he stepped aside and merely observed as the woman was "safe delivered" by Mrs. Ballard. Such cooperation had been the norm in the past as doctors conceded to the skill of the midwife. Even Dr. Alexander Hamilton, an elite physician trained in Edinburgh, had easily consulted with an "old midwife" when traveling in 1744.

Throughout the eighteenth century, the relationship between physician and midwife had been a cooperative one based on mutual dependence. That symbiosis was challenged early in the nineteenth century with the increasing presence of the physician in the labor room and his subsequent attempt to deny midwives their traditional role. The movement from midwife to male midwife can be traced in the diary of Elizabeth Drinker in Philadelphia kept from 1758 until shortly before her death in December of 1807. She details, among other events, the births of her children, those of her daughters and granddaughters as well as those of other relatives and neighbors. In the early years, especially from 1758 through the 1780s, Drinker makes no mention of either a doctor or midwife. Individuals were "brought to bed," most likely with the usual female attendants. The very matter-of-factness of her description is a comment on the reliability of natural processes. The women participating in the event may not have understood the process, but they had trust in nature. There are stillborns in Drinker's diary as there are maternal deaths, but they are the unusual events.

Drinker's first reference to a male attendant was on September 23, 1794, when the midwife thought it was necessary to call a doctor to use his instruments to deliver a dead infant. No doctors appear at any of the births noted by Elizabeth Drinker before that time. After that date there are a growing number of references to doctors, particularly Dr. Shippen. He and the midwife Hannah Yerkes appear to share responsibilities, the doctor taking charge only in the event of a difficult birth. In a portent of things to come, there was one occasion in 1797 when a Dr. Belville attended Drinker's daughter, Hannah, in the absence of the usual female companions or a midwife. By the turn of the century, doctors appear at all deliveries noted in the diary, usually with only a nurse to assist. The male attendant had become predominant; the midwife had disappeared from Drinker's diary and in her place was the nurse, a servant for the doctor.

Even the female attendants, the essentials in the "social childbirth" that prevailed for centuries, were no longer taking part. Doctors often objected to their "gossipy" presence; in particular, some of the women in social childbirth could and did comment on the doctor's techniques, what William Buchan in his popular medical work described in 1794 as offering "untimely and impertinent advice." In their place came the nurse, whose job was to follow the doctor's orders and not to take any initiative. The very culture of childbirth was changing among affluent women from a strictly intimate female group experience to one that stressed the medical nature of the event—objective, scientific, and mechanical—but in fact this did not particularly make the process safer or less painful.

Doctors promised safer and easier deliveries, convincing some women that even normal labor when protracted could be hastened with the use of the forceps. The trend toward male attendants was aided by a new "collective culture of ladies," that enjoyed "leisure and literacy." This elite group, according to Adrian Wilson, wanted to "demarcate themselves from their humbler fellow women" by choosing men to deliver their babies. That consumer-driven fashion fueled the services of men in England and America. The doctors responded by encouraging women to expect problems and to use their services instead of those of midwives. In turn, the women demanded "a guaranteed performance" from the best medical care of the time.

On the other hand, Elizabeth Drinker was mystified because her daughters seemed to experience much more "tedious" labors than she and her contemporaries had. With the growing interest in childbirth as a source of income, doctors had begun to push the idea that pregnancy and the birthing process were abnormal conditions requiring medical attention. They convinced women of Drinker's class that the doctor was essential for the process of childbirth. It may well be that the expectation of difficult births fulfilled the predictions of the doctors that their presence was necessary and thus childbirth became in fact more painful. The culture of the time also encouraged women to be more sensitive to pain than men. Their tight corsets, lack of exercise, and other changes in lifestyle for the leisured woman probably contributed to their physical discomforts. What had once been considered a natural process had become a medical problem, and physicians were happy to comply with the requests for more advanced methods of childbirth.

But was the physician's presence the best medical treatment? Skillful use of forceps permitted doctors to save the lives of babies who in the past had to be sacrificed to save the life of the mother. Clumsy application of that new technology, as in the case of Martha Ballard's young Dr. Page, often had the opposite effect: it could lacerate the birth canal or kill the child. The technology had great potential for harm. In an attempt to protect female modesty, surgeons performed their expected role without even looking at the female's genitals. The operation took place under a covering, and the surgeon used his instruments with his sense of touch only. They denied that the inability to see what they were doing was a handicap. Touch, said the doctors, was more accurate. Nonetheless, there were some complaints that men were too ready to use instruments that caused harm. Dr. Samuel Bard, although a strong advocate for medical training for men, opposed the advent of male midwives. He complained in 1769 that men often lacked the ability to discriminate about natural processes and that their free use of instruments had tragic consequences. Others argued that men were not proper for that "indelicate" branch of medicine and violated feminine modesty.

Doctors were sometimes too anxious to take advantage of other technologies that could have disastrous consequences for the women. The techniques used by doctors also became more "heroic," more focused on hastening births and expecting complications. Dr. John Stearn of New York learned about the use of ergot from a German midwife. It was a technique well known to midwives and was used both to abort fetuses when requested and also to hasten births at the end of a pregnancy. Stearn, unfamiliar with its potential, discovered to his regret that ergot worked so fast that it could rupture the uterus and kill the child. Doctors also argued that pregnant women suffered from a plethora of blood because of the cessation of menstruation and recommended bleeding in difficult cases. Benjamin Rush in Philadelphia was convinced that pain during the birthing process could be lessened by venesection and recommended taking thirty ounces of blood at the onset of labor followed by purging. Following his model, copious bloodletting became popular among male midwives to reduce pain or for any unusual symptoms. There were times when doctors bled patients to unconsciousness, which certainly did the job of reducing pain by being put them out cold. Midwives, on the other hand, scorned the practice.

Insertion of the doctor's hands into the birth canal also carried a high risk for infection. Because doctors seldom washed their hands between patients or after doing autopsies, they could bring unwanted pathogens to the woman's body, a major cause of puerperal fever or childbed fever—a wound infection of the birth passage. Midwives touched the genital area only when necessary to turn the fetus. Their job was to catch the child and tie off the umbilical cord. Unlike doctors, they seldom dealt with diseased individuals and did not carry the same threat of infection. It was not because they understood the causes of puerperal fever; it was in the nature of their practice to stand by and let nature take its course with a minimum of interference. And in the process they caused less harm.

As early as the 1790s, Scottish doctors had suggested that puerperal fever was contagious and that medical people were spreading the disease. Alexander Gordon of Aberdeen warned attendants at childbirths to wash their hands, clothes, and instruments, but the warnings were ignored. Doctors resented the notion that they were agents of contamination. They continued to assume the cause was either in the air, a miasma, clothing fads, or some moral defect in the women. Disease was often attributed to an individual character trait, and doctors regularly blamed their patients, especially women, for their illnesses. Nonetheless, in line with the Scottish study a handful of doctors began using more antiseptic practices. In Philadelphia, Dr. Rutter had tried washing thoroughly; he shaved his head and face and changed his clothes but still some patients died from childbed fever. Oliver Wendell Holmes, a young doctor in Massachusetts, read about the clinical studies and the extent of childbed fever in maternity hospitals. He took note of the incidence of fever in the patients of doctors who performed autopsies and then attended the women. He reasoned that the disease was passed by direct contact and urged physicians to change their clothes and wash their hands along with the additional warning not to deliver babies if they were ill or had conducted an autopsy.

Other American doctors viciously attacked Holmes for suggesting that they were instruments of death. Dr. Charles Meigs of Jefferson Medical College in Philadelphia accused Holmes of "filling the minds of interested people with alarm" through his "vile, demoralizing superstitions as to the nature and cause of disease." As a gentleman, said Meigs, his hands were always clean. A few years later the Austrian Ignaz Phillipp Semmelweis confirmed the earlier studies by showing statistically that medical students who did autopsies and then attended women in labor had a higher mortality among their patients than midwives who did not touch the women. After requiring birth attendants to wash their hands in a chloride of lime solution and to avoid autopsies

Dr. Charles D. Meigs, respected physician and early obstetrician in Philadelphia. He rejected the idea that a doctor's unclean hands, which had touched other sick or dead people, could be causing infection in their patients. (Courtesy of the National Library of Medicine)

for a period of time, the incidences of death declined rapidly, confirming also Holmes's suspicions. The empirical evidence appeared to be conclusive, and Holmes responded to his opponents with what Richard and Dorothy Wertz describe as "caustic reserve." For Meigs, Holmes had only the harshest reproach, accusing him of killing his patients by ignoring the warnings.

Doctors like Meigs, a distinguished physicians and longtime trainer of others, adamantly refused to take precautions. The danger from puerperal fever continued in the hands of physicians. Even those who followed Holmes's advice stood by as the women died of the fever. Neither the technology of the time nor the prevailing theories of diseases could solve or explain the problem. The exact cause was not known until Louis Pasteur demonstrated that a germ was the infecting agent when a wound was present. Americans, however, were slow to accept this germ theory of disease. Deliveries of infants, whether conducted by midwives or physicians, followed the traditional habits of each practitioner with the usual results.

The one area of experiment that obstetricians did not generally explore or exploit was the means of reducing pain with anesthesia. By the 1830s ether, nitrous oxide, and chloroform were available and were known to induce an unconscious state or, in the case of nitrous oxide, to reduce the sensation of pain. Dentists and surgeons attempted to use the painkillers during some procedures; in fact, dentists were the first experimenters. During parties it had also become fashionable among the more affluent to experiment with ether and nitrous oxide. Recreational use sparked interests in other possibilities to reduce pain. Affluent women, those who had rejected midwives in favor of the promise of easier births in the delivery room, wanted this newest technology to reduce the fearsome pain and soon began to request anesthesia. Most physicians hesitated to use these methods because they relied on the painful contractions to determine the progress of labor. In 1848 Walter Channing of Boston used ether for his patients in labor and encouraged other physicians to do the same. Few took up his challenge. No one knew how much or when during the process of delivery to use it. Ether could, in truth, have devastating effects on babies and mothers. All doctors were especially leery of chloroform, which had only recently been discovered by an American chemist and physician, Samuel Guthrie, in 1831. Unlike their enthusiastic acceptance of the forceps, in this area of female pain, doctors became very conservative. Some like Dr. Meigs thought that the pain during childbirth was a good thing, a "desirable evidence of the life forces that ensures a mother's love for her offspring." Members of the clergy, who retorted that it was God's design to suffer during childbirth, echoed the physician's distaste for the possibilities of reducing pain during childbirth. The male voice—both medical and clerical—dominated the discussion of whether women's pain could or should be reduced.

From what few records are available, it appears that not many births were accompanied by any anesthesia in the United States until the end of the century. Midwives did not use it, and it was seldom given to women in hospitals. Even though the technology was available and being tested overseas, American doctors apparently did not respond to the demand for more painless childbirth and continued to publish arguments against anesthetics for women. The British, however, were more amenable to the demands of women. In England Dr. James Young Simpson was the first to introduce chloroform into his obstetrical practice in 1847. The trend for anesthetics became more popular when Queen Victoria requested chloroform for the birth of her eighth child in 1853.

There are no reliable statistics to indicate whether the doctor's presence during deliveries had a detrimental or a beneficial result. A few studies of hospitals in nineteenth-century America (where midwives were excluded and doctors handled all childbirth cases) reported very high rates of maternal deaths and disabilities. The hospitals, however, ministered to the poor and homeless women, who may well have had other medical problems that contributed to their high mortality. But the general conclusion by historians is that the doctors fared no better than the midwives, saving some babies and injuring others, helping women with prolonged births, and damaging others with lack of skill and contaminated hands. And most deliveries, whether attended by doctors or midwives, took place in the homes of the women, away from the public eye.

Physicians had good reason to want the midwives out of the profession. They had learned that assisting in childbirth provided a lucrative and stable source of income. In general, doctors did not earn enough to support themselves and many had to have a second source of income. They coveted the business traditionally held by midwives for all gynecological complaints and infant care that could metamorphose into more comprehensive family care. They did charge more for deliveries than midwives and could expect a great deal more for difficult cases. While Mrs. Ballard charged $2.00 for a delivery, Dr. Page expected at least $6.00. There were similar disparities in New Jersey and Philadelphia. In Petersburg, Virginia, by 1850 doctors charged more than $20 for a delivery when the midwife's fee was only $3.00.

In the attempt to capture the childbirth clientele, physicians were determined to push the midwife out of the birthing room. They tried at first to discredit midwives for their failure to use more "advanced" methods. In their publications they condemned midwives as ignorant, superstitious, and lacking in judgment. They hailed their own methods as advanced and more professional. Although black midwives were often accorded a great deal of respect on southern plantations, physicians blamed slave medicine for birth complications and claimed that black women were incompetent midwives. The treatment of slaves had become an important source of revenue for southern doctors, and they worked hard to discredit competition on the plantations.

In line with the new ideal "domestic womanhood" that pushed women out of the public sphere, some doctors objected that women would lose their standing as ladies if they were subjected to the indignities of attending other women during the delivery of babies. Some argued that women were of more limited intelligence and probably incapable of doing what they had been doing, naturally, for centuries. To quote Dr. Charles Meigs (who excoriated Dr. Holmes in the puerperal fever controversy) in 1847, a woman "has a head almost too small for intellect and just big enough for love." Misogyny was very much a part of the campaign against midwives. Dr. John Gunn's popular manual *Domestic Medicine*, published in 1830, reinforced the idea that midwives were ignorant about human anatomy and too lazy to do anything else but take advantage of pregnant women. He stated that only the physician knew what he was doing. In recognition of the fact that midwives were popular, he offered advice about proper procedures with the caveat that they should always call in the physician in any hint of difficulty.

Public condemnation of midwives proved to be insufficient to eliminate the competition. Instead, in the second decade of the nineteenth century physicians tried a new tack, which focused on the abortion trade, another traditional source of income in the medical world. They began the push for licensing regulation that forbade nonphysicians from providing abortion information or procedures. The abortion issue became what James Mohr calls the "focal point" in the struggle to control the practice of medicine.

There were no laws against abortion in American until the 1820s. Abortion was traditionally criminalized only when it concealed illegal activity like fornication or adultery—sex outside of marriage—but it seldom came to the attention of the authorities unless the woman died. In one well-documented event, Cornelia Dayton describes the case of Sarah Grosvenor, who died in 1742 in Connecticut. Three years later her lover, Amasa Sessions, and her physician Dr. John Hallowell were brought up on the charge of murder—not of the fetus but of the mother. The criminal act was hiding the pregnancy and destroying Sarah's health. The doctor, however, was convicted only of a misdemeanor, not murder, and Sessions was not convicted of any crime. The casual attitude toward abortion was common at the time.

All the studies of pregnancy agree that physicians and midwives who aided the women were sympathetic to the decision of unmarried women to stop a pregnancy. Typically the women were viewed as victims. Practitioners also generally assumed that abortion was relatively safe, at least safer than child-birth. And the stigma of a baby outside of marriage was the greater concern to all parties.

Even establishing whether an abortion had been performed was difficult. There was no way to determine pregnancy before the fourth or fifth months when the fetus began to move—a moment known as "quickening." The English Common law did not recognize abortion before that time. Thus a court in Massachusetts in 1812 declared that abortion before the woman felt the fetus move (quickening) was beyond the scope of the law and could not be a crime. This theory taken from the English Common Law prevailed through the first half of the nineteenth century in America.

When other methods of contraception—such as prolonged breast-feed-ing, abstinence during supposedly fertile periods, or withdrawal—did not work, abortion became the last resort to control the number of children. Attempts at family limitation had become more frequent during the last quarter of the eighteenth century, as evidenced in the slow decline in the birthrate for white women. The crude birthrate for whites had peaked in the years between 1760 and 1789 and then began its long decline. African American women maintained a high birthrate throughout the nineteenth century until after the Civil War, when women gained greater control over their own bodies. Strangely enough the birthrate for black women did not peak until the 1820–49 period, even though there were few economic rea-sons for slave women to delay marriage. They began having children while in their teens, a much younger age than white women who had to await a male capable of supporting a family. That fertility among slave women remained low until the mid-nineteenth century may be due to women following the African practice of prolonged breast feeding for two or three years. This cus-tom changed after the end of the slave trade as southern plantation owners explored ways to encourage slave fertility. The women began to wean their babies after a year; birth intervals thus became shorter and women had more children although infant mortality remained high.

Women may not have known definitely when they were pregnant, but they often suspected long before quickening and could take action to induce labor to bring on a miscarriage by using a popular remedy for colic. Aborificents were easily available, and medical texts and newspaper advertisements regu-larly referred to methods of restoring menstruation and cures for "obstruc-tion of the menses," euphemisms for bringing on a miscarriage. Many of the remedies for abortion paralleled those for stomach ailments. Even John Gunn provided information for "obstructed menses" that included a variety of remedies, including the use of a syringe to squirt liquid into the vagina to "stimulate" the uterus as well as traditional herbal concoctions to bring on violent physical reactions normally used for stomach disorders.

By the time of the Revolution, even married white women, because of war, ill health, or financial worries, were attempting to control the timing of pregnancies and the number of children. While large families were valued during the colonial era, by the turn of the nineteenth century there was much less emphasis on conception. Elizabeth Drinker was dismayed by her daughter-in-law's fecundity in 1804. Within ten years of marriage she had had six children and buried two. "O dear!" wrote Drinker in her diary when contemplating the situation, suggesting that Hannah was not doing her duty to control her family size. Family planning was a feminine obligation and, to the despair of many white men who feared any independence from their women, it became more so as the century progressed.

In his comprehensive study of the abortion issue, James Mohr concludes that the early laws of 1821–41 reflected the general perception that abortion was a "fundamentally marginal practice usually resorted to by women who deserved pity and protection rather than criminal liability." Because the original intent was to prevent unnecessary and dangerous procedures by nonphysicians, the few states that passed laws forbidding abortion criminalized the one performing the surgery. Those early anti-abortion laws proved to be unenforceable because of the generally permissive attitude toward the practice. Under pressure from the irregular practitioners, who along with the midwives who most commonly assisted abortions, the laws were repealed in short order. The opposition had successfully argued that the laws were elitist, that they protected one class of practitioners to the detriment of others who, they could argue, caused fewer deaths and less damage to health. In fact, women were turning to the new herbal regimens of the irregulars that included large numbers of women, and regular physicians worried that they would lose the new lucrative obstetrical practice if the trend continued. Doctors continued to complain that "old women, root doctors [African American herbalists] and quacks of all sorts" were purveyors of superstition and ignorance. Thus laws to limit abortion practice were part of the medical establishment's early attempt to control medicine and the behavior of women.

The lax approach to abortion changed as the medical establishment grappled with the rapidly declining birthrate among white married women and the stubborn competition from midwives. As the least organized group outside the medical establishment, midwives were immediately vulnerable to attack. This was obvious during the second attempt by physicians to control abortion after 1840. By that time it appeared that married women, and not just poor unfortunates, were making an effort to determine family size, and as a result the native-born white birthrate declined dramatically in the decade after 1840. The blatant advertising of abortifacients taught more and more women about the possibilities of controlling their fertility with a variety of methods. And if the herbal route did not work, the advertising also offered more promising methods in the hands of abortion specialists, many of whom were women. Lurid trials of botched abortions received a great deal of publicity in the newspapers, further spreading the word about the possibility of limiting fertility. The well-known abortionist, Madame Restell, gained notoriety from a series of court cases that failed to undermine her practice until after the Civil War.

Physicians, through their nascent medical societies led the outcry against this commercialization of abortion, and a new spate of anti-abortion laws appeared in the 1840s. Supposedly the new laws were to protect women from the malpractice of unqualified abortionists. The campaign by doctors to support the laws stressed the dangers from the "quack, doctoress, and irregular" performers of abortion. The laws said nothing about banning doctors from the practice. The medical journals of the time cited cases of botched abortions but always at the hands of those outside the profession, such as midwives and botanic irregulars. The newly organized American Medical Association in 1847 joined the anti-abortion crusade ostensibly to monitor their own ranks and create a more professional code of behavior. Their rhetoric also reflected a strong antifeminine bias as they also fought the entry of women into their ranks as midwives or doctors. The attacks on midwives and the resistance to women controlling their own fertility was led mainly by physicians determined to protect and promote their own lucrative practices.

The early anti-abortion crusade did not focus on whether abortion was ethical in and of itself. That issue would not appear until after the Civil War when a moral crusade against abortion and contraception gained momentum in the 1870s. The laws of that time successfully pushed those practices into the back alleys, but they did not end them. Abortion, Rosalind Petchesky notes, had been and continued to be the "most persistent and prevalent" method of birth control regardless of the law. In the antebellum period, the moral issue regarding abortion was that of women's place in society both as mothers and the deference they were expected to give to men. Therefore, control of fertility through abortions was seen as an attack on male dominance. Birth control for some, the author Rickie Salinger argues, "stood for unchaste and unfaithful women." Doctors viewed the attempts by women to control their own fertility as threats to the traditional role of men in control of women. Abortion then was not just a physical act but, in the eyes of the medical profession, a social nuisance encouraged by midwives for their own benefit.

Not all physicians, however, believed that midwives had no place in the medical profession. In opposition to the medical establishment some doctors toward the end of the eighteenth century began to advocate more formal training for women. A handful of doctors fresh from their European training tried to establish programs for midwives, but many Americans, however, did not share the same interest in midwifery training and obstetrics as did the Europeans, and very few men or women took advantage of that instruction. Valentine Seaman led a campaign to train midwives in New York in 1791 and was successful in establishing a program eight years later at the New York Almshouse for poor pregnant women. But as in Shippen's case few women came to his course. Thomas Ewell renewed Valentine's cause in 1817 with an attempt to get the federal government to support schools to train midwives. He advocated the restoration of all "normal" childbirth cases to midwives rather than to men. His program also failed to attract interest. The physicians who did defend the midwives were in a minority and thus could do little to change the social climate that pushed women out of the public sphere, hailing domestic womanhood as the feminine ideal. This trend also meant a divergence from European practice where midwives were given training in order to improve their skills.

In the 1840s Dr. Samuel Gregory renewed the effort to train women. He gave a series of public lectures on the desirability of providing medical education for women on the grounds that most women preferred the sympathy and compassion of other women during deliveries and for gynecological problems. He helped establish the Boston Female Medical College in 1848 with a three-month course on midwifery; his emphasis soon shifted to training women physicians. Instead of following Old World practice, the American focus on the training of midwives expanded to include general medical education. Women could not attend school with men, so separate women's medical schools sprang up. In 1850 the Philadelphia Women's Medical College was founded, and by the end of the century there were about seventeen such schools, many of which (like those for men) were small and with very low standards. One exception was the New York Infirmary for Women and Children, established in 1857 by Elizabeth Blackwell, her sister Emily, and Dr. Marie Zakrewska, to give women clinical experience. The Infirmary expanded into a medical college for women in New York in 1864. Blackwell held a medical degree—the first American woman to earn an M.D.—from the Geneva (New York) Medical College, She had gained entrance to the Medical College by means of subtle tricks and no woman was permitted to follow her in that school. Because no American hospital would allow her to practice, Blackwell went to London and Paris for clinical experience and returned to America determined to train other women and to apply the knowledge being gained in European hospitals about childbirth and diseases. The number of women who could attend those schools was small, and most childbirth deliveries continued in the hands of American midwives with little formal education.

Although the medical profession had worked hard to eliminate midwifery as a profession, it had proven to be an impossible task. Most women, especially immigrants, poor isolated whites, some urban middle-class women, and blacks—in total a significant proportion of the female population—preferred being treated by other women for their deliveries and other health problems. Suzanne Lebsock, in her study of Petersburg, Virginia, found no evidence that midwives were on the decline in that city in the pre–Civil War era. As late as 1900, midwives were still delivering babies for more than half of the urban women, and many more rural white women continued to draw on those services, especially in the South.

African American women in particular were acutely aware of the danger to their health from white doctors. Like their male counterparts, black women had no choice but to submit to whatever medical treatment was ordered. They may have been the patients, but the slaveholder was a physician's client. The treatment of black women by white physicians became more of a threat to their health as the art of surgery improved. White doctors were free to perform procedures on black women that would have been socially unacceptable to white women, at the minimum violating the standard of modesty and at the worst performing highly experimental and painful surgery without anesthesia. Determined to increase slave fertility, plantation owners called on physicians to use surgery to correct any "disorded" vaginas that might inhibit conception even though the procedures were untested. Even though at this time caesarean sections were usually fatal, the majority of these operations in the nineteenth-century South were carried out on African American women. The practice of caesareans had heretofore been restricted to women who had died in childbirth, in order to save the child. In cases where the life of the mother could be saved, the fetus was destroyed. However, slave women who came under Francois Marie Prévost's knife in 1820s Louisiana experienced caesarian sections while alive. In an earlier decade in Kentucky, Ephraim McDowell, known generally for his operation to remove a tumor of a white woman at her request in 1809 without anesthetic, continued to experiment with abdominal surgery on slave women. In 1813 he removed the ovaries of four of his slave women in his first experiments with that operation. Over the next four years he continued his ovarian surgeries on black women. John Duffy admits that physicians "were far more willing to try new procedures upon slaves than upon other women."

Probably the worst violator of black women's bodies was Dr. J. Marion Sims in Montgomery, Alabama, in the 1840s. One of the dangers from a difficult or prolonged childbirth and from the clumsy use of forceps was the development of a fistula, an erosion of the vaginal wall that led to uncontrolled leakage of urine or bowel waste. Nothing could be done to heal the fistula, and many women isolated themselves because of the odor and embarrassment of such incontinence. In an attempt to solve the problem, Sims bought eleven black women slaves suffering from that condition and set out to experiment on them. In violation of feminine norms, the women were stripped of all clothing or covering of their bodies. He subjected them to forced surgeries without anesthesia, although ether and chloroform were both available. He claimed that the surgery was not painful enough and that black women did not feel pain as white women did, but the men he asked to assist and restrain the women often left the operating theater because they could not bear the sounds of the victims' shrieks. Sims afterwards kept the women on opium to control them while healing and before subjecting them to a second round of surgeries. After the horrified early assistants refused to observe these operations, Sims hired Dr. Nathan Bozman, a recent medical graduate to assist him. As he perfected the operation, Sims wrote about his work and experiments, praising the courage of his victims without revealing that they were slaves; he was soon invited to treat other women with that condition. The white women he operated on (with their consent) all received the anesthetics he had denied the black women. As a result of his success, Sims was hailed by New York and Paris with monuments, memorials, and clinics in his name.

Sims also experimented on black infants by prying apart their skull bones. He believed that tetany, a neuromuscular disorder that Harriet Washington says was a result of chronic malnutrition, was caused by the skull bones of black infants growing faster than those of white babies. Sims was convinced that the disease was caused by a displacement of skull bones and attempted to correct the condition. When the babies died, he blamed it on the ignorance of the mothers and the black midwives, a typical reaction from the physicians. Thus, there is good reason why black people rejected the medical establishment. It was not just a lack of confidence or superstitious reliance on older theories, but fear born of experience in their historical contacts with the professional medical world.

Apart from the small elite groups of white women who craved the benefits, questionable that they were, of medical advance, the birthing room remained in the hands of midwives throughout this period. Acts to expel the midwife from the profession failed because of the desire by women to be attended by other women. The physician's attempt to expand their reach led to a new set of conflicts between the goals of both women and their midwives against the medical world for control over fertility and the birthing process. Within the slave community the particular abuse of black women by white doctors added to the awareness of the perils of medical treatment. New tensions within the medical profession were apparent when a handful of concerned doctors, aware of European developments, objected to the intrusion of men into what they considered a delicate and modest practice, which should be reserved for only female attendants. In this pre–germ theory world, physicians gained little ground with the female public, except for a small number of upper-class, wealthy women.

8

The Face of Madness

On November 5, 1824, Henry Sewall of Augusta, Maine, reported in his diary that he had "a Bunk made for M. to sleep in, with a lid to shut down." The M. referred to his twenty-four-year-old daughter, Mary, who had exhibited "deranged" behavior. In an attempt to cure her insanity, she was put into a "Chair of confinement," which may have been a version of Benjamin Rush's "tranquilizer," designed to reduce all visual and auditory stimuli, and prevent any physical movement. Her arms and legs were strapped down, a head restraint covered her ears, and blinders limited her visual field. The seat contained a hole with a bucket below to catch bodily wastes so that Mary did not have to be moved during the day. Dr. Rush, who invented the chair, considered it a more humane means of restraining the deranged than the older "Mad jacket" (the straitjacket) or chains. Mary had spent her days in the chair since September, and was now to be confined at night. She continued to spend time in the coffinlike box for seventy-three more nights.

We know little about Mary's symptoms or how serious her illness was, or if she really suffered from a mental problem. Henry Sewall says very little about the behavior that alarmed him. She had developed what he called "strong convictions" and "anxiety" about her religious feelings. At the time religious enthusiasm was considered a cause of emotional distress that could bring on insanity. In late August she took to her room and refused to leave. One day in late September she was found wandering about ostensibly trying to get to a Shaker meeting thirty-five miles away. That particular behavior seems to have been the precipitating event that called for medical treatment. No other specifics were recorded.

The doctor called in to treat Mary prescribed a low diet and what had become the usual doses for such conditions: laxatives, opiates, and bleeding. The doctor approved of both the chair and the "bunk" and ordered a "seton," a needle passed through the skin on her neck to create pus, supposedly a sign of disease leaving the body. By December, she had become so debilitated that a second consultant removed the seton, took her out of the chair, and allowed her to eat a more substantial diet to no avail; Sewall noted that Mary "became so wild, restiff, & unmanageable that it was necessary to confine her again in the chair to prevent injury to herself & others." That tortuous treatment continued until February 26 when after a powerful "physic" she was so weakened that she could no longer move. Finally, she was freed from the bunk and chair and allowed to rest in an ordinary bed. On March 15, 1824, Mary Sewall died.

What caused her death? It is possible that Mary suffered from a brain tumor or some other physical ailment that could have resulted in erratic behavior and would have eventually led to her death. On the other hand, as Laurel Ulrich surmises in her narrative of this event, maybe it was the medical science of the day, the debilitating and frightening therapy, that brought on her demise. Whatever the cause, Mary Sewall's experience, horrifying as it is to the modern mind, dramatizes a change in the understanding of and the treatment of the mentally ill that began late in the eighteenth century. Insanity had become a medical problem, thought to be curable when treated at an early stage. This new medicalized approach to the mentally ill became the basis for understanding insanity during most of the nineteenth century.

Although explanations for madness, to use the more common term for the time, differed over the centuries, cures, except in rare cases of exorcism for possession, were not thought possible. For centuries it was assumed that nothing could be done to help those who were deranged. Madness, like many deviant behaviors, was also considered a transient state. It was thought that people were mad for a time, became functional, retreated into madness for a while again, and then regained their place in society in a continuing cycle without any treatment. The meaningless nature of deviant behavior was easily tolerated, posing no threat to the coherence of social life or its stability. Insanity was also considered an unfortunate occurrence that could affect anyone at any time in their lives. That fatalistic attitude toward insanity prevailed until the end of the eighteenth century.

Nor were the insane held responsible for criminal acts. They were seldom convicted of crimes but usually confined to protect the community from harm. Guardians were appointed to handle the finances of those who had lost control and provide for the welfare of their dependants. When the family could no longer provide care, public assistance was invariably available. Such unfortunates were proper objects of charity. When violent or a threat to themselves or others, the mad were restrained (sometimes in chains), isolated in distant huts or in locked rooms in a house. The very poor with no resources were kept in the local almshouse, workhouse, or jail along with other indigent people; they were often neglected and their physical needs ignored.

Mental illness was sometimes associated with demonical possession or witchcraft. Under the aegis of the Roman Catholic Church, priests developed elaborate incantation techniques of exorcism to expel the demons they believed had taken control of the soul. Protestantism had no such remedy for that malady but turned to the less dramatic spiritual practices of fasting and prayer to rid their society of the diabolical presence. Many of the so-called witches may well have been insane. Thus when a doctor declared that the peculiar behavior of a few girls in Salem during the winter of 1691/92 had no natural causes, he declined to treat them because he did not consider it a medical problem. Doctors dealt with the body; insanity or possession was of a different order. When doctors failed to cure they could blame witchcraft as a way to protect their reputations. Such may have been the case of the Dr. Griggs who refused to help the children in Salem. The girls' muscle spasms and difficulty in swallowing, their obscene comments in too rapid speech, and their apparent insubordination to adults, Griggs suggested, meant that the girls were possessed and outside the realm of medicine. When prayer and fasting did not heal, the leaders began the search for witches that supposedly were acting as the servants of the devil. To Cotton Mather, who saw a supernatural cause for many events, the devil was the moving force behind both witchcraft and all insanity.

By the beginning of the eighteenth century, mystical interpretations of insanity began to give way to a more rational, secular understanding that focused on the mind and the brain rather than the soul. The Enlightenment stress on reason put the emphasis on the proper working of the mind and also pointed to the possibility that insanity was a personal failing. Mather's

1724 *Angel of Bethesda* took a much more naturalistic approach to insanity. He continued to recommend prayer and fasting for those cases of madness brought on by demons, but recognized that other cases could be due to some "intolerable Vexation or Temporal Troubles." Among his recommendations was bleeding to "Extinguish the Fury of the Animal Spirits." Disorders of the mind he assumed were the result of immoral living, extreme stress, or possibly religious enthusiasm, a failure of will, and not just an unfortunate accident. There were too few doctors in any of the colonies then to provide the kind of medical attention that Mather suggested, and not until the end of the century would such notions of will and stress have any influence on the treatment of the insane.

At first, along with the new secular interpretation, was the assumption that loss of reason meant that the individual had reverted to some bestial level and which sometimes justified brutality and neglect. "Lunaticks," the "crazy-brained" had somehow lost the need for food and shelter, and did not feel the cold or the heat. In 1742, when Eliza Lucas Pinckney visited her friend Mrs. Chardon, she found her "quite out of her Sences." She had "ceased to be rational." Surely, Pinckney mused, "there cannot be a more dismal prospect in nature than man . . . deprived of the noblest principle of his nature and laid on a level with the beast." Many thought the insane could be beaten and starved into submission, thus the reports of the insane chained and left with little food or water, unclothed, living in their own feces. Supposedly they lacked humanity, lost the ability to reason, and therefore would not respond to humane treatment.

As the population density increased and the number of mentally ill grew during the colonial era, several communities attempted to create public facilities to care for them. In 1662, Boston unsuccessfully sought to have separate facilities in the almshouse for "Distracted persons" found wandering about and renewed those efforts in 1729. The town considered building a separate mad house in 1745, but the idea was not pursued. An increasing number of distracted "strangers" in Massachusetts led Thomas Hancock to bequeath funds in 1765 to build a separate house for those deprived of their reason, but no action was taken until the next century. Virginia was the first colony to establish some kind of institutional care. Faced with the problems of a growing number of persons of "insane and disordered minds" in the colony, Williamsburg created a hospital to confine "Idiots, Lunaticks, and other persons of unsound minds" who were "frequently found wandering." The "Eastern Lunatic Asylum" opened its doors in 1773 with a lay "keeper," a matron, and a visiting physician assigned to treat physical ills. It was built to accommodate twenty to thirty patients—whites

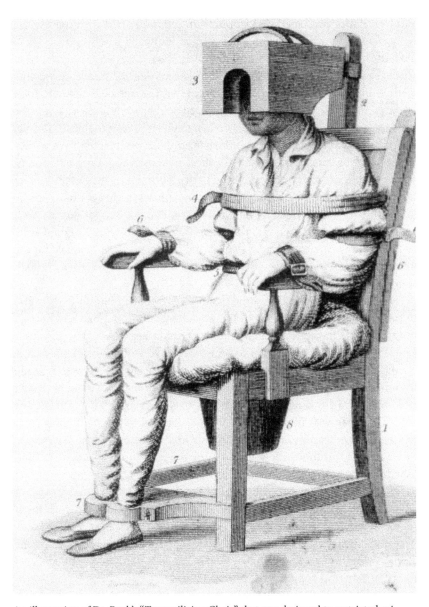

An illustration of Dr. Rush's "Tranquilizing Chair" that was designed to restrict physical movement and the visual impressions of the mentally ill in the expectation that such treatment would cure insanity. A similar contraption was used to restrain Mary Sewall. Note the bucket to catch bodily wastes. (Courtesy of the National Library of Medicine)

and free blacks, both men and women—in cells equipped with chains. The asylum's purpose, however, was custodial. The hospital setting kept them fed and sheltered and out of sight.

At the same time, new ideas regarding the care of the insane advocating medical intervention had begun to appear in various medical manuals. John Wesley's *Primitive Physician* (1747) advised herbal ointments, shaving the head and washing it with vinegar, pouring cold water on the head, fasting, temperance, and exercise. William Buchan's popular manual in 1769 also recommended forgoing spirits, tea, and coffee, and abstinence from fatty foods, as well as bleeding, purging, and cold baths. But he also suggested distraction from normal stress through music or taking sea voyages to calm the mind. Implied in these recommendations was the notion that dealing with the mind directly through entertainment or mental distraction could help. Such a therapy would later be called "moral treatment." The manuals for the first time helped to propagate the idea that madness could be cured through somatic therapies.

The earliest evidence that some doctors were considering such therapies to treat mental illness is found in the Philadelphia hospital that had opened in 1752. Unlike the almshouses that cared for both healthy and the sick indigents, the Philadelphia Hospital was the first permanent hospital built to care for the sick and insane, regardless of income or social class. Those suffering from mental woes were bled copiously and purged; their scalps were shaved and blistered. Following earlier traditions they were still chained to the cell walls and when violent put into a "Madd-shirt." Following the Philadelphia model, philanthropists in Charleston, South Carolina, lobbied the state assembly to raise funds for a hospital for the care of their "lunaticks, and other distempered and sick poor." In 1768 the South Carolina Assembly set aside funds to build a separate hospital for the poor in Charleston with an adjacent building for the insane dubbed the "city madhouse." In such institutions, the intent was to reach people during the early stages of their madness in the belief that cure might be possible if the insanity had not become chronic. The hospitals were not intended for long-term care, and patients were discharged as soon as possible.

When Philadelphia opened the doors of the first medical school in 1765, it added to its influence as a provider of medical innovation in the areas of mental health. Men from other colonies flocked to Philadelphia for their training and the chance to examine mental patients in the hospital, and whatever new ideas about treatment emanated from the school began to influence doctors everywhere. This was especially evident after the Revolution when Benjamin Rush gained stature as a physician and reformer. He maintained this influence during his long tenure as a teacher—from the mid-1770s to 1813—and his students broadcast his ideas throughout the country.

Rush had adopted a new theory of disease that emphasized the role of muscle tone or tissue irritability in poor health called "solidest." Treatment did not differ necessarily from those following the older theory. Doctors still depended on either stimulants to increase activity or sedatives and depletion to reduce irritability. Rush modified this theory to focus on spasms in the blood vessels. He argued that all fevers (whether of mind or body) were a result of excessive arterial action. Madness he described as an arterial disease, having its primary source in the blood vessels of the brain. To relieve the brain of its excess blood, he advocated a low diet, purges, emetics, hot and cold showers, and, of course, heroic bloodletting. As a substitute for the "Madd-shirt," he developed his tranquillizing chair and also a gyrator—a rotating board that spun the patient at high rates of speed to cause the blood to rush to the head and produce the opposite effect of the tranquilizer. He also advised shocking the patient through terrifying experiences and punishment. One of his therapies was a ice-cold shower bath of fifteen or more minutes. Fear of death he thought especially useful. For a man who thought himself made of glass, Rush recommended pulling a chair as he was about to sit so that he fell to prove that he was still whole. These new disturbing methods were designed to frighten the mad out of their distractions.

Rush attributed the causes of insanity to a variety of personal failings from inordinate sexual desires to intense study, joy, avarice and ambition, terror, grief, and intemperance. Enthusiastic religion (what we today call evangelicalism) in particular he thought was "calculated to induce a predisposition to madness." The second Great Awakening of the early nineteenth century, like the growing market economy and urbanization, were major social developments that reformers believed were inimical to good health. Avarice and ambition, stimulated by economic developments, were added to Rush's list. Such excesses of emotions ran counter to the Enlightenment's ideals of balance and harmony: the belief that moderation was the key to the good life. Unlike the earlier periods, when insanity was considered a mere misfortune, it had become something due to a loss of self-control and personal failings. Almanacs publicized these notions about intemperance, of physical ills causing madness, of the dangers of masturbation, and the excessive reading by women, all of which led to lunacy. Under Rush's influence, doctors at the end of the eighteenth century assumed that insanity was a moral failure that could be overcome by medical science and that treating the body would cure the mind. Such ideas were reinforced in the new medical schools in New

York and Massachusetts established after the Revolution. Dissertations on insanity written in the 1790s emphasized the strong connection between mind and body.

Thus Mary Sewall's treatment by her doctors followed the protocol initiated by the Philadelphia Hospital in the years before the Revolution, modified and exacerbated by the ideas of Benjamin Rush that had become standard by the beginning of the nineteenth century. The main difference between the Sewall case and later developments was the growing notion that cures were more likely if the patient were separated from home, from family and friends, and away from the social and emotional environment that had perhaps brought on the problems. Thus began the move to institutionalize the insane, and the nineteenth-century mental hospital was born.

The creation of formal institutions to replace the older ad hoc mechanisms of care previously provided by family and friends had become absolutely necessary in the minds of both medical professionals and lay reformers. In urban settings insanity had become more visible, and the irrational behavior of the insane could no longer be ignored. An increase of madness could threaten the social order. Physicians had begun to link mental illness with social organization, blaming it on the structure of society rather than just individual failings. The superintendents of the new institutions and the lay public alike believed that American society put unprecedented demands on mental health. They not only expected insanity to increase but also assumed that society had an obligation to take care of their unfortunates.

The social landscape had changed radically by the second decade of the nineteenth century, especially in the areas of religious and political life. The disestablishment of state churches had encouraged the proliferation of religious sects. A second Great Awakening of highly emotional religion at the turn of the century added to the religious excitement and diversity that contributed to the idea that the old external restraints on behavior no longer worked. Thus the reason for Sewall's concern about his daughter's interest in the Shakers, an offshoot of the Quakers that depended on quiet meditation but encouraged participants to shake and tremble during religious services. The elimination of property qualifications for voting and the rise of political parties created new choices in the realm of government and politics. More people voted and showed less deference to the elite, who had previously laid claim to the right to govern. Other social changes—more single people living outside of family groups in urbanized, industrialized communities, a more disparate ethnic landscape due to renewed immigration from Europe, and increasing economic opportunities—added to the sense of a rapidly changing society, which would in turn contribute to mental stress.

Philanthropists now began in earnest to sponsor hospitals devoted to the cure of the insane. The Quakers, inspired by developments in England, built the "Friends' Asylum" in Frankford, Pennsylvania in 1813, and five years later private money created the McLean Asylum in Cambridge, Massachusetts. A group of physicians sponsored another hospital in Hartford, Connecticut, in 1824; four years later Columbia, South Carolina, became the first in the Deep South to establish such a hospital. The pace to establish mental hospitals picked up after 1830 as individual states took on the responsibility for the mentally ill.

These new institutions were influenced by ideas flowing from France and England regarding the care of the insane. In France, Philippe Pinel (1745–1820) advocated what came to be called "moral treatment," a psychologically oriented therapy. Because emotional excess and social strains were held responsible for insanity, reeducation of the mind for more effective means of self-control became his objective. The idea of moral management ran counter to the eighteenth-century bestialized image of the insane and fit into the new reformist ideas about the possibility of transforming not just the social order but also man's intellectual capacity. Pinel recommended that changing the environment and regular routines of work and distractions would be more effective than confinement, physical abuses, or drugs. He laid the groundwork for the more humane treatment of the insane in Europe. William Tuke, an English Quaker merchant who opened an asylum called the York Retreat in 1792, put Pinel's ideas into practice in England. Tuke concentrated on developing greater internal means of restraint and self-control. He believed that kindness, freedom of movement, and supervised occupation and recreation were essential although with a great deal of authoritarian control.

Tuke visited the United States in 1815 and harshly condemned the Rush treatment that depended on fear, depletion procedures, physical abuse, food deprivation, and physical restraint. American doctors ignored Tuke's criticism when they adapted his version of Pinel's "moral treatment." They were committed to the notion that madness was a disease with somatic influences that originated either in the blood vessels of the brain (for the followers of Rush) or in the gastric intestinal system. Cathartics and bleeding continued to be therapeutic measures in American asylums along with the supervision and control of everyday behavior. American doctors felt threatened by the notion of an exclusively psychological treatment as advocated by Tuke. They insisted on the close connection between the mind and the body that required somatic treatment to cure mental ills. Without the orthodox depletion treatments geared to curing diseases, the doctor could claim only a small role in handling the mental ill. In time many physicians did modify their use of traditional therapies but did not abandon them. It is possible that the Pinel-Tuke influences led to more humanitarian treatment of the insane in asylums at that time.

An additional force behind the public mental hospitals was the reforming trend that was pushing for the abolition of slavery, of temperance, of more humane prisons, of women's rights. The Reverend Louis Dwight, visiting jails as an agent for the American Bible Society, wrote about the horrors of prison life for the insane. He found lunatics living under shocking conditions in the Massachusetts jails. Many were confined for years to one room with no fresh air. Horace Mann put additional pressure on the Massachusetts legislature to build a separate hospital for the insane. Their efforts led to the opening in 1833 of the first state-funded hospital for the insane in the north, the Worcester Insane Asylum. The superintendent Samuel B. Woodworth sincerely believed that prompt medical and moral treatment would cure insanity. He reported recoveries of 82–90 percent a year, but that was of recorded recoveries, not the number of inmates. Many left, supposedly cured, only to be readmitted months or years later, declared recovered again, sent home, and then readmitted. His reported successes and skewed statistics led other states to follow the Massachusetts example. Ohio and Vermont set up institutions in 1840, and within ten years Maine, New Hampshire, New Jersey, Indiana, Tennessee, Georgia, and Louisiana had such asylums.

In the meantime Dorothea L. Dix began her campaign to make public asylums the foundation of public policy. After a visit to Tuke's York Retreat in England she became an advocate for the insane. Her passionate appeals for humane treatment, her detailed description of the horrible conditions of the insane in the jails, and her indefatigable collection of petitions on behalf of the mentally ill moved legislators to provide new funds. Gerald Grob credits her huge successes to her "exaggerated rhetoric" and "embellished facts." Nonetheless, she played an important role in moving public money into hospitals for the insane. In the antebellum years each state had built at least one public asylum to house patients of every class and condition of mental derangement although there were more numerous private asylums. All were dedicated to recovery from madness. The superintendents were dedicated to providing a supportive environment where cure was thought to be possible.

The rise of the asylum and the consequent incarceration of the mentally ill was celebrated by historians as evidence of human progress. Albert Deutsch, for example, argued that the asylums were a more humane way of handling madness than the previous ad hoc methods. More recent studies, however, have shown that many of the public asylums were unable to follow through with their new notions of psychological treatment. In spite of Dix's proselytizing, a lack of funds and overcrowding in the public institutions led to mainly custodial treatment. The use of drugs, punishment, outright cruel handling by keepers, and public displays of the insane continued. The chances of dying in the mental hospital also became a threat.. The doctors excused the high death rate on the grounds of the advanced age of many patients and their generally debilitated conditions. Therefore the doctors argued such a group was more likely to die than other people. No reference was made to the kinds of treatment or physical abuse that followed the continuing heroic therapies that American doctors preferred. Little was done to prove that there were physiological causes of insanity or that the therapies actually worked. The revolving door of supposed recoveries provided some questionable statistical evidence of cures, but no useful clinical studies were attempted.

Physicians had good personal and professional reasons for supporting the asylums. Unlike most medical practitioners, superintendents of mental hospitals had guaranteed salaries and living expenses. They were protected from the insecurities of those practicing medicine in the general market, which depended on fees for service. In addition they could explore novel ways of treatment on a captive population that could not readily complain or deny therapy. Their professional status and the possibilities of finding cures were assured, and they took advantage of their protected status by establishing what Grob calls a "distinct professional identity." Psychiatry as a medical specialty thus was born in the mental hospital. In 1844 thirteen superintendents formed the first major professional organization, the Association of Medical Superintendents of America in Institutes for the Insane (forerunner of today's American Psychiatric Association). Jointly they developed guidelines and standards for treatment, and came to define the boundaries between normal and abnormal. By 1860 membership in the association had risen to eighty-three. Unfortunately, as the superintendents developed a rational for institutionalizing the mental ill, they tended to ignore empirical data and continued, as did other physicians, to conceive of disease in individual rather than general terms. They relied on visible and external signs of distress, and the categories established were merely vague definitions that varied from place to place.

The new professional identity did little to improve the quality of life for those confined in asylums. The medical model of therapy continued to be essential. To have changed their ways and refused to use what had become hallmarks of medical treatment might well have undermined the medical model of insanity and the role of the physician in such cures. Blood-letting was still used to reduce the supposed inflammation of the brain, violent patients were sedated with opium and morphine, and melancholic or depressed patients received laxatives, baths, and digitalis. Punishments for the recalcitrant who tried to resist therapy were common practices. It was a highly regimented and repressive environment designed to inculcate internal means of self-control. By the 1840s, however, the asylum also became a place of last resort, and gradually moral treatments gave way to the custodial care of growing numbers of chronic cases. The patients were at least kept clean, fed, and more comfortable than they would have been in jail, but there is no proof that people recovered except for a temporary reprieve for the lucky few.

For some patients in the asylums confinement was a tragic experience. They were isolated from family and deprived of personal liberty. They resented being forced to associate with people not of their class or culture or to contend with the bizarre behavior of the sickest patients. One Robert Fuller compared his treatment to the Spanish Inquisition because of the repressive regimen. Fuller also noted that many of his fellow patients were injured in the course of treatment. Grob, who analyzed the narratives of former patients, concluded that in spite of many complaints, there was a sense that the asylum relieved families of the financial and emotional burden of carrying for those who threatened the stability and safety of the community. Families sent their relatives to the hospital; seldom did the courts or doctors take such action. The asylum then cared for those who could not provide for themselves or who were rejected by their families.

Within the asylums, not all patients were treated equally. Because a particularly controlled environment was considered essential to the cure, patients were separated by class, ethnicity, and except in parts of the South, by race. Life in the institution followed the norms of the larger society as defined by the psychiatrists and their elite paying patients, who, it was thought, would be disturbed by the close presence of people they considered inferior. The best care in the mental hospitals went to native-born paying patients, with indigent whites, immigrants, and blacks receiving the lowest quality of care. The most recent immigrants fared the worst. Doctors were confused by differences in language and customs and made little attempt to understand the problems of the immigrants, often assuming that such deviants would not be susceptible to treatment.

The attitude toward African Americans differed dramatically from that of the rest of the population. Many were denied access to the asylum, as in Indiana and Ohio, or put into rigidly segregated quarters, as in Massachusetts, New York, and Cincinnati. Most southern hospitals usually accepted free blacks, some in segregated quarters and others integrated. South Carolina was the exception; there African Americans were refused admission. An 1848 law to permit black patients in the Charleston asylum was intended to enhance South Carolina's reputation for humanity in order to counter abolitionist antislavery propaganda, but few black people were actually admitted. The Williamsburg Lunatic Asylum treated both white and black, slave and free in integrated quarters until 1840 when the idea of moral management was introduced. The new system not only reduced the use of restraints and provided more activities for mind and body, but also segregated blacks for the first time on the theory that all should have the kind of accommodations and company to which they were accustomed. Black people, it was assumed, required less comfortable accommodations than whites and were more accustomed to menial labor. The accommodations and care reflected that racist philosophy.

The early Virginia asylum records of slaves indicate that some of their problems paralleled that of the larger population. Todd Savitt mentions the case of Dilsey in 1819 whose symptoms the superintendent attributed to the loss of her husband's affection. One man was deranged over the subject of religion, and a black woman had to be put into a strait jacket during her fits when she was refused permission to see the man she was to marry. Other doctors criticized the belief that slaves suffered from different mental diseases, identified by Samuel Cartwright as "dysaethesia aethiopsis," for what slave owners called "rascality" or the fanciful drapetamania (a propensity to run away), as mere speculation. Cartwright's ideas failed to attract much of a following among his contemporaries and now appear as a mere curiosity in most historical analyses.

For the most part slaves were not confined in asylums, and in the 1850s they were excluded even in Virginia. Insanity on the plantation often was not recognized as such. Disruptive slaves were often sold away, whipped for bad behavior, tied up to control them, given simple tasks when possible, or merely watched over by other slaves, and most probably treated by local conjurers with charms and incantations. It was not unusual for masters to free ailing or deranged slaves to avoid the cost of their care. Slave owners argued that slaves seldom suffered from insanity because they had fewer problems in everyday life than free people and that the physical labor on the plantation strengthened their constitutions. Therefore, they argued, when a slave succumbed to insanity, he or she recovered faster than whites. But Savitt contends that "though slaves escaped the tension of politics and property," they suffered from the problems associated with enslavement: anger and aggression toward the master, watching the humiliation of their parents during childhood years, and lack of control over their lives, all of which contributed to mental strain. Some slaves simply could not cope and escaped into their own worlds of erratic and antisocial behavior. Nutritional deficiencies, such as pellagra, could also contribute to bizarre behavior.

The mental ills of free blacks, like those of whites, were blamed on intemperance, religious enthusiasm, disappointed affections, and marital strife, as well as the problems of making a living. Harriet Washington suggests that some cases of insanity among former slaves were most likely due to problems that preceded their freed status. A flawed census in 1840 counted insane and idiots for the first time with a surprising number of free black people in those categories. Slave owners seized on that census to prove that free black people were more prone to insanity than slaves or whites. The statistician Edward Jarvis examined the census and found that it was in fact riddled with flagrant errors. The Worcester State Hospital in Massachusetts supposedly had 133 "colored lunatics and idiots," which was the actual number of white patients at the time. There were towns with all-white populations that had "mysteriously" acquired six insane black people. Because of those distortions there is no way to know how many free African Americans suffered from mental ills or how many were in the asylums.

Most of the insane in America remained outside the walls of the asylum. Only small numbers came to the attention of hospitals or doctors. Throughout the South, community and family care of the insane continued to be the norm. For example, the asylum in South Carolina had difficulty attracting patients, possibly because there was a widespread assumption that hospitals were for poor lunatics and the belief that insanity itself was dishonorable. Affluent families were loath to confine their relatives to the asylum, so the mental hospital became a place of last resort for their uncontrollable family members in the South. Even in the northern asylums by the 1850s, most patients were there because they were either indigent or violent. At the same time, much of the moral treatment had given way to mere custodial care. Even doctors were advising families to keep the less dangerous at home.

Among many of the folk living in small or isolated communities, the attitude toward mental ills had not changed from the older supernatural causes. David Fischer notes the widespread and persistent use of charms, omens, and spells among the backcountry people for all kinds of illnesses and problems. He found an eclectic body of beliefs with borrowing from Indians, Africans, Germans, and other cultures from the British Isles. Magical cures were especially persistent in the South where African traditions were strongest. Cases of insanity, like other illness, were still often attributed to magic. Cases of insanity rumored to be magically induced were common in reports of life under slavery compiled after the Civil War. As a result conjure doctors continued to be in demand to ply their trade and remove the spells causing mental ills.

Although the superintendents in the asylums claimed to know what caused mental illness and how to treat it, their definitions and their therapies were not always accepted by the public in either the North or the South. In South Carolina there were several incidents of conflict between the lay Board of Regents and the doctors in the asylum over whether patients were cured sufficiently to be discharged or over the use of restraints. Relatives also clashed with the doctors over treatments, sometimes interfering directly or taking the patient home without permission. And too, there were new tensions between the fledging psychiatric profession and the legal system. In 1812 the Superior Court in Massachusetts ruled that it could not accept insanity as a defense when it was defined by the doctor. The medical definition was, according to a judge, too vague and "equivocal." A similar ruling in 1831 rejected medical opinion as expert testimony, the court preferring to make use of its own personal observations of the defendant's behavior.

Over the course of three centuries the treatment of insanity had moved from one that generally ignored those with deviant behaviors to one that actively treated mental ills in a hospital setting. The best that can be said about the hospitals in early America is that they provided minimal custodial care to keep the mentally ill off the streets. There was some objection to depletion procedures, but there was no hard evidence of overt or organizational objection to the asylum. It continued to be popular as an urban institution, as the rural folk continued to care for their incompetent relatives at home. Nor did much of rural life, black and white alike, appear to have been influenced by the new medical models of insanity. Psychiatry may well have taken a move forward as a medical specialty but, as with other health problems, only a small number of the population accepted the doctor's role in the handling of the insane.

9

Democratic Medicine

William W. Dyott, a bootblack, arrived in Philadelphia from England in the 1790s. He was an entrepreneurial immigrant who demonstrated his business acumen early on by extending his bootblacking enterprise to the manufacture of the needed shoe polish. The surplus he sold to other bootblacks. So successful was this early manufacturing venture that he decided in 1807 to promote patent medicines. With some knowledge of drugs gained previously as an apprentice to an apothecary in England, Dyott concocted a new medical compound that he claimed was the creation of his grandfather, a Dr. Robertson of the University of Edinburgh, to cure "a certain disease." It was the first of many fabrications that were to propel Dyott to financial success and great popularity: there was no Dr. Robertson in the medical school at that university, but Dyott's counterfeit claims to a medical background grew as he created new combinations of chemicals to cure a variety of ailments from toothaches, itch, gout, and rheumatism to his very special "Dr. Robertson's Infallible Worm Destroying Lozenges." In short order he also invented experiences as a physician in London and the West Indies in order to claim the title of doctor.

To support his new patent medicine business "Dr." Dyott built a glass works to manufacture his own distinctive bottles. At the time, as James Harvey Young reminds us in the *Toadstool Millionaires*, manufacturers took out a patent on the labels and the bottle design. Copyright laws did not extend to the ingredients in the container. Dyott was aided in these new endeavors by an increase in the number of newspapers and their reduced prices that allowed him to advertise widely to promote his nostrums throughout the country. He touted the pleasant taste of the stuff while attacking the unpleasant therapies and high cost of regular doctors. Nonetheless, without the requirement to list the ingredients of his nostrums, Dyott could freely add the usual mercury and opium as well as alcohol in more pleasant-tasting concoctions. With such successes in manufacturing, he then turned to banking, which became his downfall in the financial panic of 1837. Dyott served four years in prison for fraudulent financial activities but afterwards returned to his patent medicine business to recoup his fortune before his death in 1861.

Dyott's story reveals a great deal about how the economic, political, and cultural changes in the United States during the second quarter of the nineteenth century helped to transform the healing arts throughout the country and contributed to the decline of orthodox medicine. In its economy the United States was an entrepreneurial paradise, making it easy for frauds like Dyott. There were few regulations imposed by either government or industry for any kind of business, including the sale of drugs or health care. The egalitarian rhetoric of political and cultural life of the Jacksonian era gave new impetus to the idea that every man was master of his own fate including that of his health. This democratic ethos elevated the common man and questioned the need for a talented elite, further undermining the importance of the doctor in medical care. Because of opposition to monopolies, weak licensing requirements for doctors put few limits on who could practice medicine or teach. As a result men of stature had little incentive to turn to the profession. A medical student in the late 1840s, Steven Smith, regretfully observed that "a boy who proved unfit for anything else must become a Doctor." The father of J. Marion Sims had nothing but contempt for the profession and tried to discourage his son from pursuing a medical education on the grounds that no reputation or honor was to be made that way. His son, known as the "Father of Gynecology" had other ideas aided by a distressing (even for his own time) set of ethics regarding his African American patients.

The proliferation of competing, low-standard, proprietary schools, owned and operated by poorly trained doctors who were themselves graduates of similar institutions, combined with the business model of the time, contributed to the declining reputation of medicine in the United States. In 1810 there were six medical schools in the country, mostly in the northeast; by 1830 there were twenty-two schools, and by the middle of the century there were forty-two. Doctors operated the new ones, scattered mostly throughout the West and South, with no association to clinics or colleges. Few required any previous education for admission not even minimal literacy. In competition, even the most prestigious medical school in Philadelphia eliminated the bachelor's degree requirement for admission. The owners of the proprietary schools watered down the curriculum in order to attract students. There was no uniform course of study or standardization of therapies, and within the schools doctors bickered about treatments and theories, leading to what James Cassedy describes as "vituperative conflicts of competing medical ideas" complicated by the "impotence of most of their therapies." The commercialization of medicine born of a cultural environment that valued income over public service did little to improve the status of the profession. Ronald Numbers had good reasons to conclude that, "midway through the nineteenth century, American medicine lay in a shambles."

There were some who tried to take action to stop the trends but ultimately failed. Daniel Drake (1785–1852), trained in Philadelphia and with a long apprenticeship, was well respected and known for his publications on the relationship of environment and disease. He fruitlessly advocated hospital-based training and a minimum of four years of medical instruction. In 1834 a proposal to charter a medical college in Louisiana was apposed by French physicians because it would have no university sponsorship. They too lost the battle to raise standards, and in 1835 when the Louisiana school opened it was left in the hands of its proprietors who were more concerned with collecting fees than providing a good medical education. The number of those claiming a certificate from those diploma mills rose from 250 in 1800 to 40,000 in 1850, a faster rate of growth than the population. With the exception of those in the larger northeastern cities, few could make a living from medical practice partly because of the abundance of doctors in small towns and the dispersed rural population of the West and South, and because fewer people were willing to pay for their services.

The "I can do it myself better than the professional" belief of this era was encouraged by new health manuals that claimed to educate the traditional domestic healing of every housewife or herbal expert in the ways of orthodox medicine. One of the more popular of the new manuals came out of the western states and was published in Knoxville, Tennessee, in 1830 as *Gunn's Domestic Medicine*. It was to be, as the subtitle extols, *The Poor Man's Friend*.

In the Hours of Affliction, Pain, and Sickness. The author, a well-trained physician, proposed to reduce the practice of medicine, "to principles of common sense" without the jargon of theories that accompanied the professional physician. Such doctors, those "impudent" pretenders "of science and quackery," he declared, deceived the public into accepting what he considered nothing but "fudge and mummery." Every man, he argued, was capable of finding the correct herbs to cure or to buy what could not be grown, to take his own pulse, to bleed, and to set a fracture. Such knowledge was not mysterious and did not require any special training. Gunn promised that his book would do away with the need for a physician. By dispensing with the physician's visit, Gunn helped to further weaken the boundaries between the nonspecialist and the professional.

Gunn's prescriptions, however, probably struck a familiar chord in the minds of his readers. They were not much different from orthodox medicine. He advocated routine "puking" with ipecac, bleeding at the first sign of inflammation (fever), opium for pain and diarrhea, and mercury purges for fever and organ problems, especially the scourge of alcoholism, "diseased liver." Unlike physicians who dealt mainly with sickness, Gunn recommended the means of preserving health through regular exercise, bathing in warm water, and moderate eating that included a mixture of vegetables and animal food with a minimum of cooking or spices. He also stressed the importance of sleep to good health. To maintain one's health would further eliminate the necessity for a physician. In rural areas where a well-educated physician was a rarity and if available too expensive to consult, such a source of information was a welcome addition to the household. The book went into its one hundredth edition in 1871, following only the Bible and hymnbooks in personal libraries. The popularity of Gunn's manual was one indication that many Americans had come to believe that they could deal with most problems of illness by using common sense and their own native intelligence. To a greater extent than the people in the colonial era, nineteenth-century Americans refused to accept the physician as the single authority in matters of health.

By the second quarter of the century, regular physicians struggled against competition not just from within their own ranks but from a growing number of patent medicine entrepreneurs, new do-it-yourself manuals, and, increasingly, unconventional ideas about healing and good health that ran counter to orthodox theories—the sectarians. These incursions into the orthodox medical profession were all aided by the peculiarly American democratic ideology that eschewed formal education, disdained monopolistic business practices, and stressed limited government action in the marketplace, in favor of a free-for-all enterprise. As that dean of medical historians,

GUNN'S
DOMESTIC MEDICINE,

OR

POOR MAN'S FRIEND.

IN THE HOURS OF AFFLICTION, PAIN, AND SICKNESS.

THIS BOOK
POINTS OUT, IN PLAIN LANGUAGE, FREE FROM DOCTOR'S TERMS
THE DISEASES OF

MEN, WOMEN, AND CHILDREN,

AND THE LATEST AND MOST APPROVED MEANS USED IN THEIR CURE,
AND IS EXPRESSLY WRITTEN FOR THE BENEFIT OF

FAMILIES

IN THE WESTERN AND SOUTHERN STATES.

IT ALSO CONTAINS

DESCRIPTIONS OF THE MEDICINAL ROOTS AND HERBS OF THE WESTERN AND SOUTHERN COUNTRY, AND HOW THEY ARE TO BE USED IN THE CURE OF

DISEASES:

ARRANGED ON A NEW AND SIMPLE PLAN,

BY WHICH THE PRACTICE OF MEDICINE IS REDUCED

TO PRINCIPLES OF COMMON SENSE.

mcC 25757

Why should we conceal from mankind
That which relieves the distresses of our fellow-beings?

Knoxville,

PRINTED UNDER THE IMMEDIATE SUPERINTENDANCE OF THE AUTHOR,

A PHYSICIAN OF KNOXVILLE.

::::::::::::
1830.

A University of Tennessee Press 1986 facsimile reprint of "*Gunn's Domestic Medicine*," was a do-it-yourself medical manual popular in the western states where few doctors were available. First published in 1830 it went through innumerable reprints and helped to blur the lines between the professional medical man and the laymen. (From the author's collection)

Richard Shryock, once remarked, Americans felt they had "inalienable rights to life, liberty, and quackery."

The first of the new challenges to regular medicine came from a back-woods New Hampshire man with a curiosity about plants and the effects of different leaves, berries, and barks on the body. His random sampling turned to more serious consideration after several members of his family were treated by physicians with the usual mercury and opium with poor results. His mother died in 1790s after that therapy, and his wife suffered dur-ing childbirth under the ministrations of a male midwife. During the next ten years, family members who turned to folk doctors survived their ill-nesses and, in Samuel Thomson's mind, such traditional botanical treatments appeared to be wiser, the orthodox treatments futile. He was especially dis-dainful of physicians attending women and advised natural childbirth with midwives. After experimenting with a variety of Native American herbal treatments and influenced by their traditional sweat baths, Thomson came up with a new theory of illness that heat was life and its extinction was death and that disease was caused by cold.

To bring the body back to health, he advised cleansing the system first using a combination of enemas; sweat baths, and a botanical emetic bor-rowed from Indian lore, *lobelia inflata*. To restore the heat he then advised the use of cayenne pepper, another American Indian product. This was fol-lowed by a regimen of teas and tonics of brandy mixed with other botanicals. The violence of the lobelia and the enemas mimicked the heroic therapies of humoral medicine and thus were familiar treatments but avoided the harsher chemicals and bloodletting. Thomson intended to rescue "medicine from the doctors" who bled and poisoned patients with mercury, opium, niter, and rats bane (arsenic). On the other hand, Thomson was brought up on charges of poisoning a woman with lobelia in 1809 but was exonerated and went on to greater fame.

Thomson's genius, like Dyott's, was in the merchandizing and distribu-tion of his system. He too took advantage of increasing newspaper publi-cations, low postal rates, and patent laws, obtaining the first patent for his techniques in 1813. After publishing a *New Guide to Health* in 1822, he sold rights to his system for families for $20.00, and established a network of "Friendly Botanic Societies." His therapies were most popular in the south-ern and western frontiers throughout the 1820s and 1830s. A sizable minor-ity of slaveholders, fed up with ineffective and expensive treatments from regular physicians, became enthusiastic followers of his system. Thomson advertised in newspapers and traveled extensively to promote his system of Friendly Societies. James Whorton attributes Thomson's success to his

Indian themes were commonly used to promote patent medicines in the nineteenth century as in this advertisement for "Old Sachem Bitters," 1859. (Courtesy of the Library of Congress)

ability to exploit public antipathy to calomel and because his marketing "res-
onated with popular prejudices against allopathic [orthodox] therapy." To
James Harvey Young, Thomson's system "was the ultimate in the democratic
approach to health," with its suspicion of too much book learning and elite
physicians who tried to monopolize the field. With the Thomson method
there was no need for doctors and for one $20 expense a family could buy a
book of directions to take care of its own for their lifetime. Thomson's heyday
was short. Except in the South, by the 1840s Thomsonianism as a system of
healing was on the way out and was replaced with other botanical advocates,
many of whom were regular physicians who called themselves eclectics, and
new unorthodox therapies, all of which made even greater inroads into the
medical profession. Remnants of Thomson's theories, however, can still be
found in modern-day botanical therapies as well as in popular health lore
such as "feed a fever and starve a cold."

A greater threat to regular medicine than Thomsonianism was homeopathy because many of the adherents were educated, orthodox practitioners.
They claimed to be more scientific than others because of clinical trials used
to test each drug, and they put forth an elaborate metaphysical doctrine
that disease was fundamentally a matter of spirit—an ethereal "vital force."
At first the New York Medical Society conferred honorary membership on
the local homeopaths in 1832 but, realizing the potential harm to orthodox
medicine, rescinded the honor a few years later. The homeopathic success in
curing patients had proven to be too much of a challenge. Those cures came
about because, unlike orthodox medicine, the treatment did not disturb the
body's ability to heal itself. Belief in the therapy had also become a powerful
placebo. In response, Dr. Oliver Wendell Holmes attacked the new therapy
as a delusion based on a false theory, which of course it was. But at the same
time Holmes claimed that patients were being denied access to treatments
that were based more solidly on science—the traditional system of depletion
that was as much a fantasy as the sectarian theories.

Homeopathy was the invention of a German physician, Samuel Hahnemann (1755–1843) who, disillusioned by the ineffectiveness of traditional
medicine, left the profession and began to translate classical works including those dealing with ancient medicine. He wondered about the effects of
those older drugs and began to experiment with them on himself. He noted
that often medicines recommended for particular diseases brought on similar symptoms in the healthy person. Cinchona bark (although not an ancient
remedy) was his prime example. From those trials he concluded that a small
dose of such drugs would stimulate the body's healing power, its vital force.
With this understanding, Hahnemann returned to medical practice to treat

patients with a gentle medicine that did not produce dramatic effects on the body. His successes attracted followers throughout Europe, and his fame spread to what Roberta Bivens calls the "fertile soil" of the United States where the "therapeutic excesses and monopolistic ambitions of orthodox medicine" had prepared the way for a more agreeable type of healing.

Hahnemann's ideas were brought to America by several European-trained physicians—at first the German immigrant Henry Detweiler in 1817 and later Hans B. Grams, a Bostonian who returned to New York after training in Denmark in 1835, and other educated immigrants who congregated in Philadelphia. Their popularity grew rapidly. During the cholera epidemics of the 1830s and 1840s, their mild and pleasant-tasting medicines of infinitesimal doses of known drugs proved to be an advantage over the purging and bleeding regimens. The homeopathic drugs also cost less and had no disagreeable side effects. Homeopathy especially appealed to intellectuals—transcendentalists and the clergy—because of its philosophical component. The homeopathic physician also listened carefully to each patient's litany of complaints rather than mechanically providing drugs and treatments based on common practice. Like Thomsonianism, the homeopaths prepared self-help kits with instructions and samples of the medications to be used at home. By 1835 fourteen American editions of the instruction book, the *Domestic Physician*, had been published in English and thirteen in German.

By 1844 there were enough homeopathic practitioners to establish a national medical society, and in 1848 Detweiler and Constantine Hering founded the first Homeopathic Medical College of Pennsylvania in Philadelphia. Unlike orthodox medical schools, homeopaths invited women to attend and to practice. Trainees then carried the ideas to New Jersey and New England but had little affect in the South where Thomsonianism was still a force. Along with the minute doses of drugs diluted in quantities of water, the homeopaths advocated proper bed rest and diet, bathing, and improved public sanitation. They also opposed common domestic remedies and patent medicines as too harsh. Their own prescriptions in their kits rarely caused any adverse effects and thus were touted as safe for all ages. Even the orthodox admitted they were safe even if misused. It was a therapeutic regimen that continued in popularity throughout the century and continues to resonate with Americans today.

As attractive as homeopathy was to Americans, hydropathy, the third major irregular medical program, was even more appealing. It too was a European import and rejected the dangerous and unpleasant drugging, purging, bleeding regimen of orthodox medicine. It went even further than homeopathy by rejecting drugs altogether and using water alone for bathing or wrapping the body and for drinking but did retain the familiar idea of depletion by sweating and cold water enemas to dissolve the so-called morbid matter of disease. Like Samuel Thomson, the creator of this new healing system, Vincent Preissnitz (1799–1851), was an unlettered peasant in Austria who turned his home into a water cure that consisted of cold water baths, packs, and wet bandages. Intrigued by the Austrian system, Drs. John Shaw and Russell T. Trall opened the first water cure establishment in New York in 1843. Within five years there were thirty such establishments in the United States and the number grew through the 1850s. Spas that stressed the use of water, usually mineral waters, were an old idea as a place of rest and recreation. The first one was established in southern Maryland in the seventeenth century, and the popularity of such a retreat continued throughout the eighteenth century. But this water cure was different. The regimen was a more dynamic, individualized program, with more personal interaction between practitioner and patient than was usual in the old-fashioned spas and had a special appeal for women.

During the cure women benefited from a respite from pregnancies and family responsibilities, and found the tactile stimulation and social atmosphere of the retreat particularly appealing. As the center of attention, their sexual, social, and psychological needs became paramount. Dr. Russell Trall, the major theorist of the movement, emphasized the natural aspects of women's reproductive cycle, rejecting the orthodox medical ideas that they were varieties of illness or that women lacked sexual passion. Trall instead spoke about female sexual urges and recognized their intent to control fertility. He suggested various means of contraception, and when all else failed considered abortion preferable to bearing unwanted children. Women were also encouraged to be active participants in the therapy. To protect their modesty, it was necessary to train and employ female practitioners, thus emphasizing an active role for women outside of the home. The first class of the American Hydropathic Institute that opened in New York in 1851 was comprised of eleven men and nine women. The succeeding classes included at least one quarter of the class as female students. As an aid to health, hydropathy also encouraged women to forgo the tight corsets and constricting fashionable clothing in favor of a loose dress worn over bloomer-type pants.

The goals of hydropathy were to remove obstructions in the body, to wash away impurities, supply nutriments, and regulate body temperature in order to aid nature's healing power. The process included wrapping in cold sheets covered with blankets to encourage sweating, followed by cold baths and drinking quantities of water, followed in turn by cold showers, sizt and foot baths, and brisk rubbing of the body by an attendant. All was accompanied with attentive nursing, fresh air, exercise, and pleasant companions. To publicize the program, hydropaths published a *Water Cure Journal* for one dollar a year; the journal continued in existence under a variety of names from 1844 to 1913. By 1852 there were 50,000 subscribers and by 1860 the number rose to 100,000, the editors claiming a million readers. The *Water Cure Journal* advocated medical simplicity, dietary changes, and techniques adapted for home use for those too far away from a regular establishment. It continually ridiculed established medical authorities and rejected all orthodox medical treatments and drugs including, unfortunately, vaccination.

Although there were many variations on the theme of water cures, not all hydropaths agreed on how it was to be used or whether it was acceptable to use warm water. The leaders did little to standardize treatments or training although various hydropathic schools did exist. Some practitioners used homeopathic drugs in small quantities; some were vegetarians; others approved of meat in the diet. It was an amorphous movement that stressed the prevention of disease and easily allied with other reform movements of the day such as dress reform, temperance, dietary changes, utopian communities, and antislavery. It had little appeal in the South, though. The stress on right living enabled patients to be their own doctors. Such an "ideology of self-control," writes Susan Cayleff, "mirrored the formula for success in economic life" and the democratic ideal of controlling one's own destiny. Like popular religions of the time hydropathy stressed self-help as an avenue of personal betterment.

Although the hydropaths encouraged the use of bathing, physical cleanliness was not the major object. There was no attempt to use soap, which was used primarily for washing clothes and floors but not the body until later in the century. Men used soap to aid in shaving, and women thought of it as a perfume or as a cosmetic to soften skin. Soap was an expensive product and thus of limited use for the larger population. The hydrotherapy movement did not generally filter down to the urban poor. Because the cost of a cure ranged from five dollars to ten dollars, it was out of the reach of poorer people. There was no running water in the tenements and thus that segment of the population lacked the means of following the prescriptions for washing, bathing, or drinking water even if they thought it important to do so. Water from public pumps was often polluted and dangerous to consume in the cities, and public bathhouses for the poor would not make their appearance until the end of the century. Although many of the sectarians advised bathing for reasons of health, the hygienic value of immersing one's body in water had not yet permeated the larger population. When installing a bathroom in

SHOWER BATH.

This page and opposite: Bathing of any kind was so unusual in the pre–Civil War years that Joel Shew included illustrations of both a shower and a tub method in his *Hydropathic Family Physician* published in 1854. (Photos by Thom Pinho. Courtesy of the University of Maryland Health Sciences and Human Services Library, Baltimore)

WASH TUB BATH.

the White House was proposed in 1851, there was a furious reaction by the public to such an unnecessary expense.

Other, less organized, self-help health movements that had captured the democratic imagination aided the sectarians. Sylvester Graham, whose legacy lingers in the Graham cracker, was a Presbyterian minister and a spokesman for the anti-alcohol crusade. He soon expanded the subject of his lectures to what he called the "Science of Human Life"—rules governing diet, physical activity, sexuality, and bathing. His "science" led to the suppression of animal appetites that, he believed, caused illness because it interfered with godliness. In effect, anything that produced pleasure and therefore lowered inhibition was morally wrong. Graham advocated bland food without spices; avoidance of tea, coffee, and, of course, alcohol, in favor of water, and absence from crowded places such as ballrooms, theaters, and gaming establishments (although attending church was acceptable). His recommended diet was based on bran and vegetables alone—no meat. He warned against any lewd imagery that could arouse sexual desire. He thought that sexual activity depleted the body and should be limited to procreation only. He contributed to the warnings against masturbation as a cause of insanity. Like the other sectarians, he encouraged women to lecture to other women on his health regimen. Apparently Graham never converted more than a few thousand adherents, but many of his ideas about diet, clothing, and bathing, and the role of women in health merged with the hydropath movement.

Graham was not the only reformer on the health circuit. John Harvey Kellogg had his own health maintenance regiment of vegetarianism and regular purging of the bowels. William Andrus Alcott, a regular physician, declared his "medical independence" in 1830, announcing that he was rejecting traditional therapies to rely on nature alone. He preached a gospel called "Physical Education." Encouraged by the public role of Graham's female followers, other women took up the cudgels of health reform on their own. Mary Gene Nichols, a Grahamite, drifted into hydropathy and clothing reform. Harriet K. Hunt, a graduate of a homeopathic institute, organized a "Ladies Physiological Society" to educate women about their health and the workings of their own bodies in a series of lectures. Harriet Austin, another homeopathic physician, demonstrated and lectured on the new style of clothing designed by Amelia Bloomer. Folk medicine with its reliance on botanics, especially Native American remedies and magical rituals had not lost their attraction and may well have gained popularity following the decline of the Thomsonian movement. There were many alternatives to orthodox medicine for those who had become discouraged by the harshness and ineffectiveness of the extreme depletion methods. A major advantage of the fads was a growing emphasis on improving life style with better nutrition, fresh air, and exercise.

Two other European imports of note influenced the medical self-help movement. Anton Mesmer, a Viennese physician proclaimed a new basis for medicine called "animal magnetism," the notion that the human being has a magnetic fluid that could be stimulated to heal the body. His idea was tested in France in 1784 by a group of scientists that included Benjamin Franklin. They decided that such a fluid did not exist and rejected Mesmer's notions. Nonetheless the idea lingered and like other unconventional medical theories became popular in America. It attracted some surgeons who experimented with a state of sleep in their patients that came to be called hypnotism (mesmerism) in the 1840s. Probably even more popular was the German-French import of phrenology. The brain, according to its theorist Frank Joseph Gall, consisted of innumerable organs responsible for specific mental or emotional traits. The shape of the skull reflected the shape and purpose of those organs. Thus one could determine the underlying personality traits and pathologies of individuals by the shape of or irregularities on the skull. A prominent forehead signified a great thinker, and a bulging temple characterized a burglar. Phrenologists advised exercises to strengthen desirable traits and weaken the undesirable. It was an idea that was difficult to accord with medical theories but had tremendous popular appeal. Lorenzo and Orson Fowler, American publishers, promoted the ideas as part of their self-improvement ideology, and Lorenzo lectured on phrenology calling it a "mental philosophy." The individual was told how to improve his positive personality while discouraging those qualities considered antisocial.

The established medical community tried several approaches to undermine the new fads. Better-trained doctors tried to fight back against the sectarians and other health fads with the creation of the American Medical Association in 1847. They had hopes that a nationwide medical society would establish higher standards for medical education and ethical behavior. The AMA began a renewed push for licensing provisions to limit the competition and oppose the role of women in medicine. Attempts at licensing failed because such laws were considered monopolistic and undemocratic reflecting the prevailing idea of economic freedom. The commercialization of medical education was too strong a trend to stop, and the few schools that lengthened their curriculum had to retreat in the face of competition. Those doctors with hospital privileges succeeded at first in denying access to hospital patients from midwives, homeopaths, and other faddists, but public outcry stymied those actions. Individual physicians and their local medical societies attacked the competition as quackery, as purveyors of superstition and irrational thinking, with dire warnings of the threat to life if patients abandoned the rational therapies that had prevailed for so long. Those arguments carried little weight. Educated doctors were unable to counter the self-help movement in health. Growing public disillusionment with their therapies and public squabbles had undermined their authority to claim exclusive knowledge of medicine.

Some of that loss of authority was due to the obstinate nature of American medical practice. In Europe, professional identity was defined by law and consequently could be more open to innovation, but in the United States the doctor's identity was traditionally based on less formal criteria—on who he was personally—his moral character and mannerisms, his elite status, his educational attainments. Most American physicians of the nineteenth century had lost those defining characteristics. What was left was a therapeutic practice that required intervention. Their professional identity was so closely tied to the humoral theory and its variations that they could not countenance any radical change or think in terms of testing those therapies. When in 1835 Joseph Bigelow of Harvard described self-limiting diseases and advised letting nature heal, his proposal was rejected as nihilism. To practice medicine without strong drugs was to admit that the doctor had no mastery over disease. In their insecurity doctors relied on what Warner calls a "rigid ideology" of therapeutics, a "shared faith in the value of bloodletting," that was the most "distinctive mark of the regular physician." To uphold that principle was a matter of professional ethics, its use a matter of professional identity. When Hughes Bennett of the University of Edinburgh declared that bleeding prolonged disease in 1857, his fellow nationals as well as Americans decried his findings. Such an idea was anathema to the professional's sense of identity. Although some historians have assumed that early Americans were progressing toward a scientific medicine, there is no evidence that such was the case until much later in the century.

The orthodoxy that had become a hallmark of the profession also translated into a medical nationalism that not only undermined the possibility of a scientific approach to medicine but also reinforced the dependence on heroic therapies. By the 1820s there was a renewed interest in Europe as a place to complete medical education. There, aspiring doctors were exposed to the French clinical studies in anatomy and pathology, and the idea of collecting statistics as a way to determine the best therapies. Proof of diagnosis was often discovered in the lesions found during autopsy. Every patient who died in the Paris hospitals was taken to the autopsy room for confirmation or repudiation of clinical observations (a practice that increased the incidence of puerperal fever in the women patients when such autopsies were followed by obstetrical care). As the French doctors began to evaluate the effectiveness of their therapies statistically, they became more skeptical about drugs and procedures. But Americans returning from France ultimately refused to accept scientific studies that relied on statistics and autopsies. Doctors rejected the statistics on the grounds that the numerical method was an assault on tradition and a debasement of the profession. Thus a Philadelphia paper in 1820 condemned hospital statistics as a "dangerous form of empiricism." The results from autopsies were similarly ignored on the grounds that American constitutions and diseases were somehow different from Europeans. They countered the French discoveries by arguing that Americans were sturdier and more energetic, and could tolerate the heroic remedies. Diseases, according to the most outspoken

American doctors, were specific to age, gender, locale, and class. Geography was uppermost. There was a strong allegiance to disease specificity—that all diseases were specific to each individual and place, and were not specific entities in themselves. What was true of hospital patients in Paris, therefore, could not apply to care in the United States.

Such medical nationalism was carried to the extreme in the South where identities and livelihoods were even more at risk than in the North. The low status of physicians propelled arguments for southern distinctiveness in medicine. Doctors claimed that the pattern of disease distribution was different there because of the large proportion of blacks, small number of European immigrants, variation in agricultural practice, and the warm climate. Given those conditions, doctors concluded that northern therapies were wrong for southerners. Venesection, they argued, was more debilitating to southerners, especially the black population, but the liver was duller and had to be stimulated by larger doses of calomel. Mercury poisoning thus became a mark of southern medicine. Southern doctors lamented their intellectual dependence on the North and blamed the emphasis on excessive bloodletting for leading to public disillusionment with regular physicians. That disillusionment, they claimed, in turn fostered the growth of quackery and gave encouragement to the Thomsonians. In a defense of the southern way of life that was dependent on slavery, the doctors urged a liberation from northern medical authority much as writers and slaveholders urged liberation from northern ideas and economic institutions.

The most insecure doctors became the most vocal in their defense of extreme treatments. In a comparison of the Commercial Hospital in Cincinnati with that of Massachusetts General in Boston, John Harley Warner found that the greater the competition from the sectarians and the lower the status of doctors, the more likely the doctors would reaffirm their allegiance to heroic treatment. It had become a device to "cope with an erosion of their professional power." In Boston the doctors were still part of the entrenched social power structure and capable of exhibiting a social and professional confidence that was not visible in western and southern areas. They could more easily give in to pressure from their middle-class patients, heavily influenced by the sectarians, to let nature heal while still giving lip service to their traditional therapies. Doctors in Cincinnati lacked the established power and the social deference of the Bostonians. The area was also a stronghold of irregulars who denounced the monopoly of medicine by orthodox doctors and advocated less intrusive therapies. Those physicians in turn refused to moderate their heroic procedures. They denounced the faith in nature as a "cruel mockery" and "total dereliction of the high and sacred function of the medical profession." They feared that to change was to give comfort to the sectarians. Their arguments, however, did not stop most people from choosing alternative forms of healing. And it certainly did not improve the credibility of orthodox medicine.

Competition from the new fads of the early nineteenth century such as homeopaths, Thomsonianism, hydropaths, eclecticism, the Graham fitness program, and the proliferation of patented medicines with their sugarcoated pills contributed to the continuing decline in confidence in traditional medical treatments and the alienation of the public. The publicity and apparent success of these new sectarian treatments convinced more and more people to distrust the extreme methods of depletion used by physicians. The lack of uniform standards among educated medical people also fed the suspicion that such physicians were no more useful than traditional home remedies. Because so many patients got well in time with no treatment, the less orthodox remedies with fewer demands on the body seemed to bring about cures. None of the new remedies had any more scientific basis than the old, but they made people feel good about themselves and gave a greater sense of control over their own lives while avoiding the miseries of purging and bloodletting.

10

Public Health

Dr. John H. Griscom, a city inspector in Manhattan, walked the streets of lower New York eyeing the drains: open sewers containing human waste, dead animals, manure, and the effluvia from nearby slaughterhouses. The stench was overpowering, the worst he had ever experienced in a summer heat. What he saw was even more horrifying. He knew that occasionally the drains were flushed with water that pushed the garbage into the river. But when it rained he saw that the drains overflowed into the streets, driving the filth from the cesspools into the open, working its way into the basements and sub-basements of houses in the slums. He suspected the overflow also contaminated the drinking water available from standpipes in the street. In an age when strong unpleasant smells from unwashed bodies and rotting garbage were commonplace, Griscom was overwhelmed by the foulness of both sight and smell in the poorer sections of the city.

The year was 1842 and Griscom's job was to report nuisances, inspect buildings, and collect mortality statistics. Few had taken the job seriously before his time, but Griscom was sufficiently offended by the immorality of people living in such disgusting conditions that he was determined to awaken public consciousness to the health problems he saw. He gathered more information from the city Tract Society, missionaries who visited the homes and knew intimately about the lives of the poor and their constant sicknesses. There was one ten-foot-square cellar room with seven-foot ceilings that was home to two families of ten people. The floor was covered with the excrement and rotting material from the sewer, and boards had been placed around to cover the slimy substance. Another two-family dwelling housed eight families. How could one expect high morals with such a lack of privacy and the filth from overflowing drains? Disease and high death rates haunted the immigrants and the African Americans who inhabited the slums. Griscom recommended that newly installed pipes bringing pure water from the Croton River reservoir to the more respectable parts of the city be extended to the slums, that new housing be provided by benefactors, and that sewer pipes be installed underground to drive the filth away from the area. Neither the plight of the poor nor the possible danger from diseases spreading to the rest of the city moved the authorities to take action. For his boldness, Griscom was fired. In his place a lawyer was appointed as city inspector. It seemed that doctors were not to be trusted with the responsibility for the poor or their health. Such decisions were repeated elsewhere, a clear indication of the low esteem with which the medical profession was held by the 1840s.

Griscom argued that filth was a cause of disease, and that poor health was not the result of impiety. Such ideas ran counter to conventional wisdom. Many physicians and the political and social leadership were convinced that low morals predisposed people to poor health; thus the poor were responsible for their own sicknesses. It was assumed that the immoral, the impious, the depraved, and the intemperate drinker, were most prone to disease. Rather than clean up the streets, the public outcry was for quarantines to keep the diseased individuals isolated. Those who could fled the cities when epidemics began. That behavior and the accompanying beliefs about the poor was unchanged. Only the living conditions of the poor changed; they had become qualitatively worse. The smelly, filthy slums became breeding grounds for all kinds of diseases and were a major cause of the declining life expectancy in many nineteenth-century American cities. In some places the mortality rates approached or surpassed that of the some European cities.

Griscom's dismissal did not stop his mission to improve the living conditions of the poor. He was acutely aware of the sanitary movement in England and on the Continent. Unlike many of his contemporaries, he did not believe that American constitutions and requirements were any different from Europeans. He had an unusual respect for science and learning, which he attributed to his father's familiarity with Europe's leading scientists and his work as a chemist and academic. The son had learned that the collection of vital statistics was the key to understanding disease. This was obvious when three years later Griscom expanded his ideas in a longer work the *Sanitary Conditions of the Laboring Population in New York* (1845). He now argued for free medical care for the indigent, improved housing, instruction in personal hygiene, and the keeping of statistics to track births and deaths based on the English model. No longer confident that philanthropy was sufficient, he called for state powers to improve the living conditions of the poor, much as the sanitary movement was demanding in England. He wanted more dispensaries (outpatient clinics) for the poor under the control of doctors, not lawyers. His efforts were fruitless; his demands were merely an irritant to municipal officials. In the meanwhile, he was in contact with others concerned about public health and helped to organize the Association for Improving the Condition of the Poor (AICP), and in 1857 was instrumental in founding the New York Sanitary Association. As a philanthropic organization, the AICP opened the first public bathhouse for the poor in 1852. It included laundry facilities, a swimming pool, and tub baths for males and females, but it was open only during the summer months. The bathhouse was not well used because the cost of five or ten cents was still beyond the means of many. It did, however, reflect Griscom's belief that cleanliness would be a means to elevate the moral sensibilities of the poor and protect their health. Such an idea would not benefit from public support until the end of the century

Everywhere tuberculosis, typhoid fever, dysentery, smallpox, pneumonia, scarlet fever, and diphtheria were a constant presence. Such diseases, along with high infant death rates, were assumed to be a normal part of life, although mortality of both children and adults was highest among the poor. The conditions in the slums continued to deteriorate after 1845 with the massive influx of impoverished Irish immigrants. They had run from famine in the Old World to face excruciatingly poor living conditions and new disease epidemics in America. The death rate in the cities increased dramatically in the next few years. Griscom reported in 1861 that while deaths in New York in 1850 had been one for every thirty-three people, that number had risen seven years later to one in every twenty-seven. Philadelphia had improved somewhat and mortality dropped from one in thirty-eight in 1850 to one in forty-five in 1857. Boston had improved only slightly. On the other hand, life expectancy had increased for the rural population in Massachusetts from thirty-five years at the beginning of the century to almost forty years in 1855, a record unmet anywhere else. The highest death rate in the country was probably in New Orleans where eight out of every one hundred people died annually (1:12.5), and yellow fever, continued to plague the New Orleans and Gulf Coast population on a regular basis.

For the most part public authorities had little interest in sanitation or the plight of the poor unless immediately threatened by an epidemic—diseases that appeared suddenly, spread rapidly, and took a heavy toll on lives in a short period of time. Outside of the South there had been no epidemics since yellow fever early in the nineteenth century, only the usual plague of diseases mentioned above. That changed in June of 1832 when cholera, a totally unfamiliar affliction, took its first victim in New York, spread to other cities, and moved west with the wagon trains, attacking small and large towns. For unknown reasons, the epidemic skipped Boston and Charleston that year but devastated Cincinnati and New Orleans, and hit the slave population in Louisiana especially hard.

Cholera had long been epidemic in many parts of Asia but did not spread beyond its traditional borders until the British began a military campaign in India in 1817. The army carried the disease to northern India and then to Arabia where a naval force landed to suppress the slave trade in 1821. Another epidemic in 1826 carried the disease overland to Russia and Turkey and reached Poland in 1830. From there it traveled by ship to England, then Ireland, and reached Canada in 1832. It spread to the United States that June and to Mexico the following year. It was a true worldwide pandemic, which followed patterns of trade and the routes of the military. and was maintained by dense populations wherever it appeared. Notice of the new epidemic disease in Europe had reached the United States in 1830 and the eastern cities began a quarantine to try to stop the infection before it reached land, but to no avail. The Medical Societies advised flushing the streets with water several times to clean the refuse and to disinfect the cesspools that held human waste with chloride of lime (bleach). Their advice was followed only sporadically and not where it was most needed.

The first case of cholera in New York City appeared in a slum building on Monday June 26, 1832. The Irish immigrant and his two children in an apartment succumbed to the disease and by Friday the mother too was dead. On July 2 doctors took the lead to announce that there had been nine cases of cholera with only one survivor. The panicky exodus from the city began. By December it had killed three thousand people in the city. It ended abruptly in New York that month with the disappearance of the dense concentration of people—many were able to leave the city and the most susceptible of those who had to remain died. The disease, however, had already started to move west and south. It was a continuing problem in West Virginia until 1833 and reached Knoxville, Tennessee, in 1834. The epidemic hit Cincinnati on September 24, 1832, and by the end of November had killed 20 percent of those who did not flee. New Orleans suffered almost as much during the month of October where the disease killed between 4,500 and 5,000 of its 50,000 residents. An estimated 15,000 people left the city. Cholera continued to strike Louisiana periodically for the next two years and then disappeared for fifteen years.

Unlike yellow fever or malaria, cholera is a disorder of the intestinal tract caused by bacteria that lives in water. Insect vectors play no role. The disease is caught when drinking the contaminated water or eating food that has been in touch with the bacteria in the water or from hands that came in contact with the stool or vomit from a victim. Overflowing privies and cesspools as well as street drains carrying the bacteria contaminated the water supply in the pumps and standpipes; unwashed hands of those tending the sick added to the spread of the disease. The germ produces a toxin that inhibits the absorption of water and salts in the body, then flushes the intestines of existing fluid, causing dehydration. Symptoms appear with no warning—sudden vomiting, cramps, and extreme watery diarrhea that has been described as resembling rice water. Because of the dehydration, victims suffer a desperate thirst for water, the face appears blue, the extremities cold, the skin on hands and feet puckered. Death can occur in a matter of hours or a day; the bacillus generally kills half of those infected.

The standard therapy of the time of calomel and ipecac and bleeding certainly added to the misery of the victims who wanted only to drink cold water. The only useful therapy would have been to satisfy that thirst and the transfusion of a saline solution to replace the lost water and electrolytes. Some doctors did try those remedies but also continued the traditional depletion. Nothing seemed to work. The best means of prevention, apart from leaving town, was probably imbibing alcoholic drinks, but the temperance movement that infused the health movements often discouraged that. The medical profession argued that such drinks added to the conditions leading to the disease. Like the usual therapies, such advice did little to help the victims. The fact that drunkards seemed to be immune to the disease was not something people talked about. Also, it appeared that tea drinkers in England benefited from the boiled water and the tannic acid that held the bacteria at bay.

Respectable city fathers were mystified by the reaction of the common folk to the authorities and the advice from physicians. People continued to drink their usual beer and whisky, and the poor, black and white alike, refused to go to hospitals. They feared, probably realistically, being used for experiments under the care of doctors. Charles Rosenberg in his study of the epidemic in New York found instances where physicians and city officials were attacked and beaten when they appeared in the slums to carry out local laws. Contrary to public health instructions, many immigrants opposed immediate burial of the dead in the desire to follow traditional mourning rituals. The common folk also insisted that cholera was contagious, the result of face-to-face contact with a diseased person, and tried vainly to prevent people from entering their communities.

Serious public health measures were expensive, and the rich refused to tax themselves for the benefit of the poor. There was no public support for public health programs. Even if some, like John Griscom, wanted to take action, they were unable to muster the necessary leadership to improve living conditions. There is no evidence that the majority of doctors took any interest in sanitary reform before the last quarter of the century. In spite of the miasma theory, the main focus of doctors was on disease therapies and not on environmental issues. A suggestion from the older historians of medicine that the cholera outbreaks awakened public consciousness to the need for community medicine does not hold up. Rather the opposite situation prevailed.

Such was the case in Baltimore during the second cholera epidemic in 1849 that raged through the city from the end of May to early September. At the time Thomas Buckler was the physician in the Baltimore almshouse, located north of the most populated area, that served both the city and the county poor. The water supply for the almshouse was not dependent on the contaminated Jones Falls that supplied the city water, but cholera still reached his patients. Treatment included the usual system of bleeding and calomel but also included chopped ice for those who complained of a dry mouth, "morphia," and valeria, a resin often used in domestic medicine. Buckler also called for a diet of fresh meat, rice, potatoes, and bread, omitting vegetables and fruit. Because cholera appeared in the summer at the beginning of the hot weather, a time when fresh fruits and vegetables were brought to town, it was thought that such foods contributed to the susceptibility to the disease; some physicians thought they were a cause. Buckler complained that the inmates did not always follow his dietary prescriptions and were found eating apples. It is quite possible that fruits eaten raw may well have been a culprit because of the closeness of farms and gardens to contaminated water supplies or when hands that picked the bounty carried the bacteria. Thus the raw food itself could have been responsible. For breakfast Buckler ordered bread with coffee or tea, and during the day one glass of whiskey, which he admitted was the habit of the inmates. Both the whiskey and the tea probably aided in resistance to the disease. His recommended diet may well have prevented a worse catastrophe.

In a matter of months, he reported that more than 240 inmates had been stricken with cholera; 86 of them died out of a population of 669. Buckler kept careful notes by gender and race of those who tended to get sick and those who died. He found that once sickened, black people and white women had a slightly higher rate of mortality. But the men of both groups, he reported, suffered a higher rate of disease than the women, an intriguing statistic that Buckler felt compelled to explore. He attributed the high death rate among African Americans to their overall poorer health. Many had suffered from typhoid fever recently. The greater incidence of disease among men he thought was due to their proximity to air contaminated by sewage in ponds and drains on their side of the building and because they worked outside during the day while women labored indoors. Therefore, he reasoned, men were more exposed to the miasma in the air.

Convinced by the numbers that cholera was a result of the "malarial" (meaning bad) air rising from the sewage, he ordered a series of tests around the drains. He was determined to consider all theories regarding the source of the pestilence including one to search for "animicular" matter, a possibility that had been suggested recently by a variety of doctors in the United States and Europe. One crude experiment—plates of glass coated with sugar and starch hanging near the drains that he thought would attract such living organisms—revealed nothing when examined under the microscope. He found no evidence for any of the other current theories. Instead he decided to rely on his limited statistics that seemed to indicate that those exposed to the drains were the most vulnerable. He ordered all windows closed on that side of the building adjacent to the source of the bad air to prevent contaminating the atmosphere inside and then set about with a general cleanup of the source. The drains near the building were covered, the ponds emptied, and all areas, both inside the building and outside, were disinfected with lime. The drastic cleanup measures had a positive result. He reported that the rate of sickness, including typhoid and dysentery as well as cholera for both inmates and the medical students caring for them, dropped dramatically.

Elated that he had found a solution to many diseases, Buckler wanted to extend his program to the larger public. Like Griscom he became a strong advocate of strict public health measures—clean the streets, build underground sewers, remove all decomposing substances from the town, disinfect cesspools, and most important, find a better source of drinking water that was not as foul as that of the Jones Falls. He argued that these problems created the conditions and to correct them would reduce the incidence of disease. The city did take some action that summer of 1849, and many of the main streets were cleaned but most of the alleys and areas behind houses continued to be sources of disease. Contaminated water from the Jones Falls continued to be pumped through the city. Buckler's campaign for permanent public health programs in Baltimore was no more successful than Griscom's was in New York, but he was just as tenacious and continued to push for his sanitary programs until action was finally started in the 1880s. But those later years represent a new era in medical knowledge and the beginning of the revival of the medical profession to an authoritative position. In the 1840s and 1850s Buckler lacked any public support, and Baltimore continued to suffer from repeated epidemics and increasing mortality from disease.

The cholera epidemics of the pre–Civil War era had little direct influence on either the state of medicine or the attitude toward public health in the United States. Emergency measures regarding the clean-up of streets and the use of hospitals lapsed after each crisis passed. As Griscom's 1845 report emphasized, the slums continued to deteriorate with their increasingly crowded conditions, which led to an even greater decline in life expectancy in the cities. The noxious materials in the drains and overflowing privies continued to flow, polluting the drinking water and food supplies. The news from London that the cholera outbreak was traced to a particular water pump in 1849, inadvertently disproving the miasma theory, had little influence in the United States. Dr. John Snow, aided by the skeptical Reverend Henry Whitehead, confirmed that cholera was a waterborne disease traced to one source of water in one section of London. They could not see the bacteria but used the tools of science and statistics to detect the cause indirectly in the pattern of deaths.

Cholera returned to various parts of the United States in 1834, 1849, and 1854, each outbreak leading to temporary emergency measures and the failure to establish any permanent means of improving public health. During intervening years boards of health in many cities disappeared or lapsed into inactivity, unable to enforce the already weak public health laws. Requirements for individuals to clean streets or remove effluence from the roads were considered infringements of private and property rights, and the local laws were easily evaded. Attempts to permanently dispose of human waste were opposed by the "night men." scavengers who collected and sold the human feces and animal manure to farmers to use as fertilizer, thus further contaminating the soil. In some places cholera epidemics seemed to occur regularly between 1848 and 1854 with little respite between outbreaks. No permanent state boards of health were established until the 1870s.

Because of the stigma associating cholera with the intemperate and impious, southern physicians denied that whites even suffered from that disease. Cholera was associated with poverty and the enslaved. Virginians believed that cholera was a "Negro disease" brought on by a penchant for eating fruits and vegetables. White people therefore were diagnosed with diarrhea, dysentery, or bilious fever, but never cholera during the epidemics. The reoccurrence of yellow fever throughout the South after 1840 sometimes overshadowed any concern for the new disease during those years; public authorities revived quarantine regulation to protect the public from yellow fever epidemics but ignored the presence of cholera. An attempt by New Orleans authorities to build a sewer system after a yellow fever epidemic in 1853 was denounced by a doctor as a waste of money.

In the more western areas, successive bouts with cholera exacerbated the conflict between regular doctors and the alternative medical sects like the homeopaths. A large number of German immigrants stricken with cholera came up the Mississippi River from New Orleans, their American arrival point, and flooded the Cincinnati hospital in 1849, adding to the patient load. In the attempt to preserve the hospital from homeopathic competition, regular doctors stood firm in devotion to their orthodox faith in depletion. In their extreme frustration and inability to prevent death, they renewed Benjamin Rush's approach during the epidemic and turned to even more extreme heroic depletion measures. The Cincinnati Board of Health in the hands of those orthodox physicians falsified statistics to reflect good care rates for the regular practitioners at the hospital. In response the sectarians, who had more success, sent their more favorable report directly to the newspapers and stepped up the campaign to denounce the special privilege and lack of integrity of the orthodox doctors in the hospital. They successfully brought public opinion to their side. The dishonesty and desperation of the hospital personnel took its toll on traditional medical practitioners. After the epidemic, regular physicians were purged from the Boards of Health and a sectarian practitioner replaced the distinguished Dr. Daniel Drake as head of the Cincinnati hospital.

Apart from the Cincinnati hospital conflict, physicians in most places did tone down the severity of traditional procedures in response to sectarian successes during the cholera epidemic. By the 1860s most orthodox physicians had either abandoned bloodletting and purging or moderated their heroic therapies. It had become obvious that their therapies worsened the symptoms of cholera, which was already depleting the body of fluids. The orthodox physicians had come to let nature heal, often limiting themselves to using quinine for fever and alcohol as a tonic, but few could admit to being wrong about their old ways. Many justified the shift in therapy on the grounds that disease and patients had changed and now required less harsh forms of treatment. They argued that the human condition had been weakened by a variety of environmental shifts, the cholera epidemics, urban life, or by electrical changes on the earth; thus people were not able to tolerate heroic treatments. Whatever the reasons, the more extreme heroic practices seemed to be on the decline. Scientific knowledge had very little to do with this shift away from traditional therapies. It was the competition from the competing sectarians and the concern for their own loss of income and prestige that forced the change. The cholera epidemics had that one positive result but gave little impetus to permanent public health measures.

There were a few physicians who refused to accept that disingenuous reasoning to explain away what was obviously a "fundamentally wrong practice." In his investigation of the reasons for the decline of bloodletting, John Haller concluded that there were a handful of orthodox-trained physicians who had become painfully aware that their supposedly tried-and-true therapies were ineffective. They publicly defected from orthodoxy and adopted selective therapies from the hydropaths, homeopaths, and other alternative healers. To distinguish themselves from all other groups, and to disassociate themselves from regular physicians, they called themselves "eclectics." Their new title added further to the erosion of traditional medical authority.

Although the medical profession was at its lowest point in both power and prestige by 1850, there had been a few improvements in technical skills, especially in the area of surgery, that kept the reputations of physicians from dissolving completely. Such surgical techniques were widely touted by the profession. They did not essentially contradict the humoral theory and thus were easier to accept than any wholesale overturning of centuries of knowledge and belief. While doctors often disagreed about therapies for a particular malady, they had no trouble as surgeons accepting that there was only one method for setting a broken bone or extracting a bullet or a breast tumor or opening an abscess or removing a bladder stone. On the other hand, while the physician's reputation depended mostly on his manners, social standing, and particular therapies, the surgeon's reputation rested on his physical strength, manual dexterity, and speed. American surgeons did not hesitate to apply what they learned in Europe about anatomy and the application of surgical techniques. They may have rejected the medical "nihilism" of natural healing, but they accepted surgical tools.

The amputation of a young boy's leg in a crowded room at the Stuyvesant Institute in New York. The 1859 print illustrates the unhygienic conditions and horrors of surgery of the time. An article complaining about the too frequent use of amputation accompanied the drawing. (Courtesy of the National Library of Medicine)

The greatest danger in the practice of surgery came from infection and pain. The patient's pain could be relieved with one of the available anesthetics: the well-known ether and nitrous oxide, or the newer chloroform developed by the American Samuel Guthrie in 1831. All were effectively used by dentists to extract teeth but were used only grudgingly by physicians. Dentistry received a tremendous boost as a profession with the early and easy acceptance of ether and nitrous oxide. In 1842 Elijah Pope painlessly extracted a tooth from the jaw of a patient using ether administered by William E. Clarke. Two years later, Horace Wells in Hartford, Connecticut, did the same using nitrous oxide. Others continued to experiment with one or another of the anesthetics, anxious to win over patients and have them return. Unlike surgeons who, as Richard Shryock once remarked, "rarely expected to treat a patient more than once," dentists looked forward to return visits.

Surgeons feared an unconscious patient, a state usually associated with shock and subsequent death. Those most practiced in surgery, moreover, prided themselves on their ability to withstand the cries and agonies of their patients, and gloried in their skills of speed and dexterity, none of which was as much a premium when the patient was anesthetized. With the use of anesthetics, more deliberate and careful techniques would eventually take the place of speed as prized abilities. Such a change eventually led to the use of more complicated procedures and greater specialization. In the antebellum era, surgeons continued to glory in their speed and dexterity, but very reluctantly explored the usefulness of anesthetics. On the other hand, though, few patients took advantage of their skills. Most people, inured to pain preferred to suffer with their disabilities than to subject themselves to the greater agonies of the surgeon's knife and the possibility of immediate death.

Infection as a result of surgery was an even more intractable problem. To prevent infection would have required a modification of medical theory, which most doctors were unwilling to make. That the doctor's hands or instruments were causing disease was an unacceptable notion. Americans resisted the news coming from Vienna and Budapest when Ignaz Semmelweis in the 1840s proved that puerperal infection in lying-in hospitals was caused by doctors with unwashed hands, which had touched other infected patients or performed autopsies. Fortunately for most Americans, surgical procedures were conducted in private homes or the physician's quarters where infection was less likely to occur than in hospitals. But the indigent who inhabited the few hospitals in America had no choice in their treatment and were more likely to die of infections after surgery.

Except for the insane asylums, lazarettos, and special quarantine facilities, hospitals housed mainly the homeless, paupers, travelers, seamen in a strange port, unmarried pregnant women—generally people without family or friends to care for them. Such institutions served not to provide the best care but as a refuge for the desperate or a temporary place to house the sick during epidemics. With few notable exceptions hospitals in the United States began as almshouses, which provided medical care for those who could not care for themselves. The Pennsylvania Hospital in Philadelphia was unusual. From the beginning it was a curing institution that included both paying and destitute patients; the Commercial Hospital in Cincinnati was erected with public funds for the specific purpose of caring for sick boatmen in the Ohio River trade as well as the destitute. It was part of the Marine Hospital system begun by the federal government in 1796 to provide medical care to sailors and for which the men were required to contribute a small sum. The hospital contracted with the federal government to treat the rivermen at a fixed price and the state paid for the local sick poor. Charity Hospital in New Orleans, the oldest such institution in the country, began in 1736 as a separate place to treat the illnesses of the working poor, transients, and the inmates of the almshouse, but it was not an almshouse itself. In all cases the physicians volunteered their services in return for the prestige that came from such appointments. They worked diligently to keep competitors such as sectarians and midwives out of those institutions. Physicians knew that association with a hospital could raise their stature in the mind of the public and help to attract more private paying patients. They could also have privileges to use the hospital as a place to acquire clinical experience. There was no law at this time to prevent them from surgical experiments on the hospitalized patients and consent was not necessary. Medical ethics were primitive and flexible, nonexistent in the case of slaves and the indigent.

No one with a choice went to a hospital. Such places were regarded with dread and stigmatized not just as a place for the poor but a place of infection and death. No attempt was made to separate patients suffering from typhoid fever, dysentery, typhus, pneumonia, or other infectious diseases. The indiscriminate mixing of patients with a variety of ailments in one ward contributed to the extraordinary death rate. Women giving birth were at even greater risk. Buckler, in his report on the Baltimore almshouse, regretted that eight out of ten such women died of puerperal fever while in the "lying-in" hospital section. Treatment was also perfunctory, often harsh; the patients were at the mercy of the doctor who did not know them as individuals as he did his private patients. Charity cases differed from the doctors by reason of class and often ethnicity. In many ways the patients were alien beings whose customs, and sometimes language, were unfamiliar to the medical personnel. Nursing was minimal, hygienic standards generally ignored, and food often inadequate. The undercurrent of hostility from African Americans, the poor whites, and the immigrant groups toward professional medical services is due to resentment from unwanted surgeries and indifferent harsh treatment by physicians. The experiments on slaves by J. Marion Sims and Ephraim McDowell were followed by more experiments on hospital patients who were poor and white. That the poor resisted being put into hospitals during the cholera epidemics was understandable. They were places of inhumane treatment, unwanted surgical procedures, and death. One went to a hospital to die not to be cured.

Throughout this period of early American medicine, science and scientific research played no role. Medical schools had no research laboratories and few clinical facilities. Generally doctors considered their practice to be an art with therapies specific to the particular patient's background, age, gender, and habits as well as the climate and population density of the area. Even as late as 1860 the more forward-thinking Oliver Wendell Holmes ridiculed the idea of science having any practical value for his profession. When William Good Gerhard returned from training in France he applied Parisian methods to distinguish between typhus and typhoid, but other Americans remained skeptical of such scientific conclusions based on careful observation and statistics. When Jacob Bigelow advised his fellow physicians at Harvard to let nature heal, he was excoriated for his "therapeutic nihilism."

In Europe in the meanwhile, science was making inroads into medicine. Because of these ongoing laboratory studies, morphine was isolated from opium in Germany in 1817 and in France quinine was extracted from cinchona bark in 1820, making exact dosages possible. In 1818 a German doctor used a stethoscope to detect a fetal heartbeat and confirmed what midwives had long known: the fetus's heartbeat was twice as fast that of the mother. But with few exceptions, American doctors ignored the stethoscope as they had the clinical thermometer. German medical schools created laboratory-based medical research where professors were paid to conduct research as well as teach; the French focused on empirical observation and statistical analysis as well as postmortem examination to determine future treatment for any disease, which led to more moderate therapies by European physicians. The interest in science and laboratory use eventually led to Pasteur's studies of fermentation in the 1850s and the discovery of microorganisms, then Robert Koch's announcement that specific organisms caused specific diseases, and finally Lister's use of the rubber glove to prevent infections during surgery. Americans, however, were for the most part slow to accept any of this new science and vociferously rejected it. As late as the 1880s President James Garfield died of blood poisoning because his doctors disdained studies tracing infection to their hands and unsanitary conditions and laughed at the idea that an unseen germ could cause disease. Held back by low educational standards, a lack of interest in laboratory studies, the commercialism of health education, an unregulated market for health care, and a nationalistic belief in American exceptionalism, little of the European scientific advances made any headway in the United States until beginning with the last decade of the century. With the exception of the few ethically questionable surgical experiments, the acquisition of medical knowledge in America had come to an abrupt stop.

In spite of the weakness in medical knowledge and paucity of scientific advance, most Americans continued to thrive. The food for all Americans, although less nutritious in the nineteenth century than the previous years, was still abundant. Meat was relatively cheap but vegetables and fruits were not as easily available. Americans were still taller than their counterparts in the Old World. If we omit the slum denizens of the major cities and the enslaved population (admittedly a significant proportion), white Americans as a group could expect an average life expectancy of forty years for men and forty-two for women, what it had been for most of the first half of the nineteenth century. There were some regional variations, though. In Salem, Massachusetts, life expectancy was only thirty-three years, and throughout the South the number was even lower. Those statistics would not change for the better until the end of the century with the advent of more reasonable medical care and public health works. It is notable that the Europeans were rapidly catching up to Americans during the first part of the century. In 1850, due mainly to sanitary improvements and a rising standard of living, life expectancy in the British Isles had come close to that of America.

One of the great dangers to life everywhere was the urban environment with its dense population living in unsanitary conditions. Because only a small proportion of Americans lived in the cities in 1850, about 15 percent of the total (compared with 50 percent in England), few in the United States suffered from those urban problems. Rural Americans, in spite of their deteriorating diet and unhygienic personal habits, continued to be protected from the worst of the epidemic diseases, at least until cholera hit. They lived as did early Americans —a dispersed population with comparatively scattered living arrangements on an expanding frontier. Medicine, of course, played no part in the existing life expectancy or quality of life during this period for either urban or rural peoples.

Unlike white Americans, the rural life did not protect slaves on the plantations where living conditions were more crowded and housing was unsanitary and inadequate. There was a rise in mortality among slaves after 1810 and the death rates of infants rose by twenty-four percent between 1820 and 1840. Southern slave life was shorter and closer to twenty-three years due to the ever-present tuberculosis and other debilitating diseases and, to a great extent, the high infant mortality. In a recent study Richard Steckel estimates that 350 black infants died for every 1,000 born (more than double the rate of white infants), a reflection of the unsanitary living conditions of the family and poor health of the overworked and often teen-aged mothers that led to smaller and more vulnerable infants. That mortality was offset by an increasing high fertility of slave women that kept the population growing. In the years after the end of the legal slave trade (in 1807) the black population grew from just over one million people in 1810 to more than three million in 1850. The white population, because of increasing immigration, grew from almost six million to over nineteen million during those years.

It is quite possible too that some of this growth in the white population was due to a shift away from the extreme practices of orthodox physicians. Many of the more affluent had switched to alternative health practices, Others continued to draw heavily on herbal remedies and local midwives. Even plantation owners were depending more on botanical and local medical lore and turning away from orthodox practices. The role of the physician had shifted to the margins of American life, a status that would continue to prevail for another half century.

The loss of respect for the medical profession had the unfortunate result of inhibiting moves to improve public health. The sanitary measures that came at the end of the century were the most important factors in extending life expectancy before the advent of antibiotics. Whether because of the belief in a miasma as a cause of disease, or the immorality of living in filthy conditions, most doctors understood that cleanliness and sanitary living conditions could improve health. They did not need the germ theory of disease to advocate services such as clean drinking water or a closed sewer pipe. But the declining stature of the profession in the eyes of the public during this early period in American history denied even the most forward looking doctor or physician any role in public policy.

CONCLUSION

The medical profession teetered on the edge of the abyss by the mid-nine-teenth century. American doctors, often caught up in their own desire for preservation as a profession and clinging to outmoded therapies, proved to be doing more harm than good. They unwittingly encouraged alterna-tive modes of treatment that successfully undermined the orthodoxies of humoral medicine. Although the cholera epidemics of the antebellum period demonstrated the futility of the physician's medicine, it did not bring forth any radical changes in theory, only a slight moderation of previous thera-pies. Unable to organize, retarded by a vast army of illiterate and incompe-tent medical personnel, stymied by a belief in American exceptionalism and superiority that precluded learning from European developments, there was little that doctors could do to recapture their earlier prestige and authority. And yet, even in the colonial era, at the peak of respectability, doctors faced opposition in many forms—from scientifically inclined laymen to the mass of people who drew on their own domestic medicine to African Americans who opposed them as surrogates for the slave master. Thus tensions and conflict between medicine and the public was a continuing aspect of life in early America.

From the very beginning of European exploration of the New World through a good part of the nineteenth century, doctors remained ignorant of the cause of disease. They could do little to cure although they could ease some symptoms. It was a time when the very idea of germs, of specific diseases caused by a particular pathogen, was a notion beyond the imagination of most people, including physicians. All healers, whether educated or of the folk variety, adhered to the theory that disease was an imbalance of the bodily humors caused by several possible factors: a miasma, a contagion, a muscle spasm, the individual's physical or mental qualities, or as Native Americans believed, a violation of a taboo or offense to a spirit.

The devastation of the Native American peoples that followed encounters with Europeans could not have been prevented or altered by the medicine of the time. Neither Indian remedies nor European practices were effective to prevent imported diseases and death. The problem was complicated by the genetic differences of the Native Americans who had had no previous contact with the pathogens that caused the worst mortality—smallpox, measles, and influenza. The lack of knowledge about diseases, the abusive treatment by Europeans, as well as social and environmental factors were all significant issues in the rapid decline of the Native American population. The diseases brought by the Old World peoples prepared the way for the devastation of the Indians and set the stage for health conditions and problems over the next four centuries.

In spite of the deficiencies of their profession, during the earliest period in British colonial history doctors were able to maintain a fairly secure position in society and tended to be circumspect in their choice of therapies. Colonial medical men were among the elite, highly educated, and polite members of society, and therefore benefited from a superior social status. Dr. Alexander Hamilton of Annapolis during the colonial era and Dr. Benjamin Rush of Philadelphia after the Revolution were respected physicians not because of any competence in healing but because they belonged to a special class of leaders. They represented the highest standards of European intellectual life for their times. They were learned men, socially and politically active, seekers of knowledge and worthy of respect from all segments of the population. The doctor's education marked him as the superior healer, whether successful or not, and the confidence in his ability acted as a strong placebo in the process of curing regardless of the therapy. In that eighteenth-century world physicians were in a strong position to shape public policy and influence the medical practice of others. When those standards of education and social position declined in the following century, so too did the status of the physician.

Colonial America benefited from an unusually healthy lifestyle because of the cheapness, variety, and abundance of food as well as the easy availability of alcoholic drinks. They not only had a longer life expectancy than their Old World forebears, but they were taller and the women more fertile. Both black and white, enslaved and free, rich and poor no longer suffered from famines. Shortages of food were usually temporary and seasonal, and did not affect long-range nutrition. Some physicians objected to that abundance, concerned that too much food led to sloth and poor health, but such advice was generally ignored. Although diets were not balanced in modern terms, the sheer quantity overcame the poor quality of many foods that had been preserved in sugar or salt. Although the quality of food deteriorated even more in later years and alcoholic consumption increased, the abundance continued to support a relatively healthy population. The growth of urban areas and increasing immigration of poor people with inadequate access to food in the nineteenth century began to undermine those healthful conditions.

Orthodox medicine played only a minor role in the health of the population except in those cases when heroic remedies, as in the case of George Washington, contributed to death. The few laymen of those earliest years who found particular therapies objectionable were small in number and had no interest in undermining the role of the physician, merely correcting what they considered to be questionable treatments in certain circumstances. Such objections did create some tension between laymen and the professionals but it was not enough to weaken the authority of orthodox medicine. Even Cotton Mather's dispute with the medical establishment and successful inoculations for smallpox in the 1720s did not damage the image of the local doctors. Nor did the colonial physician see any threats from domestic or folk medicine. All shared a common framework for explaining disease and ill health. The practices of the folk were, for the most part, complementary not competitive. Confidence in the doctor's skills and knowledge led many nontraditional and domestic healers to accept and practice the same kind of medicine as the professional and doctors were willing to learn from them. The belief that they *could* cure was the most potent medicine in anyone's medicine bag.

Nonetheless, the early American doctor plied his trade among only a small proportion of the population--the affluent and the destitute. They tried to expand their reach as male midwives by appealing to the more leisured class of women and convincing them that childbirth was a medical problem. The majority of the population, however, continued to rely on home remedies, the so-called root doctors, the black herbalists or conjurers; again, almost all women relied on the midwives. Except in the case of the enslaved, these curing traditions did not directly oppose the medical establishment, but they acted as a potential counterforce that would find its strength in the democratic thrust of the nineteenth century. Whenever the physician's remedies were uncomfortable or proved to be ineffective, laymen, both black and white, could always draw on the less professional remedies, gradually undermining the need for regular medicine.

Recognition of the physician's alliance with the plantation owner to control their behavior and support the system led African Americans, unlike the rest of the population, to distrust white medical personnel early on. Surgical experiments added to that distrust. In the attempts to promote fertility among women slaves, doctors intruded even more on the bodies of the women, increasing both their authority and professional standing among southern plantation owners. Resistance of African Americans to physicians continued and is not an artifact of twentieth-century experiments. In the aftermath of slavery, white officials complained that black people rejected medical and health regulations because such requirements reminded them of similar treatment during enslavement. Many African Americans would remain outside the mainstream of American medical developments, a continuing source of opposition to the medical establishment. In fact, the legacy of slavery and abuse by doctors lives on in the reluctance to take full advantage of Medicare offerings.

The inability of doctors to agree on specific remedies or to work together to advance one particular theory or set of therapies contributed to sporadic conflict both within the profession and with the public. The tension came to a head during and after the Revolution, and spilled over into the political arena as happened during the yellow fever epidemic of 1793. The struggle became more intense in the conflict with midwives that focused not just on the practice of abortion but also with the general public over the issue of early medical licensing laws. The nationalistic thrust of the post-Revolutionary eras combined with the highly individualistic, anti-intellectual, and commercial ambience of the first half of the nineteenth century helped shrink the authority and importance of orthodox medicine. The sectarians further exacerbated the tension between the regular physician and alternative forms of treatment. They exposed the perils of traditional therapies that had become more extreme as the nineteenth century wore on. The result was a competitive model that diminished the status of the medical profession.

In the area of mental health, however, doctors as superintendents of the new asylums achieved what most could not—a dubious professional identity.

There were a small number of doctors with such authority in this early period, but their ideas had extraordinary influence in continuing the incarceration of the mentally ill and the application of depletion therapies taken from Benjamin Rush's peculiar theories. The emphasis on the somatic element in treating insanity also continued in different guises. Rush's gyrator certainly has an offspring in the later electric shock treatments. Custodial care may have had its advantages in keeping the insane in a safer environment, and at best kept fed and sheltered, but did little to aid in curing or even ameliorating their mental conditions.

The American medical profession was retarded by a peculiar disjunction between science and medicine. The proprietary medical schools discouraged laboratory investigation and, as moneymaking institutions, competed for students by lowering standards. The few forward-looking medical people and those scientifically oriented individuals who advocated sanitary reform were hampered by the individualistic, free-enterprise attitude that prevented positive governmental action to alleviate the misery of the poor and invest in public health programs. One of the major stumbling blocks to any innovation in medical science was the reliance on the idea that Americans were somehow physiologically different from and superior to other people, and that knowledge acquired elsewhere could not be applied to this country. American physicians rejected empirical studies in Europe proving that age-old medical wisdom was wrong, that traditional therapies were dangerous, and that doctor practices could kill. Many continued to insist on the extreme methods advocated by Benjamin Rush long after his death. Few were willing to accept the idea that the doctor might have been a cause of death during the process of surgery or childbirth. American doctors denied the validity of those findings as they had denied the usefulness of statistics and the earlier clinical discoveries in Paris. When chemical studies coming out of the French and German laboratories regarding the idea that specific germs, animicular matter, could be the cause of different diseases, buttressed by Louis Pasteur's 1850s study of microorganisms and fermentation, the medical profession in America generally refused to accept that knowledge. For many years those doctors rejected both the germ theory as well as recently introduced antiseptic practices. They cut themselves off from the advancements of medicine that would revolutionize the profession in the Old World. That obstinate refusal to follow European science kept American medicine back, relying on outmoded theories. Not until the end of the century would Americans open themselves to the European scientific world. Until then, the nationalistic fervor that accompanied the New Nation and the assumption of American exceptionalism blocked the acceptance of new ideas in medicine and the understanding of disease.

Historians generally agree that with the exception of technical improvements in surgery, American medicine was a mess by the middle of the nineteenth century. Beset by internal squabbles among the orthodox, lack of agreement on particular therapies or on the cause of disease, competition from sectarians, declining educational standards, and the inability to take the leadership in mobilizing their own kind, medicine was a dysfunctional profession.

To some extent the low state of traditional medicine was an advantage for the times. If the orthodox through their medical societies and the American Medical Association had been able to control the profession through the licensing that they coveted, they could have eliminated all competing forces. That would have prevented the sectarians who did less harm from gaining adherents. They would have eliminated midwives and therefore increased the incidence of puerperal fever; they would have more successfully prevented women from entering the profession; and most probably seen to it that folk healers, that mainstay of care for the bulk of the population, could not provide the comfort of their traditional healing. Physicians might well have acquired the same power as the superintendents of asylums and extended their damage to the larger public, doggedly pursuing their painful and frightening treatments. As long as doctors were in the dark about disease, eschewing science and laboratory research, the public was in danger from their extreme therapies and fanciful theories. The alternatives, free to compete without licenses or government regulation, did less harm, were certainly less expensive, and were more successful in tapping into the body's power to heal itself.

The most intractable problem within the medical profession by the nineteenth century was one of pride and a stubborn adherence to the theories that were losing the confidence of the public. While doctors knew very little about the causes of disease, few would or could admit to their ignorance. The greater the opposition to medical orthodoxy, the more resistant and defensive, and therefore the more distasteful, the profession became to the public. It was what Stephen Johnson in his study of the cholera epidemics in London calls a "sociology of error." In the context of the cholera crises, he wonders how so many intelligent people could "be so grievously wrong for such an extended period of time." American doctors in particular were reluctant to submit their practices to scientific investigation. The result was a decline in the public respect for orthodox medicine, reflected most unfortunately in the negative responses to appeals for public health measures from the few knowledgeable doctors and the lay public.

Orthodox medicine, slowly undermined by a public disillusioned with its ineffective remedies and inadequate training, its foundering and ineptitude, was finally subverted by competition from the sectarians. The triumph of alternative medicine during the cholera epidemics represented a culmination of the tension that had grown between the lay public and the physician over the years. The epidemics of the nineteenth century may well have provided the final push into obscurity of the heroic therapies that had prevailed for too long and given the doctor his professional identity. But underlying all these problems was the refusal to heed the scientific discoveries in Europe. Not until the end of the nineteenth century would Americans accept the value of those discoveries and imitate the scientific methods developed abroad . The physician that began to emerge at the beginning of the twentieth century was a very different type of healer from that of early America described in this book. It took another fifty or so years before the medical profession attained the kind of scientific respect and authority that they have today.

The modern rise of the medical profession as leaders in health care bears little relationship to the events of the early years of this country. This has been the story of a decline, the fall of a professional to the status of an ordinary workingman, requiring no special training or education and, to many in the public, possessing no unique skills worthy of respect. Anyone could read a book and learn how to set a bone, prescribe a drug, or diagnose an illness. The lotions, potions, and pills of the physician were available to all. His magical touch had dissipated, lost in the disorderly nature of the democratic experiment, the anti-intellectualism of the time, and the rejection of European science. Mid-nineteenth-century medicine in America had reached not just its lowest point in authority and respect but was on the verge of disappearing as a profession, giving way to the more successful alternative sects. In the new medical world that appeared later doctors and physicians kept the title but not the substance of what it meant to be a physician in those long ago, tragic, and so-called good old days.

Admittedly this book has shown a gloomy picture of the early state of health care and the medical profession. The picture since then has been quite different. Medical practice did not begin to change until the 1890s with the establishment of the first endowed graduate program in medicine at Johns Hopkins University in Baltimore, an institution that drew on the model of the German universities and was staffed with German-trained physicians, which in fact reversed the trend of medical nationalism. Americans had come to accept the radical new ideas spreading from European laboratories that specific germs, not an imbalance of imaginary humors in the individual, caused disease and that the answer to medical advancement was through scientific method. With funds for research, the Johns Hopkins medical school was not dependent on student fees and could focus on the advancement of laboratory-based science and evidence-based clinical trials, which had long been practiced in European universities. The 1890s thus marked a new era in American medical history and a sharp break from the old. It was, however, only a beginning.

A report commissioned by the Carnegie Corporation and compiled by Abraham Flexner in 1910 finally led to the demise of the older type of medical school. Flexner exposed the deficiencies in medical education with such blunt language as "wretched and hopeless," "fatally defective," and "churning out an oversupply of badly trained doctors." As had been the case throughout the nineteenth century, the schools lacked laboratories and adequate dissection facilities. Admission required only the payment of fees. Flexner praised Johns Hopkins as the model for all. In a short time, at least half of the medical schools in the United States closed their doors. Unfortunately, this also reduced the number of women and blacks in the medical field and contributed to the lack of physicians in the rural and poor areas.

The good result is that medicine was finally disconnected from the older methods of learning, teaching, and practice. The new medical school model paved the way for the physician to again become an important part of American life with a new well-defined role as a leader in curing and preventing disease. Today, diseases are treated as distinct entities with discrete causes amenable to specific standardized medications (with some consideration for age, gender, weight, and genetic predisposition). This is a far cry from the earlier treatment when all diseases were considered specific to individuals and required therapies geared to that patient's particular qualities in accordance with the doctor's own personalized empirical decisions. The erosion of traditional medical authority assisted by the break with the traditions that prevailed in early America made that progress possible.

One continuous theme in medical history is the claim to the exclusive right to determine therapy and medication, a form of "medical absolutism." There is good reason for that absolutism today. In the closing years of the nineteenth century, a new range of diagnostic tools and therapies had a positive effect on life expectancy and the quality of life. Medicine was proving successful in combating diseases; newly developed vaccines (created in European laboratories in the nineteenth century) contributed to a dramatic decline in infant and child mortality—rabies, typhoid, cholera, and the plague—even in the United States. Early in the twentieth century new vaccines (also European discoveries and not American) against whooping cough, diphtheria, tetanus, and tuberculosis brought life expectancy from the low fifties at the turn of the century to the upper sixties by the 1940s in the United States. Much of that improvement in life expectancy is credited to changes in social conditions—better housing and nutrition, higher education, and the important municipal public health measures that brought in clean water and sewer pipes, but vaccinations did their part. There were also more coordinated quarantine measures under the aegis of the federal government. The creation of the Food and Drug Administration and the first National Health Service inspired by the Progressive Movement early in the twentieth century contributed to further improvement in health and the quality of food. Physicians were important in all these developments. They had regained a place in setting public policy.

Greater strides were made by the 1950s. The United States was coming of age in its use of medical science with the continual acceptance of overseas developments. European-discovered antibiotics—sulfonamides in the late 1930s and penicillin in the 1940s—reduced death from infectious diseases from 32 percent of all deaths in 1900 to 5 percent in 1960 in the United States. In the years since even more infectious diseases have been conquered with added vaccines, the elimination of smallpox from the world, more effective treatments for AIDS, and new genetic therapies. Surgical technology improved dramatically. Many of the new contributions came from American laboratories that have achieved unparalleled successes since the Second World War. Those who might have died from infectious diseases now live to a much older age and are subject to a host of problems that affected only a small number in the past—heart attacks, strokes, cancer, and psychiatric disorders. Many common chronic diseases such as diabetes, arthritis, thyroid deficiencies, and varieties of anemia can be treated successfully but not cured. These are much more intractable problems, but there are high expectations that the medical profession will someday cure all disease.

Life expectancy has risen steadily in the last seventy-five years, although the Europeans today generally outlive Americans, a reversal of the situation in the early period. The Center for Disease Control and Prevention (CDC) notes that infant mortality in the United States continues to lag behind other industrialized countries. The United States stands at twenty-nine, ranking along with Poland and Slovakia. Japan exceeds all nations with a life expectancy of about eighty-three years and is third in infant mortality. At the same time Americans spend twice as much on health care as the comparable countries. There is good reason to ask, if we are the leaders in biomedical research, why are we behind the rest of the world in our own health at such an exorbitant cost? Is there something in the medical delivery system of other countries with their superior health outcomes that we should follow? Are we again falling into the trap of American exceptionalism, believing that our system is superior to others because we think we are different from or better than others? There is a renewed tension between those who claim we have the best medical care and those who acknowledge that ours is an obviously faulty system.

In spite of—or maybe because of—the extraordinary success of modern scientific medicine, there is a growing disillusionment with the profession, its methods of treatment, its standards, its drug practices, and its focus on high-tech, expensive, impersonal, and fragmented specialties. Seldom does the doctor know the patient as an individual—the essence of old-fashioned healing. Too often unnecessary drugs with adverse or dangerous side effects are prescribed. *Consumer Reports* notes that "an estimated 10 percent of adverse drug events happen because of poor doctor-patient communication." At times both the doctors as well as the CDC and other public agencies have been hoodwinked by reports of misleading clinical trials, which have appeared in published medical literature. Helen Epstein reports on one such attempt to downplay the dangerous side effects of hallucinations in children and other reportedly "weird accidents" from Tamiflu (a supposed cure for the flu). Conflicts of interest between medical journals and drug companies obscured those side effects and have certainly misled the public. Epstein reminds us that the FDA relies on fees from the same drug companies they are supposed to regulate, a major factor that allows for the sale of drugs, which have been belatedly recalled for their dangerous effects (such as Avandia, a diabetic drug that has been linked to thousands of heart attacks, and anti-depressants that exacerbated the risk of suicide among teens). Medical mistakes that threaten lives have created a scary image of the most sophisticated treatments and deter some from taking advantage of available treatments including necessary vaccinations.

While many people still retain their faith in their physicians in spite of these disasters, it is possible that respect for the medical profession has declined from its peak in the decades after World War II. Unhappiness with the way that medicine is conveyed is one reason for the increase in malpractice suits against physicians and hospitals. Another more significant symbol of that disenchantment is the rise of alternative medical sects since the late twentieth century—a development reminiscent of what happened in the nineteenth century. The dissatisfaction with medicine as traditionally practiced has begun to resonate again with the American public, a public that has turned increasingly to self-help alternatives.

Support for the sectarians and many of those mentioned in this book went into a decline early in the twentieth century, undermined by the successes of scientific medicine, but they did not completely disappear. The older reliance on potions with special magical powers to cure disease has its counterpart in today's search for less impersonal sources of treatment, some of which ironically are based on those older unscientific therapies and practices. Few of the alternative systems have been subject to rigorous scientific investigation to give proof of effectiveness or safety. In spite of the strides made by the modern medical establishment to cure disease, heal bodies, and successfully treat all kinds of disorders, millions of people have turned to practices that have long been discredited. They ask that their bodily fluids be depleted, that they be detoxified, or look for magical rituals to accompany the ingestion of drugs, or attempt bizarre and unbalanced diets, or depend on the promise of a one-nostrum cure all, or tap into their mystical vital force. They have turned to non-Western ethnic folk remedies from acupuncture and yoga to a variety of herbal preparations, which lack quality control or reliability of dosages but emphasize holistic practices that echo the traditions of pre-germ theory medicine. There is one obvious difference between then and now, though. In the past, those potions and pills and the magical aura that went with them were part of both mainstream medicine and folk cures. Today, science has created a sharp divide between orthodox medical practice and these alternative techniques.

Like the sectarians of the nineteenth century, the new alternatives emphasize self-help, the integration of mind and body, avoiding undue medicalization, a respect for the healing power of nature, and a holistic regard for the patient. There is also a strain of anti-authoritarianism—a rejection of that orthodox medical absolutism. And like those who once abandoned orthodox medicine, the adherents of the alternative forms are mostly middle class educated people. They have been the first to take to acupuncture, faith healing, the physical fitness craze, yoga, the new homeopathy, osteopathy, chiropractics, message therapists, and a whole host of naturopath systems and nutritional supplements. And like the ancient magical practices, the alternatives are cheaper and more emotionally fulfilling than orthodox medicine. The medical profession in the early years of this country led a direct assault on such practices through ridicule, calling them pseudoscience, witchcraft, faith healing, and a relic of magical beliefs—which many of them may have been.

The American Medical Association again has been a leader in the fight against these alternative systems through legal means and publicity. In 1963 its Committee on Quackery (a term so reminiscent of the past) set out to "contain and eliminate chiropractic" and warned doctors to stay away from such "cultists." Within two years of its establishment, the Secretary of Health, Education, and Welfare (HEW) denied Medicare reimbursement for those practices. The public objected, and pressured by the popularity of chiropractors, HEW reversed its position and permitted payment in 1974. Since then virtually every major health insurance carrier has included chiropractic as a medical expense over the objections of many doctors and to the dismay of the medical associations. The AMA continued its battle against the alternatives. Chiropractors were most successful in countering those objections and managed to get an injunction to stop the association from their negative actions. When the Supreme Court refused to hear the AMA appeals against the injunction in 1990, the issue was finally put to rest. Since then, the attitude of doctors has been more hospitable, or at least less hostile, to chiropractors.

Other alternative systems soon gained recognition through political action and against the advice of doctors. Acupuncture was illegal in many states in the years after World War II. The Food and Drug Administration (FDA) ruled that acupuncture needles were experimental and that the devices were to be used only with the supervision of licensed physicians, who of course had no experience with the system. Growing popularity and testimonials of success put political pressure on states to make acupuncture more available. In 1973 Nevada was the first state to grant rights to practice acupuncture to those with ten years of experience. Then Oregon and other western legislatures followed. In response to the increasing use of homeopathic medicine, states began to establish Licensing Boards in the 1980s to gain some control over quality. Washington State gave a boost to these new systems in 1996 when it required every health insurance policy to cover claims from *all* licensed practitioners including chiropractors, naturopaths, acupuncturists, and massage therapists. Some HMOs also offered coverage of alternatives methods.

As in the past, this development, an obvious divergence between patient interests and those of the medical profession, has perplexed physicians. Many viewed the alternatives as an affront to modern medicine and the accumulated knowledge acquired through scientific experiments. Throughout the 1990s doctors questioned the value of alternative medicine, some appalled by what they dubbed the "political correctness" of state legislatures. But the popularity of those alternative practices continued to grow. In 2000 Americans spent ten billion dollars on herbs, vitamins, and other dietary supplements. Visits to alternative medical providers were double the growth of visits to physicians between 1995 and 2005. The widespread receptivity to these alternatives finally provoked the U.S. Congress to instruct the National Institute of Health (NIH) to evaluate the effectiveness of these therapies. The medical personnel heartily disapproved. Once again there was a conflict between the interests of the lay public and the medical profession, a problem that had been in abeyance for much of the century. Following its orders, in 1992 the NIH established an Office of

Alternative Medicine to set up research centers to evaluate some procedures. One of the early studies of acupuncture concluded in 1997 that it was
"clearly effective" in relieving post-operative pain and the discomforts of
some headaches and arthritis with no side effects. There was no agreement
on how acupuncture worked, just that it did.

The tone of the dispute has changed most recently as more doctors see
good results in this new self-help movement and have started to recommend yoga, meditation, and acupunctures among other "complementary"
therapies. In 2001 Congress provided a larger appropriation for the NIH,
and the Office of Alternative Medicine was renamed the National Center for
Complementary and Alternative Medicine, whose motto is "Take Charge of
Your Health." These acts recognize that nonconventional systems could and
did complement regular medical therapies and that people could indeed take
greater responsibility to improve their own health. Medical schools are also
paying more attention to alternatives, and doctors are less hostile to patient
choice.

The complementary treatments may well act as a placebo—useful because
of confidence that they work or because most sick people eventually get over
their ailments. Recovery is almost always enhanced by the placebo effect,
and even in modern scientific medicine a psychological or emotional factor
can often modify or suppress the effect of drugs. As Arthur and Elaine Shapiro have noted, for most people morphine can sedate but for the addict it is
euphoric. They also mention several studies that demonstrate that placebos
are about 55 to 60 percent as effective as active medications. The patient who
takes glucosamine for arthritis and swears that is has been a lifesaver may
well be responding to a placebo, but does that patient care?

Any Internet search of alternative medicine will bring up a host of books,
sites, and advice on how to treat a large number of ailments with a variety of
herbal remedies or food suggestions or spiritual healing. Such alternatives
are very much a part of the modern world and have been successful in forcing the medical profession to accept and work with some of these practices.
Medical absolutism is giving way to a more responsive medical establishment. This time the conflict between the public and the professional may
not undermine the authority of the physician as it did in the nineteenth century. To use the earlier term to describe this accommodation, the doctors are
becoming more "eclectic," conceding that they may not have all the answers.
They have shifted away from the nineteenth-century model of animosity
and rejection of alternatives. The result may be an improvement in medical
knowledge as experimenters investigate the possibilities of these unorthodox
methods to allow some of them to become part of regular medicine, truly

complementary and supportive. Doctors today have less reason to fear a loss of prestige than they did in the past. Their scientific methods may well disprove the effectiveness of the alternatives or they may prove their value, but whatever the result, the public will benefit. Openness to unconventional therapies and the apparently superior methods of delivering health care seen in other countries may well provide answers to the present disenchantment.

ABBREVIATIONS

AHR	*American Historical Review*
BHM	*Bulletin of the History of Medicine*
CSM	Colonial Society of Massachusetts
JAH	*Journal of American History*
JHMAS	*Journal of the History of Medicine and Allied Sciences*
NEJM	*New England Journal of Medicine.*
NEQ	*New England Quarterly*
SHP	Science History Publications
WMQ	*William and Mary Quarterly*

This section is arranged by chapter.

Introduction

The most comprehensive study of diseases during the colonial era and the source I have relied on extensively is John Duffy, *Epidemics in Colonial America* (Baton Rouge: Louisiana State University Press, 1971). An important analysis of the power of suggestion in medicine is Arthur K. Shapiro and Elaine Shapiro, *The Powerful Placebo: From Ancient Priest to Modern Physician* (Baltimore: John Hopkins University Press, 1997). Information on Dr. Adam Thomson is in Elaine G. Breslaw, *Dr. Alexander Hamilton and Provincial America: Expanding the Orbit of Scottish Culture* (Baton Rouge: Louisiana State University Press, 2008).

References to the status of the medical profession in the eighteenth century are taken from Roy Porter, "A Touch of Danger: The Man-Midwife as Sexual Predator," in *Sexual Underworlds of the Enlightenment*, ed. George Rousseau and Roy Porter (Manchester: Manchester University Press, 1987) [207]; Richard Brown, The Healing Arts," in *Medicine in Massachusetts* (Boston: CSM, 1980) [40]; David Wootton, *Bad Medicine: Doctors Doing Harm since Hippocrates* (New York: Oxford University Press, 2007); and Ronald Numbers "Fall and Rise of the American Medical Profession," in *Sickness and Health: Readings in the History of Medicine and Public Health,* ed. Judith Walzer Leavitt and Ronald L. Numbers (Madison: University of Wisconsin Press, 1985), 185–96.

On the backward nature of the American medical profession and its therapies in the nineteenth century, see especially William G. Rothstein, "Botanical Movements and Orthodox Medicine" in *Other Healers: Unorthodox Medicine in America,* ed. Norman Gevitz (Baltimore: John Hopkins University Press, 1988), 29–51; and John Harley Warner, "Power, Conflict, and Identity in Mid-Nineteenth-Century American Medicine: Therapeutic Change at the Commercial Hospital in Cincinnati," *JAH* (1987): 934–56. On the training of American medical students in Paris and of Oliver Wendell Homes's experiences see David G. McCullough, *The Greater Journey: Americans in Paris* (New York: Simon and Schuster, 2011); and John Harley Warner, *The Therapeutic Perspective: Medical Practice, Knowledge, and Identity in America, 1820-1885* (Cambridge, Massachusetts; Harvard University Press, 1986).

Chapter 1: Columbian Exchange

The story of the Pilgrims and their relationship with the Wampanoags is told by James Dietz and Patricia Scott Dietz, *The Times of their Lives: Life, Love, and Death in Plymouth Colony* (New York: Anchor Books, 2000); Charles C. Mann, *1491: New Revelations of the Americas Before Columbus* (New York: Vintage Books, 2006) [96]; and Alden T. Vaughn, *Roots of American Racism: Essays on the Colonial Experience* (New York: Oxford University Press, 1995) [Winthrop's statement is on 187].

For the early epidemics among Native Americans see Kathleen J. Bragdon, *Native People of Southern New England, 1500-1650* (Norman: University of Oklahoma Press, 1996); Timothy L. Bratton, "The Identity of the New England Indian Epidemic of 1616–19," *BHM* 62 (1988): 351–83; Esther Wagner and Allen E. Stearn, *The Effect of Smallpox on the Destiny of the Amerindians* (Boston: Bruce Humphries, 1945); William H. McNeill, *Plagues and People* (New York: Anchor Books Doubleday, 1976); and especially Alfred W. Crosby, *The Columbian Exchange: Biological and Cultural Consequences of 1492* (Westport, CT: Greenwood Press, 1972) [41]. Information on the postcolonial era epidemics is in Elizabeth Fenn, *Pox Americana: The Great Smallpox Epidemic of 1775–82* (New York: Hill and Wang, 2001); Alfred W. Crosby, *Germs, Seeds, and Animals: Studies in Ecological History* (Armonk, NY: M. E. Sharpe, Inc. 1994); and Dorothy Porter and Roy Porter, *Patient's Progress: Doctors and Doctoring in Eighteenth-Century England* (Cambridge: Polity Press, 1989).

The effect of the black death in Europe is described in Norman F. Cantor, *In the Wake of the Plague: The Black Death and the World it Made* (New York: Free Press, 2001); and E. A. Wrigley, *Population and History* (New York: McGraw-Hill, 1969).

The health problems in the Jamestown and Roanoke settlements are discussed by Helen C. Roundtree, *The Powhatan Indians of Virginia: Their Traditional Culture* (Norman: University of Oklahoma Press, 1989); John Duffy, *The Healers: A History of American Medicine* (Urbana: University of Illinois Press, 1976); Wyndham B. Blanton, "Epidemics Real and Imaginary and other Factors Influencing Seventeenth-Century Virginia's Population," *BHM* 31 (1957): 454–62; and John Sears Morgan, *American Slavery, American Freedom: The Ordeal of Colonial Virginia* (New York: W. W. Norton, 1975).

The arguments against the Mann thesis regarding genetic differences are in Paul Kelton, *Epidemics and Enslavement: Biological Catastrophe in the Native Southeast, 1492–1715* (Lincoln: University of Nebraska Press, 2007); David S. Jones, "Virgin Soils Revisited," *WMQ* 60 (2003): 703–42 [the quote by Samoset is on 72 and by John Smith on 721]; and Douglas H. Ubelaker, "Patterns of Disease in Early North American Population" in *A Population History of North America,* ed. Michael R. Haines and Richard Steckel (New York: Cambridge University Press, 2000). See also Alfred W. Crosby, "Virgin Soil Epidemics as a Factor in the Aboriginal Population in America," *WMQ* 33 (1976): 298–99. Firsthand observations of Indian medical practices and health problems are William Bartram, *Travels through North and South Carolina, Georgia . . . .* (Philadelphia, 1791); John Brickell, *Natural History of North Carolina* (London, 1737); and John Lawson, *A New Voyage to Carolina* (London, 1709).

For the most comprehensive compilation of estimates of the Native American population, see Herbert Klein, *Population History of the United States* (New York: Cambridge University Press, 2004); and John D. Daniels, "The Indian Population of North America in 1492," *WMQ* 49 (1992): 298–20.

The syphilis controversy is argued by Mann, *1491*; Crosby, *Columbian Exchange*; Kelton, *Epidemics*; McNeill, *Plagues*; Mirko D. Grmek, *History of Aids: Emergence and Origin of a Modern Pandemic,* trans. Russell C. Maulitz and Jacalyn Duffin (Princeton: Princeton University Press, 1990); and Clade Quétel, *The History of Syphilis,* trans. Judith Braddock and Brian Pike (Baltimore: Johns Hopkins University Press, 1990). See also John Tennent, *Every Man His Own Doctor: or, the Poor Planters Physician* (Williamsburg, Virginia, 1734).

Chapter 2: Epidemics

Ola Elizabeth Winslow, *Destroying Angel: The Conquest of Smallpox in Colonial Boston* (Boston: Houghton Mifflin, 1974) provides a dramatic and detailed description of smallpox and the inoculation controversy in Massachusetts. She quotes Douglass 86–87. Cotton Mather, *Angel of Bethesda,* ed. Gordon W. Jones (Barre, MA: American Antiquarian Society, 1972) describes his gradual awareness of the procedure, 107. Dr. Hamilton's comments on Douglass are in Carl Bridenbaugh, *The Itinerarium of Dr. Alexander Hamilton, 1744* (1948; repr., Pittsburgh: University of Pittsburgh Press, 1992), 116–117. Also of interest are the older works by John T. Barrett, "Inoculation Controversy in Puritan New England," *BHM* 12 (1942): 164–90; and John B. Blake, "The Inoculation Controversy in Boston: 1721–1722," *NEQ* 25 (1952):

489–506. A good source on the medical aspects of smallpox is Elizabeth Fenn, *Pox Americana: The Great Smallpox Epidemic of 1775–82* (New York: Hill and Wang, 2001). A firsthand description of the common procedures used by doctors is Mary Cary Ambler, "Diary of M. Ambler, 1770," *Virginia Magazine of History and Biography* 45 (1937): 151–70. Wyndham B. Blanton, *Medicine in Virginia in the Eighteenth Century* (Richmond, VA: Garret and Massie Inc., 1931) makes note of the riot in Norfolk, Virginia.

The British experience with inoculation is discussed in Donald R. Hopkins, *Princes and Peasants: Smallpox in History* (Chicago: University of Chicago Press, 1983); R. P. Stearns, "Remarks upon the Introduction of Inoculation for Smallpox in England," *BHM* 24 (1950): 104–22; Genevieve Miller, *The Adoption of Inoculation for Smallpox in England and France* (Philadelphia: University of Pennsylvania Press, 1957) [33]; and her "Smallpox Inoculation in England and America: A Reappraisal," *WMQ* 13 (1956): 476–92.

The Thomson-Kearsley debate is described by Alexander Hamilton, *A Defense of Dr. Thomson's Discourse on the Preparation of the Body for the Small-Pox* (Philadelphia, 1751); H. L. Smith, "Dr. Adam Thomson, the Originator of the American Method of Inoculation for Smallpox," *Johns Hopkins Hospital Bulletin* 20 (1909): 49–52; and Elaine G. Breslaw, *Dr. Alexander Hamilton and Provincial America: Expanding the Orbit of Scottish Culture* (Baton Rouge: Louisiana State University Press, 2008).

No one has improved on the study of all diseases and epidemics of the time since the appearance of John Duffy, *Epidemics in Colonial America* (1953; repr., 1971) [quotations on dysentery 216, 219]. Statistical information comes from James Cassedy, *Demography in Early America: Beginnings of the Statistical Mind, 1600–1800* (Cambridge, MA: Harvard University Press, 1969). Additional information on measles is in Ernest Caulfield, "Early Measles Epidemics in America," *Yale Journal of Biology and Medicine* 15 (1942): 531–56. Commentaries on the problems in the Chesapeake Bay are in Darrett B. and Anita H. Rutman, "Of Agues and Fevers: Malaria in the Early Chesapeake," *WMQ* 333 (1976): 31–60.

Peter Wood, *Black Majority: Negroes in Colonial South Carolina from 1670 through the Stono Rebellion* (New York: Alfred A. Knopf, 1974) provides the clearest explication of African resistance to malaria. See also James L. A. Webb Jr., *Humanity's Burden: A Global History of Malaria* (New York: Cambridge University Press, 2009). Other works dealing with disease problems faced by African Americans include Sharla M. Fett, *Working Cures: Healing, Health, and Power on Southern Slave Plantations* (Chapel Hill: University of North Carolina Press, 2002); Philip D. Morgan, *Slave Counterpoint: Black Culture in the Eighteenth-century Chesapeake and Low Country* (Chapel

Hill: University of North Carolina Press, 1998); and Todd L. Savitt, *Medicine and Slavery: The Diseases and Health Care of Blacks in Antebellum Virginia* (Urbana: University of Illinois Press, 1978).

The use of cinchona bark for malaria and the problems of dosage and quality are addressed in Andreas-Holger Maehle, *Drugs on Trial: Experimental Pharmacology and Therapeutic Innovation in the Eighteenth Century* (Atlanta: Rodopi V. B., 1999); Charles M. Posner and George W. Bruyn, *An Illustrated History of Malaria* (New York: Parthenon, 1999); and M. L. Duran-Reynals, *The Fever Bark Tree: The Pageant of Quinine* (New York: Doubleday, 1946).

Chapter 3: Tools of the Trade

The Maryland Court Records were useful for the Wooten cases (Anne Arundel County, 1744); and Thomas Bacon's inventory of possessions (Frederick County, 1769). The self-help manuals are analyzed by Lamar Riley Murphy, *Enter the Physician: The Transformation of Domestic Medicine, 1760–1860* (Tuscaloosa: University of Alabama Press, 1991) in a study of the boundaries between the professional and the public; and Mary E. Fissell, "The Marketplace of Print," in *Medicine and the Market in England and Its Colonies, c. 1450–1850*, ed. Mark S. R. Jenner and Patrick Wallis (New York: Palgrave Macmillan, 2007) with a focus on their popularity. See the comments from William Tennent, *Every Man His Own Doctor* (Virginia, 1734) [4–5].

There are innumerable works on orthodox medical practice including Whitfield J. Bell, "A Portrait of the Colonial Physician," *BHM* 44 (1970): 497–517; John Duffy, *The Healers: A History of American Medicine* (Urbana: University of Illinois Press, 1976) [3]; J. Worth Estes, "Therapeutic Practice in Colonial New England," in *Medicine in Colonial Massachusetts, 1620–1820* (Boston: CSM, 1980), 289–383; James C. Riley, *The Eighteenth-Century Campaign to Avoid Disease* (London: Macmillan, 1987); Richard Harrison Shryock, *Medicine and Society in America, 1660–1860* (New York: New York University Press, 1960) [117–18]; Charles E. Rosenberg, *Our Present Complaint, American Medicine, Then and Now* (Baltimore: Johns Hopkins University Press, 2007); and J. Worth Estes's analysis of New England ledger books, "Patterns of Drug Use in Colonial America," in *Early American Medicine: A Symposium*, ed. Robert I. Goler and Pascal James Inperato (New York: Fraunces Tavern Museum, 1986), 29–37.

The references to the dangers of drugs use are in Harriet Washington, *Medical Apartheid: The Dark History of Medical Experimentation on Black Americans from Colonial Times to the Present* (New York: Doubleday, 2006). Other criticism of medical practice include Roy Porter, "A Touch of Danger:

The Man-Midwife as Sexual Predator," in *Sexual Underworlds of the Enlightenment*, ed. George Rousseau and Roy Porter (Manchester: Manchester University Press, 1987); and Porter, "Laymen, Doctors, and Medical Knowledge in the Eighteenth Century: The Evidence of the Gentleman's Magazine," in *Patients and Practitioners: Lay Perceptions of Medicine in Pre-Industrial Society* (Cambridge: Cambridge University Press, 1985) [287].

On Dr. Hamilton's life and medical practice, see Elaine G. Breslaw, *Dr. Alexander Hamilton and Provincial America: Expanding the Orbit of Scottish Culture* (Baton Rouge: Louisiana State University Press, 2008). His conversations about doctors is in Carl Bridenbaugh, *The Itinerarium of Dr. Alexander Hamilton, 1744* (1948; repr., Pittsburgh: University of Pittsburgh Press, 1992) [95, 53–54].

Useful therapies are noted in Lois N. Magner, *History of Medicine* (New York: Marcel Dekker, Inc., 1992); Arthur K. and Elaine Shapiro, *The Powerful Placebo: From Ancient Priest to Modern Physician* (Baltimore: Johns Hopkins University Press, 1997); and William M. Emboden, *Narcotic Plants* (New York: Macmillan, 1979).

Folk and domestic remedies are described in Kay Moss, *Southern Folk Medicine, 1750–1820* (Columbia: University of South Carolina Press, 1999); Anthony Cavender, *Folk Medicine in Southern Appalachia* (Chapel Hill: University of North Carolina Press, 2003); Jane C. Beck, "Traditional Folk Medicine in Vermont," in *Medicine and Healing*, ed. Peter Benes (Boston: Boston University Press, 1992), 34–43. Indian practices are in John Duffy, "Medicine and Medical Practices among Aboriginal American Indians," *International Record of Medicine* 171 (1958): 331–47; Theda Perdue, *Cherokee Women: Gender and Social Change, 1700–1835* (Lincoln: University of Nebraska Press, 1998); and William G. Rothstein, "Botanical Movements and Orthodox Medicine," in *Other Healers: Unorthodox Medicine in America*, ed. Norman Gevitz (Baltimore: Johns Hopkins University Press, 1988), 29–51.

On the relationship of slaves and physicians, see Todd L. Savitt, "Black Health on the Plantation: Masters, Slaves, and Physicians," in *Sickness and Health: Readings in the History of Medicine and Public Health*, ed. Judith Walzer Leavitt and Ronald L. Numbers, 3rd ed. (Madison: University of Wisconsin, 1997), 313–30; and Sharla M. Fett, *Working Cures: Healing, Health, and Power on Southern Slave Plantations* (Chapel Hill: University of North Carolina Press, 2002) [171]. On slave medical practices, see Charles Joyner, *Down by the Riverside: A South Carolina Slave Community* (Urbana: University of Illinois Press, 1984); Jeffrey E. Anderson, *Conjure in African American Society* (Baton Rouge: Louisiana State University Press, 2005); Philip Morgan, *Slave Counterpoint: Black Culture in the Eighteenth-Century Chesapeake and*

Lowcountry (Chapel Hill: University of North Carolina Press 1998) [quote from Alexander Garden, 618]; and Patricia Samford, "The Archeology of African-American Slavery and Material Culture," *WMQ* 53 (1996): 87–114.

Chapter 4: Abundance

Firsthand commentaries come from Eliza Lucas Pinckney, *Letterbook of 1739–1762*, ed. Elise Pinckney with the assistance of Marvin R. Zahniser (Chapel Hill: University of North Carolina Press, 1972) [39]; John Brickell, *The Natural History of North Carolina* (1737; repr., Murfreesboro, NC: Johnson Publishing, 1968) [39, 126]; Louis B. Wright and Marion Tinling, eds., *The Great American Gentleman, William Byrd of Westover in Virginia: His Secret Diary for the Years 1709—1712* (New York: Capricorn Books, 1963); Ronald Hoffman, et al, eds., *Dear Papa, Dear Charley, the Peregrinations of a Revolutionary Aristocrat as told by Charles Carroll of Carrollton and His Father*, 2 vols. (Chapel Hill: University of North Carolina Press, 2001) [references to food are in Carroll's letters from 1770 to 1775 in vol. 2]; Andrew Burnaby, *Travels Through the Middle Settlements in North America in the Years 1759-1760* (1798; repr., New York: Augustus M. Kelley, 1970), [41–44,. 63]; Edward Miles Riley, ed., *The Journal of John Harrower: an Indentured Servant in the Colony of Virginia, 1773-1776* (Williamsburg, VA: Colonial Williamsburg, 1963), [56]; Jean A. Brillat-Savarin, *The Physiology of Taste: Meditations on Transcendental Gastronomy* (1948; repr., New York: Dover 1960) [51]. The description of meals in Tuesday Club meetings are scattered throughout the *Records of the Tuesday Club of Annapolis, 1745-56*, ed. Elaine G. Breslaw (Urbana: University of Illinois Press, 1988).

Information on the English diet and state of health was gleaned from Carl Bridenbaugh, *Vexed and Troubled Englishmen, 1590-1642* (New York: Oxford University Press, 1967); Andrew B. Appleby, "Diet in Sixteenth Century England," in *Health, Medicine, and Mortality in the Sixteenth Century*, ed. Charles Webster (New York: Cambridge University Press, 1979), 97–116; and E. Alexander Bergstrom, "English Game Laws and Colonial Food Shortages," *NEQ* (1939): 681–90. On the relationship of nutrition and population growth see Massimo Livi-Bacci, *Population and Nutrition: An Essay on European Demographic History* (New York: Cambridge University Press, 1991), trans. Tania Croft-Murry; Thomas McKeown, *Modern Rise of Population* (New York: Academic Press, 1976); and E. A. Wrigley, *Population and History* (New York: McGraw Hill, 1968).

Early famine in Virginia is described in John Morgan, *American Slavery, American Freedom: The Ordeal of Colonial Virginia* (New York: W. W.

Norton, 1975); Karen Ordahl Kupperman, "Apathy and Death in Early James-town, *JAH* (1979), 24–40; and Carville V. Earle, "Environment, Disease, and Mortality in Early Virginia," in *The Chesapeake in the Seventeenth Century: Essays on Anglo-American Society*, ed. Thad W. Tate and David L. Ammer-man (Chapel Hill: University of North Carolina Press, 1979), 96–125.

Statistical compilations on caloric intake include Ben J. Wattenberg, comp., *Statistical History of the United States: From Colonial Times to the Present* (New York: Basic Books, 1976) [esp. 1175]; James H. Cassedy, *Demography in Early America: Beginnings of the Statistical Mind, 1600–1800* (Cambridge: Harvard University Press, 1969); Evarts B. Greene and Virginia D. Harrington, *American Population Before the Federal Census of 1790* (1932; repr., Gloucester, MA: P. Smith, 1966); Robert V. Wells, *Population of the British Colonies in America Before 1776: A Survey of Census Data* (Princeton: Princeton University Press, 1975). On the relationship of diet and stature, see Richard H. Steckel, "Nutritional Status in the Colonial American Economy," *WMQ* 56 (1999): 31–52.

Specific demographic studies include Lorena S. Walsh and Russell R. Men-ard, "Death in the Chesapeake: Two Life Tables for Men in Early Colonial Maryland," *Maryland Historical Magazine* 69 (1974): 211–27; Russell Menard, "Maryland Slave Population, 1658–1733: A Demographic Profile of Blacks in Four Counties," *WMQ* 32 (1975): 29–54; Philip Greven, "Family Structure in Seventeenth-Century Andover, Massachusetts," *WMQ* 23 (1966): 234–56. See also Greven, "Historical Demography and Colonial America: A Review Article," *WMQ* 26 (1967): 438–54; and James A. Henretta, *The Evolution of American Society, 1700–1815: An Interdisciplinary Analysis* (Lexington, MA: D. C. Heath, 1973).

I am most indebted to Alfred Crosby, *The Columbian Exchange: Biological and Cultural Consequences of 1492* (Westport, CT: Greenwood Press, 1972); as well as an earlier study by Donald Brand, "The Origin and Early Distribution of new World Cultivated Plants," *Agricultural History* 13 (1939): 109–17 regarding native American flora and fauna. On the use of foods I have relied extensively on Trudy Eden, *The Early American Table: Food and Society in the New World* (DeKalb: Northern Illinois University Press, 2008) and James E. McWilliams, *A Revolution in Eating: How the Quest for Food Shaped America* (New York: Columbia University Press, 2005). Other important references are Sarah F. McMahan, "A Comfortable Subsistence, Changing Composition of Diet in Rural New England, 1620–1840," *WMQ* 42 (1985): 26–65; Alfred Crosby, *Germs, Seeds, and Animals: Studies in Ecological History* (Armonk, NY; M .E. Sharpe, Inc., 1994); William Cronon, *Changes in the Land: Indians, Corn, Colonists and the Ecology of New England* (New York: Hill and

Wang, 1983); Miriam E. Lowenberg et al., *Food and Man*, 2nd ed. (New York: John Wiley and Sons, 1974); and Lois Green Carr and Lorena S. Walsh, "The Standard of Living in the Colonial Chesapeake," *WMQ* 45 (1988): 135–59. The information on pellagra is from Daphne A. Roe, *A Plague of Corn: The Social History of Pellagra* (Ithaca, NY: Cornell University Press, 1973).

Aspects of the southern diet are noted in Joe Gray Taylor, *Eating, Drinking, and Visiting in the South: An Informal History* (Baton Rouge: Louisiana State University Press, 1982); and Kay Moss, *Southern Folk Medicine, 1750–1820* (Columbia: University of South Carolina Press, 1999). On the specific influence of African customs on the south, see Mary Tolford Wilson, "Peaceful Integration: The Owner's Adoption of His Slaves; Food," *Journal of Negro History* 49 (1964): 116–27; and Judith A. Carney and Richard Nicolas Rosomoff, *In the Shadow of Slavery: Africa's Botanic Legacy in the Atlantic World* (Berkeley: University of California Press, 2009). Information on the African diet comes from Robert Hall, "Food Crops, Medicinal Plants, and the Atlantic Slave Trade," in *African-American Foodways*, ed. Anne L. Bower (Urbana: University of Illinois Press, 2007), 17–44; William O. Jones, *Manioc in Africa* (Stanford, CA: Stanford University Press, 1959); Frank Willett, "The Introduction of Maize into West Africa—An Assessment of Recent Evidence," *Africa* (1962): 1–13.

There is an extensive literature and debate on the nutritional value of the slave diet, but I have relied mostly on Allan Kulikoff, *Tobacco and Slaves: The Development of Southern Cultures in the Chesapeake, 1680–1800* (Chapel Hill: University of North Carolina Press, 1986); Daniel C. Littlefield, *Rice and Slaves: Ethnicity and the Slave Trade in Colonial South Carolina* (Urbana: University of Illinois Press (1991); Philip D. Morgan, *Slave Counterpoint: Black Culture in the Eighteenth-Century Chesapeake and Low Country* (Chapel Hill: University of North Carolina Press, 1998); Todd L. Savitt, *Medicine and Slavery: The Diseases and Health Care of Blacks in Antebellum Virginia* (Urbana: University of Illinois Press, 1978); and Robert William Fogel and Stanley L. Engerman, *Time on the Cross: The Economics of American Negro Slavery* (New York: Little, Brown, 1974). Michael Tadman, "The Demographic Cost of Sugar: Debates on Slave Societies and Natural Increases in the Americas," *AHR* 105 (2000): 1534–575 reviews that debate with an extensive bibliography.

Important archeological studies are Henry Miller "Archeological Perspective on the Evolution of Diet in the Colonial Chesapeake, 1620–1745," in *Colonial Chesapeake Society*, ed. Lois Green Carr, et al. (Chapel Hill: University of North Carolina Press 1988), 176–99; Patricia Samford, "The Archeology of African-American Slavery and Material Culture," *WMQ* 53 (1996): 87–114;

and Anne Elizabeth Yentsch, *A Chesapeake Family and Their Slaves: A Study in Historical Archaeology* (New York: Cambridge University Press, 1994).

Kevin Sweeney, "High-Style Vernacular: Lifestyle of the Colonial Elite," in *Of Consuming Interests: The Style of Life in the Eighteenth Century*, ed. Cary Carson et al. (Charlottesville: University Press of Virginia, 1994); and Richard L. Bushman, *The Refinement of American Persons, Houses, Cities* (New York: Alfred A. Knopf, 1992) deal with the genteel style of eating. W. J. Rorabaugh, *The Alcoholic Republic: An American Tradition* (New York: Oxford University Press, 1979) is an early treatise on the drinking habits of Americans. That work is supplemented by Sharon V. Salinger, *Taverns and Drinking in Early America* (Baltimore, Johns Hopkins University Press, 2002); and David W. Conroy, *In Public Houses: Drink and the Revolution of Authority in Colonial Massachusetts* (Chapel Hill: University of North Carolina Press, 1995).

Chapter 5: Wartime

The tribulations of Ezekiel Brown are told by Robert Gross, *The Minutemen and Their World* (New York: Hill and Wang, 1976). Brown's "Memoirs" were published in *The Centennial of the Social Circle in Concord*, ed. Ralph Waldo Emerson (Concord, MA, 1882), 9–85.

The most important sources of information on the formation of the Medical Department during the Revolutionary War include Mary C. Gillette, *The Army Medical Department, 1775–1818* (Washington, DC: Center of Military History, United States Army, 1981) [the quote by Biney on 29, 66]; Howard L. Applegate, "Medical Administrators of the American Revolutionary Army," *Military Affairs* 25 (1961): 1–10; V. R. Allen, "Medicine in the American Revolution," *Journal of the Oklahoma State Medical Association* 64 (1971): 377–81; V. R. Allen, Philip Cash, *Medical Men at the Siege of Boston, April, 1775–April, 1776* (Philadelphia: American Philosophical Society, 1973) [71, quote by Washington on 35]; and William Frederick Norwood, "Medicine in the Era of the American Revolution," *International Record of Medicine* 171 (1951): 391–407.

Biographies of the principle administrators were especially useful in illuminating the personal animosities that hindered effective actions. Those include Whitfield J. Bell, *John Morgan Continental Doctor* (Philadelphia: University of Pennsylvania Press, 1965) [119]; David Freeman Hawke, *Benjamin Rush: Revolutionary Gadfly* (New York: Bobbs-Merrill Company, Inc., 1971); and Morris H. Saffron, *Surgeon to Washington: Dr. John Cochran (1730–1807)* (New York: Columbia University Press, 1977).

Medical treatment and diseases during the war are detailed in John Duffy, *The Healers: A History of American Medicine* (Urbana: University of Illinois

Press, 1976) [83, 77, Sullivan's quote on 78]; Stanhope Baynes-Jones, *The Evolution of Preventive Medicine in the United States Army, 1607–1939* (Washington, DC: Office of the Surgeon General, Department of the Army, 1968); Elizabeth Fenn, *Pox Americana: The Great Smallpox Epidemic of 1775–82* (New York: Hill and Wang, 2001); and Benjamin Quarles, *The Negro in the American Revolution* (Chapel Hill: University of North Carolina Press, 1961). James Kirby Martin, ed., *Ordinary Courage: The Revolutionary War Adventures of Joseph Plumb Martin* (New York: Brandywine Press, 1993) provides a personal account of medical care. "Diary of M. Ambler, 1770," *Virginia Magazine of History and Biography* 45 (1937): 152–70 is a firsthand account of the inoculation process.

The most important work on women during the war is Joan R. Gundersen, *To Be Useful to the World: Women in Revolutionary America, 1740–1790*, rev. ed. (Chapel Hill: University of North Carolina Press, 2006). See also Walter Hart Blumenthal, *Women Camp Followers of the American Revolution* (Philadelphia: George S. MacManus Company, 1952). On Deborah Sampson see also William Frederick Norwood, "Deborah Sampson, Alias Robert Shirtliff, Fighting Female of the Continental Line," *BHM* 31 (1957): 147–61. Herman Mann, ed., *The Female Review: Life of Deborah Sampson* (1797; repr., New York: Arno Press, 1972) includes a remnant of her diary.

There are enumerable studies of medical education in the colonial era, but I have drawn mostly on Whitfield J. Bell, "Medical Practice in Colonial America," *BHM* 31 (1957): 442–53; Genevieve Miller, "Medical Education in the American Colonies," *Journal of Medical Education* 31 (1956): 82–94; William Dosite Postell, "Medical Education and Medical Schools in Colonial America," in *History of American Medicine: A Symposium*, ed. Félix Marti-Ibañez (New York: MD Publications, 1959), 48–54; and Lamar Riley Murphy, *Enter the Physician: The Transformation of Domestic Medicine, 1760–1860* (Tuscaloosa: University of Alabama Press, 1991).

Chapter 6: New Nation

Most of the information on the epidemic in Philadelphia is taken from John H. Powell, *Bring out Your Dead: The Great Plague of Yellow Fever in Philadelphia in 1793* (Philadelphia: University of Pennsylvania Press, 1970) [109, 78, 115]; with additional details from Elaine Crane, ed., *The Diary of Elizabeth Drinker: The Life Cycle of an Eighteenth-Century Woman* (Evanston, IL: Northwestern University Press, 1994, abridged) [112]; Technical details about the disease is from Peter Wood, *Black Majority: Negroes in Colonial South Carolina from 1670 through the Stono Rebellion* (New York: Alfred A. Knopf, 1974). The political ramifications are in Martin S. Pernick, "Politics, Parties, and Pestilence: Epidemic Yellow Fever in Philadelphia and the Rise of the First Party System," *WMQ* 24 (1972): 559–86. Additional information on Benjamin Rush is from John Duffy, *The Healers: A History of American Medicine* (Urbana: University of Illinois Press, 1976); and David Freeman Hawkes, *Benjamin Rush: Revolutionary Gadfly* (New York: Bobbs-Merrill, 1971).

On the limitations of science and medicine at the time I have drawn on Brooke Hindle, *The Pursuit of Science in Revolutionary America* (Chapel Hill: University of North Carolina Press, 1956); Russell Blaine Nye, *Cultural Life of the New Nation, 1776–1830* (New York: Harper and Row, 1960); David Ramsay, "A Review of the Improvement, Progress and State of Medicine in the Eighteenth Century," delivered January 1, 1800, *Transactions of the American Philosophical Society* 55 (1965): 96–217. References to statistical compilations by the early Americans come from James H. Cassedy, *Demography in Early America: Beginnings of the Statistical Mind, 1600–1800* (Cambridge: Harvard University Press, 1969).

Sources on the vaccination issue include Whitfield J. Bell, "Dr. James Smith and the Public Encouragement for Vaccination for Smallpox" in *The Colonial Physician and Other Essays*, ed. Whitfield J. Bell, (New York: SHP, 1975), 131–47; John Duffy, *The Sanitarians: A History of American Public Health* (Urbana: University of Illinois, 1990); John Greene, "The Boston Medical Community and Emerging Science, 1780–1820," in *Medicine in Colonial Massachusetts, 1620–1820* (Boston: CSM, 1980), 187–98; and John B. Blake, *Benjamin Waterhouse and the Introduction of Vaccine: A Reappraisal* (Philadelphia: University of Pennsylvania Press, 1957).

George Washington's last days are described in Volney Steele, *Bleed, Blister, and Purge: A History of Medicine on the American Frontier* (Missoula, MT: Mountain Press Publishing Company, 2005); James Thomas Flexner, *The Indispensable Man* (Boston: Little, Brown, 1974); and Joseph Ellis, *His Excellency George Washington* (New York: Alfred A. Knopf, 2004).

Information on the western areas comes from David Dary, *Frontier Medicine: From the Atlantic to the Pacific, 1492–1941* (New York: Vintage Books, 2008) [87]; Kay Moss, *Southern Folk Medicine, 1750–1820* (Columbia: University of South Carolina Press, 1999); Thomas A. Horrocks, *Popular Print and Popular Medicine: Almanacs and Health Advice in Early America* (Amherst: University of Massachusetts Press, 2008); and Daniel Drake, *A Systematic Treatise . . . on the Principal Diseases of the Interior Valley of North America* (Philadelphia: G. Smith, 1854), [648]. Conevery Bolton Valencius, *The Health of the Country, How American Settlers Understood Themselves and their Land* (New York: Basic Books, 2002) focuses on the Missouri and Arkansas territories [quotes by Breckenridge 128 and Pope 173]. Comments on the filth are in Suel-len Hoy, *Chasing Dirt: The American Pursuit of Cleanliness* (New York: Oxford University Press, 1995) [quotation by Faux, 7-8]. Specific commentaries on food habits are in Michael and Ariane Batterberry, *On the Town in New York: A History of Eating, Drinking, and Entertainments from 1776 to the Present* (New York: Charles Scribner's Sons, 1973) [46]; Dary, *Frontier Medicine*; Sarah F. McMahan, "A Comfortable Subsistence: Changing Composition of Diet in Rural New England, 1620–1840," *WMQ* 42 (1985): 26–65; and Frances Trol-lope, *Domestic Manners of America* (London, 1832) [159-60]. Information on the Lewis and Clark expedition is from Drake W. Will, "Medical and Surgical Practice of the Lewis and Clark Expedition," *JHM* 14 (1959): 273–79.

The medical abuse of slaves is treated in Steven M. Stowe, *Doctoring the South: Southern Physicians and Everyday Medicine in the Mid-Nineteenth Century* (Chapel Hill: University of North Carolina Press, 2004); Sharla M. Fett, *Working Cures: Healing, Health, and Power on Southern Slave Planta-tions* (Chapel Hill: University of North Carolina Press, 2002); Harriet A. Washington, *Medical Apartheid: The Dark History of Medical Experimenta-tion on Black Americans from Colonial Times to the Present* (New York: Dou-bleday, 2006); Todd L. Savitt, "Black Health on the Plantation: Master, Slaves, and Physicians," in *Sickness and Health: Reading in the History of Medicine and Public Health,* ed. Judith Walzer Leavitt and Ronald L. Numbers, 3rd ed. (Madison: University of Wisconsin, 1997), 313–30; and Savitt, *Medicine and Slavery: The Diseases and Health Care of Black in Antebellum Virginia* (Urbana: University of Illinois, 1978). For the reference to present-day issues see Marian E. Gornick, *Vulnerable Populations and Medicare Services: Why Do Disparities Exist?* (New York: Century Foundation Press, 2000).

On the problems of the urban poor I have drawn mainly on recent stud-ies by Seth Rockman, *Scraping By: Wage Labor, Slavery, and Survival in Early Baltimore* (Baltimore: Johns Hopkins University Press, 2009); and Gary P. Nash, "Poverty and Politics in Early American," and Susan E. Klepp, "Mal-thusian Theories and the Working Poor in Philadelphia, 1780–1830: Gender and Infant Mortality," in *Down and Out in Early America,* ed. Billy G. Smith (University Park: Pennsylvania State University press, 2003), 1–40, 63–92.

Chapter 7: Giving Birth

Martha's Ballard's diary was edited and abridged with commentary by Laurel Thatcher Ulrich, *A Midwife's Tale: Life of Martha Ballard Based on her Diary, 1785–1812* (New York: Random House, 1990) [162-63, 178]; Elaine Forman

Crane edited *The Diary of Elizabeth Drinker: The Life Cycle of an Eighteenth-Century Woman* (Boston: Northeastern University Press, 1994). The references to *Gunn's Domestic Medicine* (1830,) are in the facsimile edition edited with an introduction by Charles E. Rosenberg (Knoxville: University of Tennessee Press, 1986).

On the entry of men into the field important sources are Jane B. Donegan, *Women and Men Midwives: Medicine, Morality and Misogyny in Early America* (Westport, CT: Greenwood Press, 1978); Jean Donnison, *Midwives and Medical Men: A History of Inter-Professional Rivalries and Women Rights* (New York: Schocken Books, 1977); and Adrian Wilson, *The Making of Man-Midwifery* (Cambridge: Harvard University Press, 1995). Adrian Wilson, "Midwifery in the 'Medical Marketplace,'" in *Medicine and the Market in England and Its Colonies, c. 1450–c. 1850*, ed. Mark S. R. Jenner and Patrick Wallis, (New York: Palgrave Macmillan, 2007), 153–74 focuses on Great Britain. Two earlier studies that highlight the importance of men midwives are Edwin M. Jameson, "Eighteenth Century Obstetrics and Obstetricians in the United States," *Annals of Medical History* 10 (1938): 413–28; and Herbert Thorns, "The Beginning of Obstetrics in America," *Yale Journal of Biology and Medicine* 4 (1932): 665–75. Suzanne Lebsock highlights one community in *The Free Women of Petersburg: Status and Culture in a Southern Town, 1784–1860* (New York: W. W. Norton Company, 1984).

The descriptions of childbirth practices consulted for this study include Jacques Gélis, *History of Childbirth: Fertility, Pregnancy and Birth in Early Modern Europe*, trans. Rosemary Morris (Boston: Northeastern University Press, 1991); Virginia G. Drachman, "The Loomis Trial: Social Mores and Obstetrics in the mid-nineteenth Century," in *Health Care in America: Essays in Social History*, ed. Susan Reverby and David Rosner (Philadelphia: Temple University Press, 1979), 667–83; Susan E. Klepp, "Revolutionary Bodies: Women and the Fertility Transition in the Mid-Atlantic Region, 1760–1820," *JAH* 74 (1998): 920–42; and Richard W. and Dorothy C. Wertz, *Lying-In: A History of Childbirth in America*, rev. ed. (New Haven: Yale University Press, 1989) [Meigs quoted on 58 and Holmes on 122]. Judith Walzer Leavitt, *Brought to Bed: Childbearing in America, 1750–1950* (New York: Oxford University Press, 1986) focuses on the transformation of birth from a natural to a technological event. On the puerperal issue, see also Sherwin B. Nuland, *The Doctors' Plague: Germs, Childbed Fever, and the Strange Story of Ignac Semmelweis* (New York: W. W. Norton, 2003). Information on the use of anesthetics is from Leavitt, "'Science' Enters the Birthing Room: Obstetrics in America Since the Eighteenth Century," *JAH* 70 (1983): 281–304; Lawrence G. Miller, "Pain, Parturition, and the Profession: Twilight Sleep in America," in Reverby and Rosner, *Health Care in America*, 19–44; and John Duffy, *The Healers: A History of American Medicine* (Urbana: University of Illinois Press, 1976).

On birth control methods and statistics see Dorothy McLaren, "Fertility, Infant Mortality, and Breast Feeding in the Seventeenth Century," *Medical History* 22 (1978): 378–96; Patricia A. Watson, "The 'Hidden Ones': Women and Healing in Colonial New England," in Medicine and *Healing*, ed. Peter Benes (Boston: Boston University, 1992), 25–33; Herbert Klein and Stanley L. Engerman, "Fertility Differentials Between Slaves in the United States and the British West Indies: A Note on Lactation Practices and Their Implication," *WMQ* 35 (1978): 357–74; Richard H. Steckel, "African American Population of the United States, 1790–1920," in *A Population History of North America*, ed. Michael R. Haines and Steckel (New York: Cambridge University Press, 2000), 433–82; and James Reed, "Doctors, Birth Control, and Social Values, 1830–1970," in *The Therapeutic Revolution: Essays in the History of Medicine*, ed. Morris J. Vogel and Charles E. Rosenberg (Philadelphia: University of Pennsylvania Press, 1979), 109–33.

Information on obstetrical training came from Kay Moss, *Southern Folk Medicine, 1750–1820* (Columbia: University of South Carolina, 1999) [quote by Buchan, 140]; Steven M. Stowe, *Doctoring the South: Southern Physicians and Everyday Medicine in the Mid-Nineteenth Century* (Chapel Hill: University of North Carolina Press, 2004); and Lamar Riley Murphy, *Enter the Physician; The Transformation of Domestic Medicine, 1760–1860* (Tuscaloosa: University of Alabama Press, 1991).

For the American Indians I relied on John Duffy, "Medicine and Medical Practices Among Aboriginal American Indians," *International Record of Medicine* 171 (1958): 331–47; Ann Marie Plane, "Childbirth Practices Among Native American Women of New England and Canada, 1600–1800," in Benes, *Medicine and Healing*, 13–24; and Theda Perdue, *Cherokee Women: Gender and Social Change, 1700–1835* (Lincoln: University of Nebraska Press, 1998).

The most complete source of information on the abusive treatment of female slaves is Harriet A. Washington, *Medical Apartheid: The Dark History of Medical Experimentation on Black Americans from Colonial Times to the Present* (New York: Doubleday, 2006). Much of what she says is confirmed by Todd L. Savitt, *Medicine and Slavery: The Diseases and Health Care of Blacks in Antebellum Virginia* (Urbana: University of Illinois Press, 1978); Marie Jenkins Schwartz, *Birthing a Slave: Motherhood and Medicine in the Antebellum South* (Cambridge: Harvard University Press, 2006); and to a lesser extent by William D. Postell, *The Health of Slaves on Southern Plantations* (Baton Rouge: Louisiana State University Press, 1951).

The clearest descriptions of the abortion issue are in James C. Mohr, *Abortion in America: The Origins and Evolution of National Policy, 1800–1900* (New York: Oxford University Press, 1978), [37, 44]; Rosalind Pollack Petchesky, *Abortion, A Woman's Choice: The State, Sexuality, and Reproductive Freedom*, rev. ed. (Boston: Northeastern University Press, 1990); and Rickie Salinger, *Pregnancy and Power: A Short History of Reproductive Politics in America* (New York: New York University Press, 2007). On methods of abortion, see Sharla M. Fett, *Working Cures: Healing, Health, and Power on Southern Slave Plantations* (Chapel Hill: University of North Carolina Press, 2002); Susan E. Klepp, "Lost, Hidden, Obstructed and Repressed: Contraception and Abortive Technology in the Early Delaware Valley," in *Early American Technology*, ed. Judith McGaw (Chapel Hill: University of North Carolina Press, 1994), 68–113. The 1742 abortion incident is analyzed by Cornelia Hughes Dayton, "Taking the Trade: Abortion and Gender Relations in an Eighteenth-Century New England Village," *WMQ* 48 (1991): 19–49.

Chapter 8: Face of Madness

Laurel Thatcher Ulrich, "Derangement in the Family: The Story of Mary Sewall, 1824–1825," in *Medicine and Healing*, ed. Peter Benes (Boston: Boston University Press, 1992), 168–87, describes the selection from Henry Sewall's diary relating to his daughter's treatment. Eliza Lucas Pinckney's comments are in her *Letterbook of Eliza Lucas Pinckney, 1732–1762*, ed. Elise Pinckney with the editorial assistance of Marvin R. Zahniser (Chapel Hill: University of North Carolina Press, 1972) [46].

On the witchcraft aspects of insanity, I have drawn on Norman Gevitz, "The Devil Hath Laughed at the Physicians: Witchcraft and Medical Practice in Seventeenth-Century New England," *JHMAS* 55 (2000): 5–36 and my own work in *Witches of the Atlantic World: A Historical Reader and Primary Sourcebook* (New York: New York University Press, 2000); and *Tituba, Reluctant Witch of Salem: Devilish Indians and Puritan Fantasies* (New York: New York University Press, 1996).

One of the earliest histories of the treatment of the mentally ill in America is Albert Deutsch, *The Mentally Ill in America: A History of their Care and Treatment from Colonial Times* (Garden City, NY: Doubleday, Doran and Company, Inc. 1937). Deutsch's thesis that the mad benefited from hospitalization was first questioned by Michel Foucault, *Madness and Civilization: A History of Insanity in the Age of Reason*, trans. Richard Howard (New York: Pantheon, 1965). Gary Williams, *Age of Agony: the Art of Healing, c. 1700–1800* (1975; repr., Chicago: Academy Chicago Publishers, 1986) is also very critical. For more recent works that view the asylum in the context of changing social conditions, see Mary Ann Jimenez, *Changing Faces of Madness: Early American Attitudes and Treatment of the Insane* (Hanover, NH: University Press of New England, 1987) [60–61, 128, 79]; David J. Rothman, *The Discovery of the Asylum: Social Order and Disorder in the New Republic* (Boston: Little, Brown, 1971); and Gerald Grob, "Abuse in American Mental Hospitals in Historical Perspective: Myth and Reality," *International Journal of Law and Psychiatry* 3 (1980): 195–310. See also Grob, "Class, Ethnicity, and Race in American Mental Hospitals, 1830--1875, in *Theory and Practice in American Medicine,* ed. Gert H. Brieger (New York: SHP, 1976), 227–49. Information on the incidence of death in the asylums is from Barbara G. Rosenkrantz and Maris A. Vinovskis, "Sustaining the Flickering Flame of Life: Accountability and Culpability for Death in Ante-Bellum Massachusetts Asylums," in *Health Care in America: Essays in Social History,* ed. Susan Reverby and David Rosner (Philadelphia: Temple University Press, 1979), 154–82.

Most useful for understanding the influence of Benjamin Rush on the treatment of the mentally ill are David Freeman Hawke, *Benjamin Rush: Revolutionary Gadfly* (New York: Bobbs-Merrill, 1971); Tomas A. Horrocks, *Popular Print and Popular Medicine: Almanacs and Health Advice in Early America* (Amherst: University of Massachusetts Press, 2008); Ida Macalpine and Richard Hunter, *George III and the Mad Business* (New York: Pantheon Books, 1969); and Jimenez, *Changing Faces of Madness.*

The mental problems and treatment of African-Americans is detailed in Sharla M. Fett, *Working Cures: Healing, Health, and Power on Southern Slave Plantations* (Chapel Hill: University of North Carolina Press, 2002); William D. Postell, *The Health of Slaves on Southern Plantations* (Baton Rouge: Louisiana State University Press, 1951), Todd L. Savitt, *Medicine and Slavery: the Diseases and Health Care of Blacks in Antebellum Virginia* (Urbana: University of Illinois, 1978) [249]; and Harriet A. Washington, *Medical Apartheid: The Dark History of Medical Experimentation on Black Americans from Colonial times to the Present* (New York: Doubleday, 2006) [148]. Magical practices are described in Jeffrey E. Anderson, *Conjure in African American Society* (Baton Rouge: Louisiana State University Press, 2005); Charles Joyner, *Down by the Riverside: A South Carolina Slave Community* (Urbana: University of Illinois Press, 1984); Elliott J. Gorn, " Black Magic: Folk Beliefs of the Slave Community," in *Science and Medicine in the Old South,* ed. Ronald L. Numbers and Todd L. Savitt (Baton Rouge: Louisiana State University Press, 1989), 295–312. David Hackett Fischer, *Albion's Seed: Four British Folkways in America* (New York: Oxford University Press, 1989) deals with white folklore.

Graham Richards, *Mental Machinery: The Origins and consequences of Psychological Ideas*, Part I: *1600–1850* (Baltimore: Johns Hopkins University Press, 1992) deals with the philosophical and practical issues of insanity. Also of interest is Anne Digby, *Madness, Morality and Medicine: A Study of the York Retreat, 1796–1914* (Cambridge: Cambridge University Press, 1985). On psychiatry as an early specialty, the most useful works were Charles E. Rosenberg, *Our Present Complaint: American Medicine, Then and Now* (Baltimore: Johns Hopkins University Press, 2007); and Gerald Grob's larger work, *The Mad Among Us: A History of Health Care of America's Mentally Ill* (New York: The Free Press, 1994) [27, 46, 75].

One excellent and comprehensive treatment of the mentally ill in the south is Peter McCandless, *Moonlight, Magnolias, and Madness: Insanity in South Carolina from the Colonial Period to the Progressive Era* (Chapel Hill: University of North Carolina Press, 1996) [98]. Other useful sources of information on southern asylums are Shomer S. Zwelling, *Quest for a Cure: the Public Hospitals in Williamsburg, Virginia, 1773–1885* (Williamsburg: Colonial Williamsburg Foundation, 1985); Wyndham B. Blanton, *Medicine in Virginia in the Eighteenth Century* (Richmond: Garret and Massie Inc., 1931); Steven M. Stowe, *Doctoring the South: Southern Physicians and Everyday Medicine in the Mid-Nineteenth Century* (Chapel Hill: University of North Carolina Press, 2004); and Samuel B. Thielman, "Southern Madness: The Shape of Mental Health Care in the Old South," in Numbers and Savitt, *Science and Medicine*, 256–75.

Chapter 9: Democratic Medicine

William Dyott's patent medicine career is described in James Harvey Young, *The Toadstool Millionaires: A Social History of Patent Medicine in America Before Federal Regulation* (Princeton: Princeton University Press, 1961). Additional information on Dyott's life is in R. Daniel Wadhwani, "The Demise of Thomas Dyott: Experimenting with Popular Finance in Jacksonian Philadelphia," paper prepared for "Panic of 1837 Conference" at the Library Company of Philadelphia, October, 2007.

Important sources of information on John Gunn and Western medicine in general are in the facsimile of the first edition of *Gunn's Domestic Medicine* (1830) edited with an introduction by Charles E. Rosenberg (Knoxville: University of Tennessee Press, 1986) [98–99]; Lamar Riley Murphy, *Enter the Physician: the Transformation of Domestic Medicine, 1760–1860* (Tuscaloosa: University of Alabama Press, 1991) [104]; and David Dary, *Frontier Medicine: From the Atlantic to the Pacific, 1492–1941* (New York: Vintage Books, 2008).

The most useful works on the state of medical practice, licensing provisions, and the training of physicians include: Paul Starr, *Social Transformation of American Medicine* (New York: Basic Books, 1982), [17]; Richard H. Shryock, *Medicine and Society in America, 1660–1860* (New York: New York University Press, 1960) [149]; John Duffy, *The Healers: A History of American Medicine* (Urbana: University of Illinois Press, 1976); James Cassedy, *Medicine and American Growth, 1800–1860* (Madison: University of Wisconsin Press, 1986); and Ronald L. Numbers, "The Fall and Rise of the American Medical Profession," in *Sickness and Health: Readings in the History of Medicine and Public Health,* ed. Judith Walzer Leavitt and Ronald L. Numbers, 2nd ed. (Madison: University of Wisconsin, 1985), 185–96.

Probably the most comprehensive work on the various irregulars and the self-help movement is James C. Whorton, *Nature Cures: The History of Alternative Medicine in America* (New York: Oxford University Press, 2002) [32]; which is supplemented by the more recent Roberta A. Bivins, *Alternative Medicine?: A History* (New York: Oxford University Press, 2007), [95]. Of particular note are a variety of chapters in Norman Gevitz, ed., *Other Healers: Unorthodox Medicine in America* (Baltimore: Johns Hopkins University Press, 1988) that includes the editor's introduction, "Three Perspectives on Unorthodox Medicine," and William Rothstein, "The Botanical Movements and Orthodox Medicine," 1–28 and 29–51.

All the above works contributed to an understanding of Thomsonianism, but additional information was gleaned from J. Worth Estes, "Samuel Thomson Rewrites Hippocrates," and Michael G. Kenny, "Democratic Medicine of Dr. Alias Smith," in *Medicine and Healing,* ed. Peter Benes (Boston: Boston University Press, 1992), 113–32 and 133–41; Sharla M. Fett, *Working Cures: Healing, Health, and Power on Southern Slave Plantations* (Chapel Hill: University of North Carolina Press, 2002); Todd L. Savitt, "Black Health on the Plantation: Master, Slaves, and Physicians," in Leavitt and Numbers, *Sickness and Health,* 313–30. Additional information on homeopathy is from Martin Kaufman, "Homeopathy in America: The Rise and Fall and Persistence of a Medical Heresy," in Gevitz, *Other Healers,* 99–123. On hydropathy I found Susan E. Cayleff, *Wash and Be Healed: The Water-Cure Movement and Women's Health* (Philadelphia: Temple University Press, 1987) [98] to be especially insightful. On the question of cleanliness and the use of soap, I drew on the study by Richard L. Bushman and Claudia L. Bushman, "The Early History of Cleanliness in America," *JAH* 74 (1998): 1213–38. The early spas are described in Carl Bridenbaugh, "Baths and Watering Places of America," *WMQ* 3 (1946): 151–81.

Other self-help movements especially on Graham and Alcott are detailed in James C. Whorton, "Patient, Heal Thyself: Popular Health Reform

Movements as Unorthodox Medicine," in Gevitz, *Other Healers*, 52–81; Murphy, *Enter the Physician*, [115]; and John R Betts, "Mind and Body in Early American Thought," *JAH* 55 (1968): 787–805. Additional information on Kellogg is in Anthony Cavender, *Folk Medicine in Southern Appalachia* (Chapel Hill: University of North Carolina Press, 2003); and Carl Degler, "Women's Sexuality," *AHR* 79 (1974): 1467–90. On phrenology and Mesmerism see Graham Richards, *Mental Machinery The Origins and Consequences of Psychological Ideas*, Part I, 1600–1850 (Baltimore: Johns Hopkins University Press, 1992).

For insight into the relationship between medical therapies and the physician's sense of identity, I am indebted to John Harley Warner, *The Therapeutic Perspective: Medical Practice, Knowledge, and Identity in America, 1820–1885* (Cambridge: Harvard University Press, 1986) [5]; as well as Charles E. Rosenberg, *Our Present Complaint: American Medicine, Then and Now* (Baltimore: Johns Hopkins University Press, 2007); and his "The Therapeutic Revolution: Medicine, Meaning, and Social Change 1 Nineteenth-Century America," in *The Therapeutic Revolution: Essays in the History of American Medicine*, ed. Morris J. Vogel and Charles E. Rosenberg (Philadelphia: University of Pennsylvania Press, 1979), 3–26. John S. Haller, "Decline of Bloodletting: A Study in 19th-Century Ratiocination," *Southern Medical Journal* 79 (1986): 469–74 provided the reference to Hughes Bennet. The study of the Cincinnati hospital is in John Harley Warner, "Power, Conflict, and Identity in Mid-Nineteenth-Century American Medicine: Therapeutic Change at the Commercial Hospital in Cincinnati," *JAH* 73 (1987): 934–56.

On medical nationalism and the resistance to European developments, see David Wootton, *Bad Medicine: Doctors Doing Harm Since Hippocrates* (New York: Oxford University Press, 2007); John Harley Warner, "The Idea of Southern Medical Distinctiveness: Medical Knowledge and Practice in the Old South," in Leavitt and Numbers, *Sickness and Health*, 2nd. ed., 53–70; and his "From Specificity to Universalism in Medical Therapeutics: Transformation in the Nineteenth-Century United States," in Leavitt and Numbers, *Sickness and Health*, 3rd ed., 87–101; and Elizabeth Barnaby Keeney, "Unless Powerful Sick: Domestic Medicine in the Old South," in *Science and Medicine in the Old South*, ed. Ronald L. Numbers and Todd L. Savitt (Baton Rouge: Louisiana State University Press, 1989), 276–94.

Chapter 10: Public Health

The major sources consulted for all aspects of public health include: John Duffy, *The Sanitarians: A History of American Public Health* (Chicago:

University of Illinois, 1990) [66]; Richard Harrison Shryock, *Medicine and Society in America, 1660–1860* (1960; repr., Ithaca, NY: Cornell University Press, 1972); Margaret H. Warner, "Public Health in the Old South" in *Science and Medicine in the Old South,* ed. Ronald L. Numbers, and Todd L. Savitt (Baton Rouge: Louisiana State University Press, 1989), 226–55; and Paul Starr, *Social Transformation of American Medicine* (New York: Basic Books, 1982).

Information on John H. Griscom is taken from Suellen Hoy, *Chasing Dirt: The American Pursuit of Cleanliness* (New York: Oxford University Press, 1995); Charles E. Rosenberg and Carroll Smith-Rosenberg, "Pietism and the Origins of the American Public Health Movement: A Note on John H. Griscom and Robert M. Hartley," *JHMAS* 23 (1968): 16–35; and Gert H. Brieger, "Sanitary Reform in New York City: Stephen Smith and the Passage of the Metropolitan Health Bill," *BHM* 40 (1966): 407–29. Details taken from Griscom's works include his *Sanitary Conditions of the Laboring Population of New York* (New York, 1845); and his description of his father in *Memoir of John Griscom* (New York, 1859). The death rates are in his *Sanitary Legislation, Past and Future: The Value of Sanitary Reform* (New York, 1861).

Statistics regarding death and life expectancy in the nineteenth century are taken from Ben J. Wattenberg, *Statistical History of the United States* (New York: Basic Books, 1976); Robert William Fogel, *Without Consent or Contract: The Rise and Fall of American Slavery* (New York: Norton, 1989); E. A. Wrigley, *Population and History* (New York: McGraw-Hill Company, 1969); and Michael R. Haines, "Fertility and Mortality in the United States," (EH.net Encyclopedia, 2008) based on his chapter on "The White Population of the United States, 1790–1920," and that of Richard H. Steckel, "African American Population of the United States, 1790–1920," in *A Population History of North America,* ed. Michael R. Haines and Richard H. Steckel (New York: Cambridge University Press, 2001), 305–70 and 433–82. A good summary of recent demographic studies is Herbert Klein, *Population History of the United States* (New York: Cambridge University Press, 2004).

On the march of cholera in the world, see William H. NcNeill, *Plagues and People* (New York: Anchor Books Doubleday, 1976); Irwin W. Sherman, *Twelve Diseases that Changed Our World* (Washington, DC: ASM Press, 2007); and Robert D. Morris, *The Blue Death: Disease, Disaster, and the Water Drink* (New York: Harper Collins, 2007). The hunt for the source of the disease in London is told by Steven Johnson, *The Ghost Map: The Story of London's Most Terrifying Epidemic and How it Changed Science, Cities, and the Modern World* (New York: Riverhead Books, 2006). On the appearance of the disease in New York, the most important source is Charles E. Rosenberg, *The Cholera Years: the United States in 1832, 1849, and 1866* (Chicago:

University of Chicago Press, 1968; repr., 1987); for cholera's appearance in Cincinnati, John Harley Warner, "Power, Conflict and Identity in Mid-Nineteenth Century American Medicine: Therapeutic Change at the Commercial Hospital in Cincinnati," *JAH* 73 (1980): 934–56; and in the South, Anthony Cavender, *Folk Medicine in Southern Appalachia* (Chapel Hill: University of North Carolina Press, 2003); Todd L. Savitt, *Medicine and Slavery: The Diseases and Health Care of Blacks in Antebellum Virginia* (Urbana: University of Illinois Press, 278); and Steven M. Stowe, *Doctoring the South: Southern Physicians and Everyday Medicine in the Mid-nineteenth Century* (Chapel Hill: University of North Carolina Press, 2004). Thomas H. Buckler describes his experience and experiments in *The History of the Epidemic Cholera as it Appeared at the Baltimore City and County Alms-House in the Summer of 1849* (Baltimore, 1851).

The backward nature of American medicine and the rejection of science during this period is detailed in James H. Cassedy, "The Flamboyant Colonel Waring: An Anticontagionist Holds the American State in the Age of Pasteur and Koch," *BHM* 36 (1962): 163–76; Ronald L. Numbers and John Harley Warner, "The Maturation of American Medical Science," in *Sickness and Health: Readings in the History of Medicine and Public Health,* ed. Judith Walzer Leavitt and Ronald L. Numbers, 2nd ed. (Madison: University of Wisconsin Press, 1985), 185–96; Ronald L. Numbers, "The Fall and Rise of American Medical Profession," in Leavitt and Numbers, *Sickness and Health,* 3rd ed., 130–42; Phyllis Allen Richmond, "American Attitudes Toward the Germ Theory of Disease," in Gert H. Brieger, ed., *Theory and Practice in American Medicine* (New York: SHP, 1976), 58–84; and David Wootton, *Bad Medicine: Doctors Doing Harm Since Hippocrates* (New York: Oxford University Press, 2007). On the devastating medical treatment of James Garfield see Candice Millar, *Destiny of the Republic: A Tale of Madness, Medicine, and the Murder of a President* (New York: Doubleday, 2011).

Useful sources on the changing nature of American therapies at mid-century include John S. Haller, "Decline of Bloodletting: A Study in 19th-Century Ratiocination," *Southern Medical Journal* 79 (1986): 469–74; Martin Kaufman, Homeopathy in America: The Rise and Fall and Persistence of a Medical Heresy," in *Other Healers: Unorthodox Medicine in America,* ed. Norman Gevitz (Baltimore: Johns Hopkins University Press, 1988), 99–123; and James C. Whorton, *Nature Cures: The History of Alternative Medicine in America* (Oxford: Oxford University Press, 2002).

Important sources on the public attitude toward cleanliness and the use of soap is Marilyn Thornton Williams, *Washing "The Great Unwashed": Public Baths in Urban America, 1840–1920* (Columbus: Ohio State University Press,

1991); and Richard L. Bushman and Claudia L. Bushman, "The Early History of Cleanliness in America," *JAH* 74 (1998): 1213–38. The most recent work by Kathleen M. Brown, *Foul Bodies: Cleanliness in America* (New Haven: Yale University Press, 2009) focuses on the prescriptive literature regarding cleanliness for the genteel.

On hospital development and surgical practices, see Josiah C. Trent, "Surgical Anesthesia, 1846–1946 in Brieger, *Theory and Practice*, 193–202; Morris J. Vogel, "The Transformation of the American Hospital, 1854–1920"; and Charles E. Rosenberg, "Social Class and Medical Care in Nineteenth-Century America: The Rise and Fall of the Dispensary," in *Health Care in America: Essays in Social History*, ed. Susan Reverby and David Rosner (Philadelphia: Temple University Press, 1979), 105–16, 250–72; Edward C. Atwater, "Touching the Patient: The Teaching of Internal Medicine in America," in Leavitt and Numbers, *Sickness and Health*, 2nd ed., 129–47; and Kay Moss, *Southern Folk Medicine, 1750–1820* (Columbia: University of South Carolina Press, 1999).

Conclusion

The quotation from Steven Johnson is in his *The Ghost Map: The Story of London's Most Terrifying Epidemic and How it Changed Science, Cities, and the Modern World* (New York: Riverhead Books, 2006) [15]. The rejection of European laboratory discoveries is described by Phyllis Allen Richmond, "American Attitudes toward the Germ Theory of Disease, 1860–1880," and Curt Proskauer, "Development and Use of the Rubber Glove in Surgery and Gynecology;" in *Theory and Practice in American Medicine*, ed. Curt H. Brieger (New York: SHP, 1976), 58–84 and 203–11.

Epilogue

The report on the medical schools is in Abraham Flexner, *Medical Education in the United States and Canada* (New York: Carnegie Corporation, 1910). Sources on the founding of and importance of Johns Hopkins University Medical School include: Paul Starr, *Social Transformation of American Medicine* (New York: Basic Books, 1982); John Harley Warner, "From Specificity to Universalism in Medical Therapeutics: Transformation in the 19th-century United States," and Ronald L. Numbers and Warner, "The Maturation of American Medical Science," in *Sickness and Health: Readings in the History of Medicine and Public Health*, ed. Judith Walzer Leavitt and Numbers, 3rd ed. (Madison: University of Wisconsin Press , 1997), 87–101 and 130–42.

On medical science I found D. I. Weatherall, *Science and the Quiet Art: The Role of Medical Research in Health Care* (New York: W. W. Norton, 1995); and James H. Cassedy, "Medicine and the Learned Society in the United States, 1660–1850," in *The Pursuit of Knowledge in the Early American Republic: American Scientific and Learned Society from Colonial Times to the Civil War,* ed. Alexandra Oleson and Sanborn C. Brown (Baltimore: Johns Hopkins University Press, 1976), 261–78 additionally informative.

Most of the information on mortality and vital statistics comes from Herbert Klein, *Population History of the United States* (New York: Cambridge University Press, 2004). Other statistics come from Arthur K. and Elaine Shapiro, *The Powerful Placebo: From Ancient Priest to Modern Physician* (Baltimore: Johns Hopkins University Press, 1997). See also Marian F. MacDorman and T. J. Mathews, "Recent Trends in Infant Mortality in the United States," NCHS data brief, no. 9 (Hyattsville, MD: National Center for Health Statistics, 2008).

On the present dissatisfaction with medical care, I found the following particularly insightful: Charles E. Rosenberg, *Our Present Complaint: American Medicine, Then and Now* (Baltimore: Johns Hopkins University Press, 2007); Edmond D. Pelligrino, "The Sociocultural Impact of Twentieth-Century Therapeutics," in *The Therapeutic Revolution: Essays in the History of Medicine,* ed. Morris J. Vogel and Charles E. Rosenberg (Philadelphia: University of Pennsylvania Press, 1979), 245–66; Thomas McKeown, *Role of Medicine: Dreams, Mirage or Nemesis?,* 2nd ed. (Princeton: Princeton University Press, 1979); Steven A. Schroeder, "We Can Do Better—Improving the Health of the American People; and Daniel Callahan, "Role of Complementary and Alternative Medicine: Accommodating Pluralism," *NEJM* 357 (2007): 1221–28 and 860–68; Helen Epstein, "Flu Warning: Beware the Drug Companies," *New York Review of Books,* May 12, 2011, 57–61; and *Consumers Reports on Health,* November 2004, [6].

On the nature of the new alternatives, James C. Whorton, *Nature Cures: The History of Alternative Medicines in America* (New York: Oxford University Press, 2002); and Robert A. Bivins, *Alternative Medicine: A History* (New York: Oxford University Press, 2007) are the most detailed. Also of use are Martin Kaufman, "Homeopathy in America: The Rise and Fall and Persistence of a Medical Heresy," in *Other Healers: Unorthodox Medicine in America,* ed. Norman Gevitz (Baltimore: Johns Hopkins University Press, 1988), 99–123; and Susan E. Cayleff, *Wash and Be Healed: The Water-Cure Movement and Women's Health* (Philadelphia: Temple University Press, 1987). There is also a proliferation of websites including the NIH itself and the Mayo Clinic with sources of information on every type of alternative medication and the results of experiments.

Chocolate, 63, 66, 69.
Cholera, 181, 183, 190, 194; cause of, 173, 176;
  epidemics of, 159, 172–78, 181, 185, 191;
  symptoms of, 173–74; treatment for, 174,
  177–78
Church, Benjamin, 82–83
Cider, 63, 69, 74, 102
Cinchona bark, 50, 158, 182; medical use of,
  37–38, 43, 45, 81, 99, 107, 110. *See also*
  Quinine
Cincinnati Hospital, 146, 167, 172, 173, 177,
  180
Clarke, William E., 179
Clarkson, Mathew, 97
Clergy in medicine, 30, 54, 159
Clinical trials, 158, 166, 193, 196; in Europe,
  103, 122, 189; lack of, 47, 145
Cobbett, William (English reformer), 111
Cobbett, William (in Philadelphia), 98
Cochran, John, *84*, 85, 87
Coffee, 63, 95, 140, 164, 174
Colden, Cadwallader, 34
College of Physicians (Philadephia), 100, 105
Columbus, Christopher, 9, 19, 22, 24, 65
Conjurers, 2, 52, 58, 147, 187. *See also* Magic
Connecticut, 63, 78, 90, 126; dentists in, 179;
  doctors in, 105; hospitals in, 143
Continental Army, 70, 78, 80, 81–82, 89–90,
  91; women in, 86–88
Continental Congress, 78, 79–80, 81, 83,
  85–86, 91, 93, 94; complaints to, 82, 83,
  92. *See also* U.S. Congress
Contraception, 127, 129, 160
Cookbooks, 66, 68, 70
Cooper, James Fenimore, 111
Copyright, 152
Corbin, Margaret, 88
Corn. *See* Maize
Cortez, Hernando, 21
Cotton gin, 108
Creeks, 56
Crosby, Alfred, 13, 18, 65
Crowd diseases, 13, 15
Cupping, 43, 44, 45, 57, 80, 107, 140
Currie, William, 99, 104

Daniels, John, 23

Dayton, Cornelia, 126
Deer, 22, 62, 66, 71; used in medicine, 40, 53
Dehydration, 46, 173
De La Salle, Robert, 22
De Léon, Ciéza, 21
Democratic ideology, 59, 152, 154–58, 161,
  165, 188, 191
Demography. *See* Population changes
Demonic possession. *See* Witchcraft
Dentists, 124, 179
Depletion procedures, 2, 37, 39, 44, 45, 53, 55,
  141, 158, 160, 173, 189, 197; extreme use
  of, 4, 46, 107, 164,177; rejected, 50, 143,
  149, 164, 168. *See also* Bleeding: Cupping;
  Purging; Vomiting
Dermer, Thomas, 12
De Soto, Hernando, 21–22
Detweiler, Henry, 159
Deutsch, Albert, 144
Devéze, Jean, 99
Diet, 93, 175; American, 62, 66, 73, 183, 187,
  197–98; English, 70; and health, 1, 62, 68,
  92, 183; in medicine, 4, 34, 68–69, 136,
  141, 159, 161, 163, 164; of the poor, 70, 71,
  174–75; of servants, 62; of slaves, 37, 67,
  68, 71–73; of the wealthy, 69–70
Digitalis, 48, 52, 110, 146. *See also* Foxglove
Diphtheria, 2, 14, 40–41, 46, 54, 171, 19
Diseases. *See* Crowd diseases; *individual
  diseases by name*
Diuretics, 45, 55
Dix, Dorothea L., 144–45
Dogwood bark, 37
Domestic medicine, 44, 51, 103, 107, 108, 110,
  153, 159, 174, 185, 187
"Domestic womanhood," 126, 130
Douglass, William, 32–34, 35, 39, 41
Drake, Daniel, 111, 153, 177
Drake, Francis, 23
Drinker, Elizabeth, 95, 119–20, 128
Drinking water, 1, 73, 87, 138, 164, 170, 184,
  194; contaminated, 56, 63, 74, 75, 161,
  169, 173–74, 175–76; in medicine, 56, 99,
  159–60
Dropsy, 48, 53, 81, 110
Duffy antigen, 37
Dunmore, Lord John Murray, 89–90

Elaine G. Breslaw, retired Professor of History at Morgan State University (Baltimore) and Adjunct Professor of History at the University of Tennessee, Knoxville, is the author of the acclaimed *Tituba, Reluctant Witch of Salem: Devilish Indians and Puritan Fantasies* (also available from NYU Press).

CPSIA information can be obtained
at www.ICGtesting.com
Printed in the USA
LVHW020826290721
693949LV00012B/1496

9 781479 807048